POLISH WITNESSES TO THE SHOAH

Polish Witnesses to the Shoah

Conceived by

MARIAN TURSKI

VALLENTINE MITCHELL
LONDON • PORTLAND, OR

First published in 2010 by Vallentine Mitchell

Middlesex House,
29/45 High Street, Edgware,
Middlesex HA8 7UU, UK

920 NE 58th Avenue, Suite 300
Portland, Oregon,
97213-3786, USA

www.vmbooks.com

British Library Cataloguing in Publication Data

Polish witnesses to the Shoah.
1. Holocaust, Jewish (1939-1945)--Poland--Personal
narratives. 2. World War, 1939-1945--Personal narratives,
Polish. 3. Poland--History--Occupation, 1939-1945.
I. Turski, Marian.
940.5'318'09438-dc22

ISBN 978 0 85303 980 8 (cloth)
ISBN 978 0 85303 459 9 (paper)

Library of Congress Cataloging in Publication Data

Printed by The Good News Press Ltd, Ongar, Essex

Contents

PART 2: CRUELTY AND INDIFFERENCE

PART 3: CHILDREN OF THE SHOAH

Foreword

Antony Polonsky

This moving and poignant collection of memoirs documents the feelings of some of those in Poland who sympathized with the Jews persecuted by the Nazis and threatened with mass murder. It also provides valuable accounts of those who, at the risk of their lives and those of their families, attempted to provide them with assistance. In Poland, as everywhere in Europe, the response of those who witnessed the marking off, ghettoization, deportation and murder of their neighbours was complex. There were those who assisted the Nazis by pointing out Jews or by taking possession of their property. Most people were terrorized by the brutal Nazi rule and were only concerned with their own survival, showing an indifference to the fate of others. But there were also those who, for moral or religious reasons, risked their lives to assist those who faced death at Nazi hands.

In Poland, the effort to assist was both organized and the work of private individuals. In April 1943 the Government Delegate, the representative of the Polish exile government in Poland, issued an appeal calling on Poles to hide Jews. Before this, at the end of 1942, a Council for Aid to the Jews (Rada Pomocy Żydom, code name *Żegota*), which was set up by representatives of the Front for the Rebirth of Poland and some underground socialist and left-wing groups, was able to obtain a degree of support from the government of the United Kingdom. Between 1942 and the end of the war it was granted a total of nearly 29 million zlotys (over £5 million) which it used to provide monthly relief payments for a few thousand Jewish families in Warsaw, Lwów and Kraków. According to one of its historians, Teresa Prekerowa, by the middle of 1944 between three and four thousand were benefitting from its financial support. In addition, it provided Jews with the false documents they needed to survive on the Aryan side,[1] and established a network of 'safe houses' where those who had an 'unfavourable appearance' could hide.i It was particularly active in Warsaw. Here it has been estimated that up to 30,000 Jews were able to find shelter on the 'Aryan side', of whom some 12,000 survived.[2]

The successes of *Żegota* (which was able to forge false documents for 50,000 persons) suggest that had it been given a higher priority by the Government Delegation and the UK Government it could have done much more. According to the testimony of one of its members, Władysław Bartoszewski, the organization was regarded as a 'stepchild' by the central underground authorities.

Most of those who hid Jews were individuals acting on their own initiative, whether impelled by moral considerations or hopes of financial gain. It is difficult to establish how many Jews were saved in this way. The records of the Central Committee of Jews in Poland (*Centralny Komitet Żydów w Polsce* – CKŻP) the principal Jewish body in post-war Poland, reveal that 20,000 Jews survived on the 'Aryan' side.[3] This figure is certainly too low, because many Jews either retained their new identities or, for other reasons, did not register with the CKŻP. It should probably be doubled or even trebled. This would give a figure of 40–60,000 Jews who survived thanks to Polish assistance (between 1.2 per cent and 1.8 per cent of the estimated Jewish population in 1939 of 3,300,000). Not all hidden Jews survived the war, because of denunciations or because they were discovered in random searches. Teresa Prekerowa has estimated that only half of those who moved to the 'aryan side' lived to see liberation. She has also attempted to assess how many Poles were involved in the rescue of Jews. According to her reckoning, because it took more than one Pole to save a Jew, in order to reach a figure for how many Poles were involved in the rescue of Jews one should multiply the number of survivors by two or three.[4] This gives a figure of between 160,000 and 360,000 Poles who, at the risk of their own lives and those of their families, helped rescue Jews. Some of them did this for monetary inducements, but others did it out of pure altruism. We do not know how many people died trying to save Jews; Yisrael Gutman has argued that the number is probably in the 'hundreds'.[5] Over 6,000 Poles have been officially recognized by Yad Vashem as 'Righteous among the Nations'.

How is one to assess these figures? Only one who was prepared to risk his life in this way is in a position to do so. Such a person is Władysław Bartoszewski, who has written:

> The moral issue remains. From a moral point of view it must be stated clearly that not enough was done either in Poland or anywhere else in occupied Europe. 'Enough' was done only by those who died.[6]

In response to this statement, Yisrael Gutman, one of the leading historians of the Holocaust who participated in the Warsaw ghetto uprising and survived imprisonment in Auschwitz, has observed:

> Sometimes I hear Jews accusing the Poles of deliberately not helping

them even though they could have done so. Such observations are expressions of pain, which eclipse a sensible attitude. More could certainly have been done to save Jews, but the Poles in the conditions of the occupation could not fundamentally have changed the fate of the Jews. The Allies could perhaps have done so, but even that is not certain in the final phases of the murderers' insanity. I shall permit myself to say more – there is no moral imperative which demands that a normal mortal should risk his life and that of his family to save his neighbor. Are we capable of imagining the agony of fear of an individual, a family who selflessly and voluntarily, only due to an inner human impulse, bring into their home someone threatened with death? Are we capable of understanding the pressure of those fears when a fugitive had to be kept out of sight of neighbors and relations, when a neighbor or friend dare not hear the cough of a sick person nearby, and those hiding the fugitive lived in an unending fear, when all that was needed was one house search for both hider and the hidden to have an end put to their lives? The Poles should be proud that they had so many just lights, of whom Ringelblum spoke, who are the real heroes of the deluge. And we can never do enough to thank these rare people.[7]

This collection of memoirs documents the behaviour of these heroes. Its publication is an inadequate attempt to thank them.

NOTES

1. Teresa Prekerowa, *Konspiracyjna Rada Pomocy Żydom w Warszawie 1942–1945* (Warsaw: Państwowe Wydawnictwo Naukowe, 1982); Teresa Prekerowa, 'The Relief Council for Jews in Poland, 1939–1942', in Chimen Abramsky, Maciej Jachimczyk and Antony Polonsky (eds), *The Jews in Poland* (Oxford: Basil Blackwell, 1986), pp.161–76.
2. On Warsaw, see Gunnar S. Paulsson, *Secret City: The Hidden Jews of Warsaw 1940-1945* (New Haven, CT: Yale University Press, 2002).
3. Józef Adelson, 'W Polsce zwanej Ludową', in Jerzy Tomaszewski (ed.), *Najnowsze Dzieje Żydów w Polsce* (Warsaw: Wydawnictwo Naukowe PWN, 1993), pp.388–9.
4. Teresa Prekerowa, '"Sprawiedliwi" I "bierni"', *Tygodnik Powszechny*, 29 March 1987.
5. Yisrael Gutman and Shmuel Krakowski, *Unequal Victims. Poles and Jews During World War Two* (New York: Holocaust Library, 1996), p.196. Others have given much higher figures but these do not seem believable.
6. Władysław Bartoszewski, 'Polish-Jewish Relations in Occupied Poland, 1939–1945', in Abramsky, Jachimczyk and Polonsky (eds), *The Jews in Poland*, p.160.
7. Yisrael Gutman, 'Contribution to Discussion on Ethical Problems of the Holocaust in Poland, held at the International Conference on the History and Culture of Polish Jewry in Jerusalem, 1 February 1988', reprinted in Antony Polonsky (ed.), *My Brother's Keeper? Recent Polish Debates About the Holocaust* (London: Routledge, 1990), pp.296–8.

Introduction

Marian Turski

We are asking those of you who still remember the circumstances of the Time of Humiliation to summon up scenes and images from memory. We are appealing to Poles who helped rescue Jews, to Polish witnesses of the persecution of the Jews and of the Holocaust, to those who let a Jewish child stay for the night, for an hour, or for longer. We are also appealing to those who closed that door because they feared for the lives of their own families. We are appealing to the Polish Jews who were then imprisoned in the ghettos, or who were in hiding on the Aryan side. We are appealing to concentration camp prisoners, to children of the Holocaust, and to those who joined the resistance movement.

The drama of scenes that cannot be forgotten is what defines the history of the twentieth century, the shadow of the Holocaust, the epoch of the furnaces, The aim is to recount events, including those whose narrators would rather forget about them, or never return to them.

The Warsaw weekly *Polityka* (where I have been editor of the historical section for decades) issued this appeal to its readers on the fiftieth anniversary of the Warsaw Ghetto Uprising. The idea came from the Children of the Holocaust Association. The people who were born before or during the war and who found themselves on one side or the other of the ghetto wall are the last participants in and witnesses to their history – or rather our history, for I, too, am of that generation. Our biological time is passing. We therefore have an obligation to preserve the memory of the Holocaust for future historians, and for the generations that will follow us.

We issued an appeal for the summoning up of those scenes that, as *Polityka* put it, 'cannot be forgotten'. The magazine received a total of 225 submissions, of which eighty-two have been included in this volume, in some cases, abridged.

Why did many of our respondents wait as long as half a century to submit their testimony, to bear witness? The reason was different for every case and for my part, I can say that, after my stays in Auschwitz and several similar places, I was afflicted with amnesia for fifteen years.

Only on the prompting of a friend and fellow sufferer in the camps did I begin retrieving from my memory a certain dramatic episode in which l played a significant role. Psychologists have shown that we consign cruel or painful scenes to oblivion, particularly if these scenes are associated with a feeling of guilt – even if that feeling of guilt is frequently unjustified. One of the reasons, or perhaps the main reason, is self-preservation. I am convinced that our appeal for 'scenes that cannot be forgotten' has helped many people to reach into themselves, and to free themselves from pain, from agonizing concealed thoughts, and from that very sense of guilt with which the authors of these reminiscences have burdened themselves.

The author of one of the accounts speculates that his parents lacked the courage to shelter Jewish children whose parents they knew. 'For fifty years', he writes, 'I have refrained from speaking about this matter with anyone. Nor do I think my parents ever discussed it. I have never forgotten it. It remains vivid, shameful, and burning to this day.' While recalling a scene over which he did not have, nor could have had, any influence, another author admits: 'I cannot recall that it particularly concerned me at the time, but the tears come when I think of it today. That is simply the way it was.'

The woman who submitted the briefest episode in this collection recounts the fate of Chajka and her two children:

> At the height of the Holocaust campaign, she came to us. After all, we were the owners of the village. Wasn't there something we could do to help? Did we have any advice? ... If you can imagine, we only shrugged our shoulders and uttered a few words of sympathy. Today, such indifference is incomprehensible. Yet it is a sample of the mentality and realities of the eastern marches in those times. In the days before our own catastrophe, the slaughter by Ukrainian bands and the exodus of all Polish families under German escort, those poor children of Chajka's were only a small element of the great Apocalypse.'

Here is one more admission: 'Now, in my last years, these events keep coming back more frequently and causing me pangs of conscience. "You should have saved the lives of those two children. You could have done it. But you were a coward. You thought only of yourself"'

A scholar, who today has an international reputation, writes that he 'was unable, or perhaps above all feared to help a stranger boy who was facing death only because his people had become the object of hatred'. The scholar was only 12 years old at the time. Today, he writes that the episode involving 'the little fugitive who could look forward only to death in the closed district' is what prompted him to grow up into a historian specializing in the history of the Jews and issues of national minorities in Poland.

Half a century later ,when the eye-witnesses' reports were written – and sixty-six years later, when we publish them in English – we are revealing dilemmas, emotions and doubts about our own attitudes and the behaviour of our loved ones that we concealed for all that time. I am convinced that there is an element of catharsis, which will help us to throw off a burden that has been crushing us – often without our being fully aware of it – for decades.

There is another sort of courage that evokes my admiration, even though I am not sure that everyone will share my assessment. This is the courage to forgive the guilty. One of the most harrowing narratives in this book is the story of a little girl, 10 years old in 1939, who was the daughter of a Jewish village cobbler. The Germans murdered most of her large family. The girl took shelter with Christian neighbours, while the only other surviving member of her family hid in the forests. He found the girl, and then: 'Polish outlaws killed my twenty-year-old brother. The pain and despair broke my heart. The necessity of keeping silent made it worse. I could cry only in my heart.' The author of that account still lives in the same village where those events occurred. She married there, and was widowed. Many years after the event, she learned who had killed her brother. 'I could even give the names of those bandits today', she writes, 'but I will leave the judgement to God'. Yet she described her tragic fate, including its post-war sequel. Why only now? 'Time heals all wounds ... it is nevertheless good that the time has come when all those things that were painful can be spoken about. The time of pain and silence has ended.'

There is another issue that brutally pushes its way onto the pages of this book: Did the Jews go like lambs to the slaughter? First, here are a few quotations showing how our respondents saw this question. One writes that,

> At around eleven, a large procession emerged from the city. Soon afterwards, the yellow stars on their clothing could be discerned. It was amazing: about two thousand people varying by age and gender, some of them here and there with children in their arms, being escorted by only a few armed guards. The people marched calmly. They were obviously downcast and resigned to their fate.

In another account, we read that, 'it was simply unbelievable how quietly they walked along'. Here is the most dramatic account. It concerns the transportation of the Jews of Hrubieszów to Belżec:

> One thing was appalling and completely incomprehensible to me then. (Today, I see things differently.) I did, of course, realize that none of those unfortunate Jews had the least chance of any sort of defence. I also realized that they all had to die martyrs' deaths. Yet I could not conceive how these people, including those who were young and strong, men and women, could so passively allow themselves to be led to the slaughter by a lone gendarme like the proverbial flock of sheep (please excuse the simile), bound with a single piece of wire or, as sometimes happened, with string, without the slightest reflex of resistance, attempt at escape, or anything of that kind. This was simply incredible, atrocious and dreadful. But perhaps these people were really so permeated with fear that they felt nothing, not even that they were part of that macabre procession of death. Who can say?

The penultimate sentence contains one answer to the question we have posed. Years ago there was a Hollywood film about two hoodlums who terrorized several dozen passengers on a New York subway train. The criminals would not have had a chance if the passengers had dared to stand up to them. But when a terrorist pointed his knife or pistol at a single individual, no one wanted to be the first one to fall victim. This is the quintessence of terror: the intimidation of a whole group.

What happens when that group is an entire family? Fear for one's spouse, children, or aged father or mother is paralyzing. The desire to stay with them and to watch over them until the last moment takes precedence over natural defence mechanisms and the impulse to stand up to violence. One more very important factor is that, while we know today that this was indeed the last moment, the ultimate stage in the 'Final Solution of the Jewish Question', people like these Jews from Hrubieszów may not have known as much as we do. They may not have realized it at the time.

I am writing about this in a telegraphic mode even though I have personally carried out extensive research into what the Jews knew during the *Endlösung*. Initially, no one knew anything. When they found out about the Holocaust, they did not want to believe, or were simply incapable of believing. Information did not travel as rapidly in those times as at present. The first people to learn were those connected with the resistance movement and in touch with the outside world, that is, those in contact with the Polish underground. Afterwards, or simultaneously, knowledge reached the official elites (the Beirat, the Jewish administration, the Jewish police) who had an interest in keeping their community as calm and orderly as possible. But when did knowledge sweep through the whole ghetto community, if ever? How many days, or how many hours, before people were herded into the gas chambers or before the execution squads arrived?

There were, of course, many factors that undercut any decision to put up a fight. I have already mentioned family bonds, in both the literal and metaphorical sense. It sounds appalling, but I can affirm that the uprising in the Warsaw ghetto was made possible by the fact that the there were hardly any old people or children left there. The families had been deported to Treblinka. Only young people, relatively strong and healthy, alone, determined and desperate, had the physical and psychological resources necessary to take up arms. It is hardly an accident that the people who decided to tunnel out from the ghetto of Nieśwież, as we learn in one account, were healthy, strong 'skilled workers' who were relatively well fed by the Germans. 'It was a downright Herculean task', we read. 'Everything connected with the tunnel was done in absolute secrecy. The Germans became furious when they learned how the Jews had tricked them.'

Other respondents also indicate that the Jews were not all quiet and submissive. There is an account from Zwierzyniec of a Jew who wrestled away a gendarme's rifle, only to be shot immediately. The respondent who used the phrase 'like sheep to the slaughter' admits that, during the second phase of extermination in Nieśwież (when there perhaps were no families left),

> the Germans encountered active but insignificant resistance. When people were ordered to come out of the ghetto, they set the buildings on fire. The fire raged in the most densely built-up part of the town as it spread through the centre towards the eastern outskirts. This enabled some residents of the ghetto to escape under cover of the smoke, through the Radziwiłł Park and into the forest. In the end, however, only a very few managed to save their lives – only the most energetic individuals.

The respondent goes on to say that 'the decided majority of the residents of the ghetto refused to leave, and stayed behind in the burning district'. It is worth noting that the Jews in nearby Kleck barricaded themselves in their houses. They defended themselves with hatchets, axes and pitchforks until most of them had been killed. Some individuals escaped to the forest.

Just so – and, even if they managed to escape, what could they do next?

If they had their families with them, how could they expect to provide for them in the forest? Would they find anyone to help them? How many informers would they encounter first? One respondent touches on this theme, asking bitterly:

> Did the Poles help the Jews of Hrubieszów in their hour of trial? I do not know. I never heard of any such cases. In my opinion, knowing the reality of the times, help from Poles to Jews was rather impossible and not always eagerly rendered. Did the Jews, or even a small number of them, have any chance of escaping from Hrubieszów, for instance to the forests, to the partisans? Decidedly not.

Obviously, there were many reasons for the passivity of the Jews in the face of the Holocaust. In many cases, the reason was an acceptance of the verdict of Providence. In the Jewish tradition, after all, there is the phenomenon known as *Kiddush Hashem* – circumstances fulfilling the requirements for immolation in accordance with the will of God. There is no space here for a complete and thorough examination of the reasons for passivity. I have only skimmed the surface of a few of these reasons. Yet there is one thing that must not be forgotten! This is something about which normal people – satiated people, or at least people who are not starving – can have no idea, and that they cannot even imagine. I am talking about starvation sickness – something that was studied in the Warsaw ghetto by a team of physicians and scientists directed by Dr Milejkowski. Dr Milejkowski was the physician responsible for public health in the Warsaw ghetto and was a member of the Warsaw *Judenrat*, but he was not spared deportation to Treblinka in January 1943. The manuscript of their findings was, however, smuggled out of the ghetto to Professor Orlowski of Warsaw University. He buried it until it could be safely reclaimed. For an introduction and translation of the survey, see, M. Winick, *Hunger Disease – Studies by Jewish Physicians in the Warsaw Ghetto* (New York: John Wiley & Sons, 1979). Starvation sickness destroys people physically and psychologically, forcing them to move slowly and to conserve energy. It reduces them to a state of complete passivity and apathy. It is no accident that the only people who stood up and fought in the ghettos and camps were the better fed.

And, perhaps, one final reflection: in this book, the reader will come across many complicated, entangled issues in Polish-Jewish relations. The reader should bear in mind the words of the former German chancellor Willy Brandt, himself an anti-fascist: 'Even if we accept the statement that Jews encountered anti-Semitism in Poland, we should not forget that the Nazis were Germans.'

Acknowledgements

The publication of this book would not have been possible without the generous support of Craig Gottlieb, and of the Irena Kozlowska-Fiszel and Edmund Kon Fund.

Vallentine Mitchell would like to thank Barry Davis for his editorial assistance, and Ben Helfgott for his vision and drive in supervising the English edition of this collection of testimonies.

PART ONE

THE WARSAW GHETTO

Introduction

Warsaw on the eve of the Second World War was the second largest Jewish city in the world (after New York) and had a Jewish population of about 360,000, 30 per cent of its total population. With the German occupation, Jews were randomly seized for compulsory labour and generally humiliated, followed by the confiscation of their property. A Jewish Council, the *Judenrat*, were established at the end of November 1939, as a tool of German administration. The rationing allocated to the Jews was very low indeed, 253 calories per Jew, compared to 669 calories per Pole and 2,613 calories per German, though those working for the Germans were allowed a larger ration. The possession of work passes eventually became a matter of life and death.

As elsewhere in Poland, the Germans lost little time in creating the Ghettos, the only areas in which the Jews were allowed to live. The first ghetto in Poland was in Piotrków Trybunalski in October 1939. Apart from Warsaw the largest ghettos were in Łódź, 1940–44 and Białystok, 1941–43. One plan had been to settle the Jews in Praga, on the east bank of the River Vistula, but in the end the Germans decided, in October 1940, to confine the Jews of Warsaw to a part of the area to the north and east of the old city centre, where the Jewish population had already been concentrated. Since Jews were brought in from the surrounding areas, the Jewish population of Warsaw at first grew, and was about 400,000 when the ghetto was sealed off from the rest of Warsaw in November 1940. Over 30 per cent of the population of Warsaw was thus concentrated in 2.4 per cent of its area. About 100,000 Jews died from hunger, disease (particularly typhus) and random killings, before the deportation and murder of 300,000 Jews (mostly in Treblinka) between July and September 1942, leaving about 55–60,000 in a much reduced area. The final liquidation of the ghetto, on 19 April 1943, the eve of Passover, provoked the Jewish Uprising. The Germans were assisted by the 'Szaulis', the Lithuanian Militia mentioned in some of the accounts (5, 7). Andrzej Czajkowski also describes the role of the Szaulis in the massacres at Ponary (57). Another non-German group involved which is mentioned in the accounts was General Vlasov's 'Russian' army. [The activities of the Latvian auxiliaries in Radom are mentioned later (69)].

What the Germans expected to take a few days lasted a month, but with few survivors. The Uprising could not fail to impinge on the consciousness of the non-Jewish people of Warsaw, as is indicated by many of the accounts here. One of the most poignant stories (4) is that of the 10–11 year old boy, Stanisław, who came back to Warsaw because he could no longer bear to be apart from his family, and in order to fight in the Warsaw Ghetto uprising. The grotesque image of the merry-go-round, mentioned in the account by *Michał Wiesław Hajdo* (10), against the background of the burning ghetto has found its place in Polish literature, in Czesław Miłosz' poem *Campo dei Fiori*. Almost all of the Warsaw Jews deported to Lublin/Majdanek, Poniatowa and Trawniki were murdered in November 1943 in 'Operation Harvest Festival' (*Unternehmen Erntefest*).

1. Scenes from the Ghetto

Wiktoria Śliwowska

This account ought to have been written by my aunt. She was the sister of my father, Wacław Zawadzki, who after the war was known by his many friends as 'Pooh'. She and I survived nearly two years together in the Warsaw ghetto, from the sealing of the walls in November 1940 to the moment in early September 1942 when, after the death of my mother, she was the one who led me past the check-point to the 'Aryan' side, leaving me in the hands of friends there. (Fifteen members of our family were in the Warsaw ghetto; four people survived with the help of non-Jewish friends.)

When the Children of the Holocaust Association and *Polityka* launched their appeal [for memoirs] in the period leading up to the fiftieth anniversary of the Warsaw Ghetto Uprising, we found ourselves again asking: Why were we so reluctant to speak of those experiences for so many years, and why do we return to them so unwillingly today? Why did neither she nor my family ever write anything, although both of them would have had plenty to say? The reason was undoubtedly their shared distaste for all those posing as veterans. Yet there was more. 'I think', my aunt said, 'that the hardest experiences for anyone to speak about are those associated with humiliation, the loss of dignity, abjection in the extreme'. And she added: 'Yet the "subject" that you've set summons up at once several scenes that I can never forget. A multitude of facts, events and experiences have evaporated or faded. Yet these scenes give me no peace. They return in dreams and in the waking hours, as if they had happened this morning.'

* * *

Summer, 1942. A cloudless, sunny day. A period of moving endlessly from place to place, flat to flat, an additional torment for the exhausted inmates of the shrinking 'closed district'. Empty streets, silence, not a living soul about. Another 'action' must have just ended. In the rays of sunshine that illuminate abandoned possessions and papers blown about by a breath of wind, an infant a few months old crawls across the cobblestones at the intersection of ulica Krochmalna,

Nowolipka and Dzielna: it raises the cucumber it holds in its tiny hand to its mouth, sucks it, takes it away and begins crying. Over and over again. It crawls on without letting go of the cucumber.

*   *   *

I am standing beside my brother, who was rescued from the *Umschlag-platz* and then from the hospital on ulica Leszna, in a column waiting to be marched off to the workshops. We are holding 'right to life' chits. We have been standing there for a while, and a 'blockade' is under way inside the walls of the neighbouring building. We can hear gunshots, shouts, laments, more shots, someone's loud sobbing and the sound of monotonous blows, not ceasing even for an instant, from a whip. The echo of each blow is amplified a hundred times in our brains. It all lasts forever. I have the impression that night is falling. I ask my brother what time it is. Eleven. And so only a few hours have passed since they lined us up in this courtyard.

*   *   *

It must be 1943. My brother and I are again standing together after another action, in a column of fortunate ones who have not yet been assigned to the gas. A young man standing beside us and wearing a knapsack whispers something over his shoulder. From the knapsack comes the muffled, lisping voice of a little boy, 'Daddy, do you want to make me happy?' Experienced over many months at concealing his presence, the child recklessly pesters his father: he knows that talking is not allowed under any circumstances.

This account ought to have been written by my aunt. She was the sister of my father, Wacław Zawadzki, who after the war was known by his many friends as 'Pooh'. She and I survived nearly two years together in the Warsaw ghetto, from the sealing of the walls in November 1940 to the moment in early September 1942 when, after the death of my mother, she was the one who led me past the check-point to the 'Aryan' side, leaving me in the hands of friends there. (Fifteen members of our family were in the Warsaw ghetto; four people survived with the help of non-Jewish friends.)

When the Children of the Holocaust Association and *Polityka* launched their appeal [for memoirs] in the period leading up to the fiftieth anniversary of the Warsaw Ghetto Uprising, we found ourselves again asking: Why were we so reluctant to speak of those experiences for so many years, and why do we return to them so unwillingly today? Why did neither she nor my family ever write anything, although both of them would have had plenty to say? The reason was undoubtedly their shared distaste for all those posing as veterans. Yet there was more. 'I think', my aunt said, 'that the hardest experiences for anyone to speak about are those associated with humiliation, the loss of dignity, abjection in the extreme'. And she added: 'Yet the "subject" that you've set summons up at once several scenes that I can never forget. A multitude of facts, events and experiences have evaporated or faded. Yet these scenes give me no peace. They return in dreams and in the waking hours, as if they had happened this morning.'

* * *

Summer, 1942. A cloudless, sunny day. A period of moving endlessly from place to place, flat to flat, an additional torment for the exhausted inmates of the shrinking 'closed district'. Empty streets, silence, not a living soul about. Another 'action' must have just ended. In the rays of sunshine that illuminate abandoned possessions and papers blown about by a breath of wind, an infant a few months old crawls across the cobblestones at the intersection of ulica Krochmalna, Nowolipka and Dzielna: it raises the cucumber it holds in its tiny hand to its mouth, sucks it, takes it away and begins crying. Over and over again. It crawls on without letting go of the cucumber.

2. Through a Hole in the Wall

Weronika Tajak

A shop on the ground floor of our house sold imported foodstuffs. The owners were Jewish. They were a large family, with perhaps five children, the mother, Pani [Mrs] Sara, her parents and some additional relatives. They occupied the whole ground floor, and they were all engaged in commerce. I sometimes asked, 'Where did they all come from?' and my mother answered, 'They're a big family and they must love each other, for they live together without fighting the way you and your sister do – and there are only two of you.' I would then cry out, 'But we don't mean it!' and my sister and I would hug each other tight, the way we were supposed to.

'Mommy, what about Rózia?'

'You know better than anyone what Rózia's like. She never fights with you.' Rózia was our best friend ...

The days, the months, the summers and winters passed. And then, one spring, they were gone. The flats on the ground floor were vacant and crossed boards were nailed across the windows.

They had all gone to the ghetto.

'We won't be gone long', Rózia said to console us. 'They say that there are even nicer houses there than here, because they're all built of brick instead of wood. There will be shops, and we'll all live together just like here. I'll be coming to visit you. I'll be allowed.'

I could not comprehend what that word 'ghetto' meant or implied.

My sister and I often ran to ulica Chłodna and ulica Żelazna [in Warsaw]. We saw people walking and riding trams, cars and rickshaws on the other side of the wall. Children were running around just like us, except that they were behind a wall. Why? My head was full of the word 'why', and seldom did I know the answer.

Rózia came to visit. They were all happy, selling things and not badly off. 'Except we have to wear stars on our sleeves.'

'Why?' I asked again.

'Because the Germans make us. But when I come to see you, I'll take mine off, because it'll be easier for me to get out then.'

She came back a few more times, but she was no longer so happy and no longer wanted to play. 'What happened, Rózia?' my mother asked.

'It's worse and worse there', she replied politely. 'I think I'm going to escape.'

'Where will you go?'

'I'll come here.' We hugged each other tight at the very idea that such a thing might happen.

Rózia stopped visiting. I overheard my parents talking about how bad things were in the ghetto, and how there were mass deportations. But where to? ...

They evicted us from our home in March, 1943. We had to move from the Wola district to ulica Dzielna, which had previously been part of the ghetto. I saw things that terrified me.

All the houses on the right side of the street were sealed off by a wall that stretched to the tobacco factory and beyond.

'Are we going to be living in the ghetto now?' I asked my father.

'No.'

'What about the wall?'

'In a few days, the wall will be taken down in front of our house.'

'And further down the street?'

'The wall will stay there, because that will still be the ghetto.' ...

We ran to the wall and looked through a hole to see into the ghetto. The streets were different and the people seemed different, too. The life that had once been there was gone. People were walking the streets, but in fact they only dragged one leg after the other. They sat in front of the houses, covered in some sort of rags that could not be called clothing. Skinny, dirty children wore shoes several sizes too large. They had shiny eyes; they wore the armband with the star. Germans with rifles on their shoulders, leading huge furry dogs, were everywhere.

We could not stay at the wall long because the German sentries threatened us and aimed their rifles our way. We had to run home.

There was, however, one older, moustached guard who said in Polish that he was Silesian. He allowed us to stay longer and talk with the children in the ghetto. Once, he said, 'They can't eat words. It would be better if you brought bread or something else to eat, because they're starving to death in there.' And so it began.

There was a tearful scene at home. Mother sobbed that she did not have enough to fill her own pot, while we cried that all we wanted was a tiny piece, a tiny little piece of bread and a couple of potatoes. Wringing her hands, mother agreed.

I once overheard my parents talking. Mother said, 'They run there all the time and sooner or later, some German is going to shoot them. You've heard about how many children are killed on both sides.'

'Of course children are dying, but you know well what's happening in the ghetto. They're not stupid, they'll know when to run away.'

'But bullets are faster than they are.'

'Our turn will come soon enough. In the meantime, share what you have. They're people, too.'

Hearing this, I felt ashamed of having doubted my mother.

We were no longer alone at the wall. More and more children gathered there. We played hopscotch, the boys kicked a football around, and those who had brought something passed it through the wall. We set up a rotation of those who played and those who passed things through, and the hole that we squeezed our food through seemed to be getting bigger. We always looked for our Rózia among the children who gathered on the other side. 'Ask them about her', I urged my sister. But no one knew her.

We reported to our parents in the evening. To make us feel better, they said that we might see Rózia one of these days.

We spent less time playing in our courtyard, and more time sitting around talking about the other side and how we could help the children there. Some of our playmates started keeping their distance from us. We heard: 'My father says that all you think about is helping the Jews.' The words that some of the children repeated after their parents hurt me and made me cry. My sister and I would run away to avoid having to listen.

'You see what they're like', my sister said. 'We'll only go around with children who do not say such things. They might tell children from the other courtyards about us. Then nobody will want to play with us. Did you hear how one boy called us 'the Jew twins'?' my sister asked. Because we really were twins.

'I'll beat them up and then they'll remember', I vowed. My sister knew I could beat up any of the boys.

But we never got into a fight.

The days passed. 'Our' German was no longer on sentry duty and the others would not let us come so close to the wall. Even though the days were still warm, we sat inside reading books that mother borrowed from her friends. We did not go to school; our education had stopped halfway through the second form. We must have known how to count, because we went to the shop, and to read, because we could finish a whole book in one day ...

A girl interrupted our reading one day. 'Come quick. Our Silesian is there!' Being referred to as a German enraged him. He had been ill. He was pale, changed, with sunken eyes. His moustaches drooped somehow. He looked at us sadly and nodded that we could go to the wall. He said something under his breath about 'the end'. The end?

We were the first ones to reach the wall, and when we looked through, I felt dizzy. There was the face of our Rózia, right next to mine. Dear God, was it a dream?

Her big black eyes had a feverish shine to them, and they got bigger and bigger. They looked like they would pop out of her head. 'Rózia, is it you?' I reached in to touch her hand. My sister looked on in wonderment. Rózia said nothing. We started to give her what we had brought. Bread, potatoes, carrots, an onion. She quickly stuffed the food into the pockets of her apron and a big bag she carried over her shoulder. She broke off a piece of bread and raised it to her mouth. She touched my cheek. Her hand was hot and moist. My sister tried to grasp her hand.

'Thank you, thank you', she whispered. 'I'll be here the day after tomorrow.' Then she ran away from the wall. The other children also scattered, like a frightened flock of pigeons.

We saw a patrol at the end of the street, and we, too, fled.

There was no end of telling the story at home. My sister and I kept interrupting each other as we recounted it to our parents. 'She seemed small, somehow', my sister said, puzzled. 'Maybe it wasn't Rózia at all, but just another girl who looked like her. She was so small and dirty, and I don't think she had any hair.'

'She wouldn't have taken you by the hand', I said. 'Right, Daddy?' We always wanted him to back us up.

'I'm sure it was Rózia', he said. 'It had to be.'

Evening was falling, the curfew was drawing near, and we had no desire to go outside. Those two days passed quickly and we went back to the wall. She quickly took what we had. We did not have much. It was harder and harder to get anything from home. Daddy was out of work. He would leave early each morning, and sometimes did not come back until just before the curfew. Once, he said something to mother, and she replied, 'But that won't help us get anything to eat'. We received some food from our aunt who lived next door, and from the neighbours who suspected where we took our food.

Rózia was pale. She wore large men's slippers and had a scarf tied around her shoulders and head. A crowd of children pushed her away from the wall, and a dozen hands stretched out in our direction. They were frightened, and so were we. We kept glancing at the sentry post. There had been times when the sentries had lost their temper and sent us running home with a solid kick, with a lump on our heads ...

One day before Easter, there were an especially large number of us playing near the wall, and the Germans seemed not to take any notice. Twilight was slowly falling when a boy shouted, 'Run for it!' I grabbed

Rózia's arm and I do not know what happened next. I heard her let out a deep gasp, and then I heard her footsteps running beside me. Or was it some kind of illusion? No. My sister was running on one side of me, and Rózia on the other. We were close to home, and we ran all the way up the stairs to the first floor. We're lucky it's no higher, I thought. The corridor was long and dark; five families lived here.

We entered our flat. Mother froze, and father stood up from his chair. 'Is somebody chasing you? And what's this?'

'Not what', my sister and I shouted in unison. 'Who! It's Rózia!' We stood terrified near the door. 'We pulled her through the wall. She's so skinny, she just came through.' She nodded.

'Now what?' my mother asked fearfully. 'It's almost the curfew.'

'She'll stay here', I said, shrugging my shoulders.

Mother looked at father. 'Do you hear what she's saying?' We did not move; we stood closer together. 'Look at her.' Tears were running down our cheeks.

'The best thing would be for you to be quiet right now', my mother said. I wanted to say that we weren't making any noise, but my father gave me a knowing glance. I kept my mouth shut. People said I took after my father, and this was why.

'She needs caring for', he said to my mother. 'She should be bathed and given something to wear. Just look at her.'

And now we did take a close look at her. Her hair was cropped, her body was covered with scabs, her legs were swollen, and she was so horribly thin that every bone was visible beneath her skin. And her clothes? How could anything so ragged and dirty be called clothing?

Rózia was washed in the big basin that was our only bathtub, combed, and put into one of my dresses. We competed in giving her things. A vest, pants – from me, from my sister. We sat on the bed while mother prepared a supper of potato pancakes, black coffee, and bread with lard and marmalade. After my sister and I had washed and eaten, Rózia began telling us about her family. Her grandfather had died, and her father and little brother were also gone. Her older sister, still alive, had married and moved in with her husband. Rózia had been left with her mother, grandmother and brothers, who often went into hiding.

Things had not been so bad at first. They kept moving to new flats. People were being moved out to work camps, as the Germans said. The ghetto became more and more crowded. People fell sick, and illness and hunger claimed many victims. They ran out of things to sell, and had nothing to live on. Many families were in a similar situation. 'My brothers were in hiding, my grandmother sat in the street all day, mama stayed at home, and I went around looking for anything I could find to take home to her. Sometimes my brothers came with something to eat, and then they would disappear again for days at a time. The Germans were chasing everyone, including children. Someone told me that children were passing food in here on ulica Dzielna, so I came.'

Mother cried and cried, and so did we. Father sat with his head down.

It was late. The blankets over the windows masked the light of the carbide lamp; we made sure that the shadows of our heads fell on the walls [rather than on the windows]. Her voice was quiet, and so was our sobbing. We three girls slept in one bed, hugging each other tight. I heard my parents whispering long into the night.

In the morning, my parents said, as always, that they were going out to look for work. We were supposed to stay at home, not go outside, think of some way of amusing ourselves, and not tell anyone who was with us.

We were hardly so stupid as to go boasting about who was at home with us, although we would have liked to do so. Father reminded us: 'For concealing a Jew, the Germans kill not only the fugitive but also everyone in the building.' We were terribly frightened, and I did not even want to go to the window when I heard my friends calling from outside ...

We were lucky that no one came to visit. My parents locked the door when they went out. We went [out] to the shop or to get water from the corridor or to go the toilet on the landing. Rózia used a bucket. Only late at night did my mother wrap her in one of her scarves to take her there, pretending that she was one of us.

Several days later, father brought a friend home. 'I'm going to take you with me, little one', the man told Rózia, and we made such a scene that we were within an ace of a fearful beating.

'You see, she can't go back through the wall', my father said, 'because something's going on there in the ghetto. The Germans are getting ready for something. They're bricking up all the holes in the wall.'

'But ...'

'I know what you want to say.' Mother cut me off. 'No, she cannot stay. They're making terrible searches of people's flats because more and more people are crossing over.'

'But, Daddy, she'll still come to see us. Say she will.' I looked at him imploringly.

The two men looked at each other, and one of them said, 'If only I can, I'll bring her here to you. And for a long visit.'

Mother prepared food for her to take. She was dressed in our clothes, but had to wear those big men's shoes because we didn't have an extra pair. She put on a sweater that mother had got from our aunt next door, which covered her bag stuffed with food. She went off trusting the man who was supposed to lead her back through the gate of the ghetto, and not through the hole that we had used to pull her out. We all followed them into the street. Dusk was falling. They walked hand-in-hand towards ulica Okopowa. She only turned back once to wave.

'Will they get there before the curfew?'

'I'm sure they will', Father said.

'Will she come back, Daddy?' My sister was hugging Mother. We were both crying.

'Will she come back?' I asked him, looking him straight in the eye. He never lied.

He stroked my head. 'No, I don't think so. I don't think anyone will be getting out of there any more.'

The sky over the ghetto turned red on 19 April. The glow from the fires shot high above the roofs of the houses, and we could hear salvos not only from rifles, but also from cannon. The uprising had begun in the ghetto.

My father died in May. The Germans killed him.

3. The Testament

Zenobia Wikło

1942, the Occupation, a few days before Easter. I was 10. Daddy and I were going home. We lived at 12 ulica Graniczna in Warsaw. On the other side of the street stood a high wall topped by a few strands of barbed wire and with sharp fragments of glass set into the concrete. The wall divided ulica Graniczna from ulica Grzybowska. The street was congested with pedestrians on our side. High above, at the top of the wall, a barefoot man was carefully walking along the broken glass. Blood ran from his feet. He was a Jew, no longer young, and he was swaying. Two Germans in black uniforms stood at the foot of the wall, doubling over with laughter. They had ordered the Jew to walk the whole length of the wall after removing the string he wore around the waist of his trousers instead of a belt. He was holding his trousers up with one hand, and holding onto the barbed wire with the other. He was singing 'Poor Rebecca'. I could not look. I turned around and saw other faces, some in tears and some amused.

My father spun me around. I rubbed my eyes against his hand. He took hold of me and whispered, 'Watch, dear. I don't expect to live to tell the world about what we are seeing, but you've got a chance. Human baseness knows no limits.'

Now, writing about these events, I feel as if I am passing on my father Jan Szczepański's last will and testament.

4. To Die Among One's Own

Teresa Szymczak

I lived with my parents in the big building, with several courtyards, at aleja Niepodległości 227/233 [in Warsaw]. The small shop at the intersection with ulica Nowowiejska kept us supplied with bread, flour and kasha. We went to the indoor market on ulica Koszykowa for meat.

But a Jewish family supplied the whole neighbourhood (ulica Sędziowska, ulica Filtrowa and ulica Langiewicza) with milk that they brought from a village outside Warsaw in a cart drawn by a horse called Dereś.

Where they lived, I do not know, and what their name was I do not remember. (I was 9 when the war broke out.) They were a numerous family and the delivery of milk supported them all.

There came a day when they had to sell the cart and the horse Dereś, and give up their canisters of milk and their clients: they had to go to the ghetto. My father purchased the milk business, as we would call it today. From then on, Dereś was our horse, and at five o'clock in the morning my mother and I had to deliver the milk that my father brought in the cart.

The original owners of the business were behind the walls. But not all of them. The mother had managed to place one of her sons with a peasant somewhere not far from Warsaw. Months passed. Increasingly dire news reached us from behind the walls. Then, finally, came April 1943.

* * *

I met him early one morning in our courtyard. He was rummaging in a dustbin looking for food scraps. He was a chubby blue-eyed boy my age with a shaved head, dressed in village garb. He did not look Jewish.

I wanted to find out why he was digging in the rubbish and I wanted to make some sort of contact with him. I didn't succeed at first. He was terrified. 'Don't you know who I am?' How well I remember that question which dropped from his lips one morning when he finally stopped running away at the sight of me. His hunger kept driving him back to the nourishing dustbin, and I waited stubbornly for him right there.

'No, I don't', I answered truthfully. I led him home and there, as we talked, it turned out that he was the son of the previous owner of our milk business, that he was called Stanisław now, and that he lived (or more pre-cisely, had lived until recently) in a village. He had wandered to Warsaw upon hearing about the outbreak of the Ghetto Uprising. He had decided to fight together with his own people. Longing for his family, for his mother, had not moved him. It was only when he heard about the Uprising that he set out. But he did not know where the ghetto was. The only thing he had been able to find in Warsaw was this house where he and his mother had once delivered milk. Washed and fed, he found a temporary haven in our one-room flat. We tried, however, to convince him to return to his protec-tors, where he had a roof over his head and the certainty of a slice of bread. All our urging was futile.

I would never again in my life encounter such determination. He had decided to go to his own, to fight in the Uprising. And he was only thirteen.

That was when we decided to lead him to the wall so that he could see for himself … Our guide was a friend from the courtyard, 14-year-old Mirek Miłosz. The three of us set out.

I remember the high wall, a burning house behind the wall, and a woman who jumped to the cobblestones with her infant in her arms from the flaming third floor.

I do not know what was happening in our Stanisław's soul, and even if I knew, I would be unable to describe it. I only know what I felt then and what I feel today, when I think back to those times.

Stanisław came home with us. He was pensive and silent, but was he convinced? We kept on urging him to return to the village.

And then one day he left. He disappeared from our lives as unex-pectedly as he had entered them. Did he return to the village, or go to die with his own? I do not know. Did he survive? A little Jewish boy who wanted to die with his people. Mirek, do you remember him?

5. The Little Smugglers

Józef Szeląg

I do not remember the exact date. It might have happened over the winter of 1942–43; it was certainly before the liquidation of the small ghetto in Warsaw. The north ghetto was large, while the south ghetto was smaller. They were connected by a wooden footbridge over ulica Chłodna near ulica Żelazna. I was a food buyer for the Europejski Hotel in Warsaw and I had a rickshaw and a bicycle at my disposal to transport goods purchased at bazaars, warehouses and in shops. My helper, a worker from the Powiśle neighbourhood, was the rickshaw driver and I rode the bicycle. We spent whole days cruising around the city making purchases and transporting them to the hotel. Thanks to spending so much time in town and talking to people, we were very well informed about what was happening in Warsaw – where the police were stationed, where the Gestapo was sniffing around, where a round-up was being prepared, where the Germans were getting a firing squad ready for the next group of prisoners or hostages, what was going on in the ghetto, and so on.

We passed our information on to our acquaintances so that they could stay abreast of the situation. Our work was not particularly safe for the city was constantly at war, but we got through somehow.

That fateful day, Antoś Draganowski and I rode to the pickling warehouse on Grzybowska to pick up two barrels of sauerkraut for the hotel. Antoś was on the rickshaw, and I was on my bike. It was around five in the afternoon. We turned from ulica Chłodna into Żelazna, which was the border street between the 'Aryan' side and the small ghetto. The three-metre-high ghetto wall did not run here. Instead of the wall, there was a barbed-wire fence running between the tram tracks down the middle of the street. Of course, there were no trams running on Żelazna. Armed Wehrmacht units marched along the barbed wire on the 'Aryan' side, as did groups of the bestial Lithuanian collaborationist 'Szaulis' troops with their white belts crossed on their chests.

Everyday life continued on both sides of this villainous boundary. The Jews were confined in their prison-city, where four hundred thousand people found themselves oppressed by overcrowding, hunger, filth and the unimaginable cruelty of the 'masters of the world'. Animated living skeletons of men, women and children could be seen from the

'Aryan' side. The dreadful hunger led children to dramatic steps – in the quest for any nourishment, they threw themselves onto the barbed wire, trying to reach the other side. This site on ulica Żelazna was not the only crossing point for the Jewish children. They also crawled through the storm drains near Hala Mirowska or through the sewers. Their daring cost many of these children their lives. The 'expeditions' in search of food normally took place in the early morning, with the return to the ghetto in the evening. They did not always make it back, and spent the nights in rubble or cellars on the 'Aryan' side.

The way things worked on ulica Żelazna was that the children gathered in small groups at certain points on the ghetto side and, if a survey of the situation indicated that a rush at the barbed wire could succeed, they made a run for it and reached the other side together. After such operations, children injured by the barbed wire often ran through the streets dripping blood. They tried to melt as quickly and as deeply as possible into the 'Aryan' zone. But they did not always succeed. The sentries guarding the ghetto opened fire mercilessly, frequently leaving dead or wounded children lying on the barbed wire or in the street.

Those who made it across tried to get food by begging. They had to be very cautious, always keeping out of sight of the Germans. The majority of the children begged among the vendors at the various street markets. They wandered around the city trying any possible means to get food – they even picked scraps out of dustbins. There were also many good people who aided these unfortunate children.

In the late afternoon, at around five or six o'clock, the children reassembled in the doorways of the buildings on the streets perpendicular to ulica Żelazna on the 'Aryan' side, loaded down with the acquisitions they concealed carefully under their clothing. Thus prepared, they all moved out towards the barbed wire on an agreed signal and tried to get back to their starving families on the ghetto side.

Now, Antoś and I arrived at this time and looked on in horror at a tragic spectacle.

Flocks of children ran into ulica Żelazna from the side-streets and began struggling through the barbed wire barrier like birds caught in a snare. The sentries shouted and fired their rifles while some of the children made it through to the ghetto, others were left hanging on the wire, and still others turned back to the 'Aryan' side. An open German utility vehicle suddenly drove up from ulica Chłodna (it was beautiful weather). An elegant young officer of about 25 sat beside the driver. The vehicle stopped. A small group of children who had not made it to the other side began disappearing into the nearby streets. Seeing what was going on, the officer began shouting at a 'blue' policeman [Polish police who worked under the Germans] to catch the fugitives. However, the policeman, no longer a young man and rather overweight, could not lay hands on the nimble children. Confronted with this display of police inefficiency – which may well have been intentional – the officer gave an order to his driver. That healthy young soldier leapt out and set off like an Olympic sprinter. He ran down his 'prey' in one of the side-streets and proudly led her back to his master by the scruff of the neck.

The victim was a little girl of about 8 and, for all I know, she may have been named Raja or Salcia.

She had unpinned dark hair, a bright face and large, dark eyes.

The terrified child stood bawling and helpless before her executioner. I can remember every detail of this abominable scene.

The officer wore a brand-new green uniform decorated with death's heads and high patent-leather boots. His face seemed gentle and benevolent. He smiled with angelic beauty. That was why I thought for one naive instant that he was going to stroke the child on the head and console her tears. I could not have been more mistaken – this was a well-trained beast from the Nazi stables. With a flick of his hand he summoned the 'blue' policeman, took his rubber truncheon, and drubbed him repeatedly over the head and neck. The policemen jerked himself to attention and calmly bore this castigation of his sluggishness. The little girl stood there the whole time with her head hanging down. In a long grey-black dress tied at the waist with a string, she looked as if she were pregnant. She carried the day's catch, food for her starving family, against her belly under her dress. Now it was her turn. The officer turned to his driver and said something. The driver instantly drew a knife from his pocket and cut the girl's dress open. Potatoes, onions, scraps of bread and carrots spilled to the ground. The soldier did this so violently that I had the impression he had ripped the girl's belly open and her innards had spilled out. She stood crying and trembling in fear before the Germans.

This handsome young officer with the angelic face clenched his teeth in a malevolent grimace and began beating the little girl over the head and shoulders with terrifying self-control. The poor thing raised her hands in defence, and he went on beating her with all his might. He beat those frail little hands with which she attempted to shield her head, until they dropped limply under his onslaught. The girl fell fainting onto the scattered potatoes, vegetables and bread. She lay on the ground with blood flowing from her forehead and lips. The officer straightened up and made an imperious gesture summoning a Jewish policeman standing on the ghetto side. The Jewish policeman hurried over and reported. The German ordered him to take the little girl to the ghetto. The policeman picked up the girl, who was moaning in pain, and started carrying her towards the Jewish side. The officer screamed an order to drop the girl on the cobblestones and whipped the policeman across the face and head with the rubber truncheon, after which he waved him away and summoned a second Jewish policeman. He ordered this one, too, to take her to the ghetto. The second policeman understood the German's intentions. He grabbed her long, dark hair and dragged her across the cobblestones. We could hear the agonized cries of the girl as she thumped along, and then those cries died out somewhere in the ghetto side-streets. The German officer was contented at last. Fully satisfied with his mastery and his accomplishment, he climbed back into the vehicle along with his driver and drove off with a beaming face, tossing out the instrument of his crime, the 'blue' policeman's rubber truncheon — now spattered with the blood of a Jewish child. Polish and Jewish eyes watched his exit in hatred, while the Lithuanians and *Wehrmacht* soldiers smiled obsequiously.

6. In a Tram Car

Barbara Rendzner-Rogozińska

I remember one short scene that could not have lasted more than ten or fifteen minutes. It took place in 1940 or perhaps 1941, when the ghetto had been established in Warsaw but was not yet completely closed. Trams ran through it, regular city trams, carrying passengers from the Żolibórz district to the city centre.

I was then taking part in a clandestine outing in the Kampinos Forest for older girls from our Tenth Warsaw Girl Guides' Group, under the direction of Jadwiga Zwolakowska. There were about ten of us, and we were gathering herbs.

We were on our way home by tram after spending the whole day and evening in the forest. It was very crowded, because it was Sunday and the trams ran seldom. The tram stopped at the boundary of the ghetto and, as was 'normal', armed Szaulis –occupation police, the most terrifying characters amongst all the police – took up positions at each of the tram car's doors. Then the tram moved off. It was going slowly, and all the passengers were trying to see as much as they could of ghetto life. Naturally, I did the same. People in stripes were walking along the streets, trading, begging. Suddenly, I noticed a child lying on the pavement. It was more of a skeleton than a child. It might have still been alive or it might have been dead, because people were walking past indifferently. The child lay peacefully, not moving, and the tram continued on. I kept watching and watching, and then I heard someone shouting, 'This girl has fainted! This girl has fainted!' I was the girl. I woke up sitting next to the closed window; the passengers had carefully placed me there. The tram kept rolling slowly along, while I bent to gather up from the floor my bouquet of field flowers and herbs.

7. The Ghetto Uprising

Alina Szczypińska

I lived on ulica Hoża in Warsaw and was running an errand to my grand-mother's on ulica Warecka. It was a lovely day, rather warm, with a breath of spring in the air. Walking along Krucza and Marszałkowska, I had just reached the intersection with aleja Jerozolimskie, when two powerful explosions, one after the other, jarred the city. I could hear people around me saying, 'The Germans have blown up the Citadel'. A huge geyser of smoke, fire and earth rose at the end of Marszałkowska, behind the Saxon Gardens. It was a horrible sight. I ran quickly down ulica Bracka, and at ulica Szpitalna we could hear the roar and the sirens of approaching German vehicles. These were not the usual army field lorries, but rather two special, low lorries with three rows of benches and a machine gun in the middle, full of Lithuanian 'Szaulis' troops under German command. Soldiers from Vlasov's army rode in the three vehi-cles that followed, and a normal lorry full of German soldiers brought up the rear. We were already aware that something was happening in the ghetto. An uprising! A real uprising, an outburst of desperation against murder, deportation and the destruction of the whole Jewish popula-tion. This made a profound impression on me. Gunfire and explosions could be heard all day and at night. The ghetto was surrounded and the Germans did not allow anyone to approach the walls. Fighting, or more precisely the murdering of people, was going on inside. We walked to the Saxon Gardens and watched the destruction from a distance, pow-erless ourselves. People we knew, and whom we would never see again, were dying there. You must surely be interested in how Warsaw really reacted to these events. While there had been many people holding the extremist right-wing views of the ONR [Obóz Narodowo Radykalny (The National Radical Camp) a Polish anti-Semitic party, formed in 1934] before the war, there was not a single person in Warsaw during the Ghetto Uprising who failed to sympathize with the Jews who were fight-ing, and whose heart did not go out to them. People said aloud on the street that this was a regular slaughter, barbarity and so on. It was as if they sensed that the same thing waited in store for us and that a year later all Warsaw would lie in ruins. Just after the war I walked through the still-living remains of the ghetto, that gigantic cemetery of Heroes, and thought that perhaps the world would never again know such brutality, such bestiality, never again!

For me, however, those nameless Heroes of the Ghetto earned eternal commemoration and glory.

Living in Warsaw throughout the Occupation and travelling to Otwock (where my father was director of the hospital until 1943) I saw many dreadful things associated with the martyrdom of the Jewish people, but I do not know if I would be able to describe them in a way that did justice to the horror of the situation.

8. My Father

Antoni Marianowicz

It was obligatory in the Warsaw ghetto to remove one's hat before all uniformed Germans. This was unpleasant but, in comparison with the other horrors of ghetto existence, rather childish. I always tipped my hat first to everyone, often to people hardly deserving of respect. What is more, I tipped my hat even to strangers, or rather to those I was not sure I knew, since my short-sightedness made me fear committing a gaffe. Why, living as I did in a world of shame and lawlessness, should I regard removing my hat before strangers as any great humiliation?

Things were different with my father. For him, it was a question of principle. This man with the heart of a lamb did nevertheless have his temperament and an inborn inclination to fighting, which had been exacerbated by his years as a student in Germany. As everyone knows, the student brotherhood codex of honour demanded active intervention in the case of the slightest infringement, which was regarded as including not only inappropriate gestures and words, but even the manner of looking at someone (the so-called fixed stare). In this atmosphere, tipping one's hat to German soldiers took on downright mystical aspects. We therefore did all we could to make our father spend most of his time at home, especially in winter when it was impossible to go without a hat. In any case, Father did not feel well and was hardly eager to walk the infernal streets of the ghetto. He spent most of his time in his armchair, lost in thought, smoking one cigarette after another.

One winter day I went out with him on an errand near home. Despite his advanced age, he still looked imposing in his fur hunting coat and soft grey cap. As always, he carried his cane. A German soldier, a boy of perhaps 20, suddenly appeared before us. The soldier stood in the middle of the pavement carefully observing the passersby – he was evidently enforcing the tipping of hats. I removed my hat without thinking and then, at the same moment, stole a look at my father. I went stiff with fright because his facial expression clearly foretold a catastrophe. The German took a step in our direction and they stood facing each other, staring each other down: my 50-year-old father and an adolescent in a Nazi uniform. How long it lasted I cannot say, but to me it seemed like ages. At last, the German bellowed: *'Du, nimm ab dein kapelusz!'* [You, take off your hat!]. (I cannot imagine why he used the Polish word *kapelusz*, to which he gave an incorrect stress.) My father did not flinch. I glanced in horror at the German's pistol and my father's cane. And then the German turned around and walked away. To this day I cannot comprehend his loss of nerve. Was he cowed by the elderly gentleman's gaze? Or could some human instinct have been awakened in him?

9. What I Saw from my Balcony

Teresa Augustynek

My family consisted of my parents, one son and three daughters. I was the youngest; I was 14 at the time of the Uprising. My brother, a junior cadet in General Kleberg's army, had died at Wola Gułowska during the last two hours of the battle on 5 October, 1939. The death of a fine and talented son was a grave blow to my parents. From that moment on, the atmosphere at home was consistently opposed to force and the senselessness of war.

The Ghetto Uprising made a great impression on my father. There was an atmosphere of mourning at home, just as there had been after my brother's death. One day, my father lay down with us on the floor between the open double balcony doors of our third-story flat on ulica Sierakowska. A square in the ghetto was visible from there. Fighting was still under way, there were exchanges of fire, and we could see exactly what was going on from our vantage point. I remember it as if it were yesterday. It was high noon and the street was completely empty. The outlines of partially burned houses loomed. The houses that hadn't been burned looked abandoned. The whole view was dreadfully depressing: complete desolation in the bright sunshine. Every so often, a distant shot rang out.

At a certain moment, a group of fully armed and outfitted Germans came into sight. They walked into a doorway of which we had a good view. They returned a moment later shoving a small group of women and children along with the barrels of their rifles. One of the women held something, shielding it. She tripped and staggered as if she had too little strength to keep going. A German took whatever she had been carrying and threw it on the ground at the foot of a streetlamp. The woman fell to the ground, bent in a tragic pose with her arms stretched above her head, leaning over what was now clearly visible as a tiny child. She would not let the German, who was poking at her with his rifle muzzle, push her away. We broke into spasms of weeping. However, our father did not allow us to leave, to crawl away. He spoke those terribly prophetic words: 'You have to remember what they are doing in the ghetto today. It is the beginning of the destruction that the Germans are planning.' Our mother stood inside the room trembling and begging our father to let us go. We kept crying, and it was a nightmarish evening full of that fire-glow, the blazes and the desperate helplessness of being unable to do anything. One of my sisters came down with a 104-degree temperature from the shock and lost consciousness for a while. Little more than a year later, on 1 August 1944, the Warsaw Uprising broke out. My father died. He was probably shot at Stawki like the rest of the men from the Wola district, all of whom vanished without trace. For my mother and sisters and me, our own turn came to be herded along by Germans using their rifle butts to drive us through the burned-out squares of Warsaw to Pruszków on 26 August. Our mother said then, 'Your father was right. Keep your eyes open and remember. You will never have the right to forget.'

10. The Fun Fair

Michał Wiesław Hajdo

I began my work in the Organization for Aid to the Jews by delivering food allowances and money to those who were sheltering Jews. All of my 'clients' were Poles, and I visited their flats during my working day. They ranged from a 'blue' policeman on ulica Krochmalna to an engineer in Żolibórz [a district of Warsaw].

On 19 April 1943, when the Ghetto Uprising began, I had a morning appointment in Żolibórz. My route took me along ulica Miodowa, through Krasińskich Square.

As I entered Krasińskich Square I could hear individual shots and series of machine-gun fire. But aside from those sounds of the fighting, I also heard blaring fairground music. I saw a moment later that a 'fun fair' was operating, with a rotating carousel, other rides and booths crowded with merry onlookers.

This was probably the first and certainly the last time in that grim period that I lost control. Rage overwhelmed me. I began screaming and cursing – people were dying in an uneven battle a few metres away. The merrymakers reacted immediately. They grabbed hold of me, and shouted, 'Now we'll teach you a lesson, you lackey of the Jews', and dragged me towards ulica Bonifraterska. I did not resist. We were close to the gate at the Court building. Through the gate, I could see an SS crew operating a heavy machine gun. They were firing at the windows of a building just inside the wall.

I realized that I had to do something, that I could not remain passive in the clutches of my tormenters. I had to break free. Surprisingly, it was the machine gunners who came to my aid. Noticing our group approaching, they swung the barrel towards us.

I gave a sudden jerk, tore free and ducked behind a pillar.

A burst from the machine gun scattered not only my tormenters, but everyone in the vicinity.

On the way to Żolibórz I kept wondering whether my tormenters from Krasińskich Square could really have been authentic residents of occupied Warsaw.

11. A Letter to my Mother

Marian Liwa

Fifty years have passed since I left the ghetto! Half a century, which is a long time, because we have had only had twenty centuries in this present era. Everything seems 'normal' to children; they know no other life and have nothing to compare it with. Today, on the other hand, summoning up those memories and those images is difficult and sometimes borders on the painful ...

I am not sure of the date, but it was probably 8 March. I do not know which day of the week it was. I can only remember how father had taken me for a walk the day before, in the late afternoon, on Nowolipki Street [in Warsaw]. It was dark then, and only the snow that had not been shovelled made things any brighter. Things that had been thrown away – 'the corpses of things', a writer would later call them – littered the street and the pavement. After going out the gate, we turned left towards the *Wache* [the sentry-post], on the corner. We could hear the banging of windows that had been left open in now-vacant flats. Those windows open in the winter – black eye-sockets of what had once been alive – were an uncanny and enthralling sight. A group of gendarmes stood at the post, a bonfire was burning, and a woman was screaming horribly somewhere out of sight. Was she being beaten? Tortured? The terrifying scream of an anonymous woman concluded my final walk with my father. Yet why had he taken me for that walk? Did he want to familiarize me with the route I would have to follow the next day? Did he simply want to go for a walk with his son when he alone knew that it could be the last walk? My father was only 38 ...

The next day – I cannot remember what time it was – my father called me to say goodbye to my grandfather. I was playing in the courtyard with other children, as if it were a normal day. There were not many children left by then, but the moments when my friends had disappeared were not fixed in my memory, for that, too, was something normal. I do not recall the last time I saw the older friend who wore plus fours and glasses. In his flat (through the second gate and to the left), he and his whole family glued envelopes. That was their source of income. One day, I saw him with his hair clipped almost to his scalp. 'That's the fashion now', he told me. I do not recall our last meeting, but today I am happy that I remember a child who had the dignity to present as a matter of style, and therefore aesthetics, what was simply a preventive measure against typhus-bearing lice.

So I broke off my game with the other children – I did not think that the break would last for years – and ran to say goodbye to my grandfather. I did not know that it was forever. There must not have been much time left, for I said goodbye to my grandfather 'across the threshold'. I still remember his good, tender face bending to kiss me. Then things started happening so quickly that I can no longer recount them. I remember dashing between a wall and a gendarme who had his back turned. I can still see his broad shoulders in his green uniform. Those couple of metres that I had to cross were like jumping into an abyss, and I well remember the horrible feeling of fear and loneliness that overcame me. From today's perspective, it was like being born again: a brutal abandonment of childhood, a passage into solitude – and I was not in the least prepared for any of it.

In the entranceway across the street, 'on the other side', a strange man was waiting for me, as arranged. As I had been instructed, I quickly turned out the fur collar that had been folded under the neck of my coat. A moment ago, it had been illegal to wear fur. And, as instructed, I said nothing about the little watch that my aunt Saba had concealed in my coat. I was 7 – the time when children started attending the first form in school, wearing blue smocks with white collars.

The stranger led me through a gate and into a street the name of which I do not recall. So I was 'on the other side', and the first thing that surprised and delighted me was the sight of women in hats! Then I found myself in a flat. Another stranger, a lady, appeared and showed me a photograph – another agreed signal. That little square of paper had a miraculously calming effect: I felt as if I were no longer alone, as if I were at home again, loved, protected. I went to the tram stop with that lady. What I saw and thought about then – I cannot recall. Perhaps, under the spell of your photograph, I thought of one of our walks together. It had been perhaps a year earlier that we walked down ulica Orla towards Leszno in the Warsaw ghetto. A small, undernourished child sat on the step of a food shop. Without hesitating, you went into the shop and returned with a roll, which you gave to that child. But he did not eat it. I remember the pain in your voice as you said, 'He can no longer eat'.

When we got onto the tram, that lady took a seat and stood me facing the window. The idea was for the other passengers not to see me, because I 'resembled ...' and had bad 'looks'. As polite and obedient as always, I turned towards the window, too small and too frightened to ask myself why a child's face had to be concealed as if it were the face of a monster. From that moment on, I became a hostage to those 'looks' which threatened me first with death and later with real or imagined exclusion. Only twenty years later did I free myself, but at what a horrible price: abandoning my home, my family, and you, mother, once again!

On that memorable March day of 1943, half a century ago, that memorable tram dropped me near ulica Chłopicka, where I found you waiting.

We have parted many times since over that terrible half-century, but we have always managed to find each other afterwards.

12. Nightmares

Tadeusz Niewiadomski

I stayed in the Warsaw ghetto from 23 February to 22 June 1943. I was an inmate of the Pawiak prison, situated in the heart of the Jewish district. On 22 April I was transferred to the penal camp at 24 ulica Gęsia. Every other day for a period of two months beginning on 25 April, I was led through the ghetto under escort by German, Ukrainian and Polish police to the 'Aryan' part of town, where I had to work. What I saw on the march from the camp to the gates of the ghetto, and returning the same way, still returns to me in my dreams ...

Early in the morning of 19 April, most of the prisoners in Pawiak were surprised by the sound of gunfire and explosions outside the walls, apparently close by. Volleys of machine-gun fire were punctuated by the explosions of shells or grenades. Was it an execution? Probably not, for executions were never held in the ghetto. In any case, the shooting went on too long. Perhaps our resistance fighters were trying to take Pawiak to set the prisoners free. Less than a month earlier, after all, there had been a successful attack on a prison's Black Maria on ulica Długa. But something similar now seemed unlikely. Even if such an attack were to be mounted, it would take place during the night and not, as now, at dawn. So what could it be? The continuing firing indicated that some sort of battle was underway. The shooting grew more intense, then faded, but it kept going on without a break. Hours passed, and the Pawiak inmates grew more tense. The prisoners who brought some swedes for dinner at last relieved our curiosity. They had learned in the kitchen that the Germans had started the pacification of the ghetto and the Jews were defending themselves. We became hopeful. Perhaps help would come from the 'Aryan' side and we, too, would be freed.

The sounds of combat almost died away overnight. In the morning, they intensified again. We thought that we could hear artillery or mortars. On the third day, the fighting was more subdued.

At about nine in the morning of 22 April, Krzysiek and I were unexpectedly removed from our neighbouring cells. At 24 ulica Gęsia, we found ourselves on the grounds of a work camp that had been founded several weeks earlier. No one at Pawiak had even suspected the existence of such a camp. It was subordinated to Pawiak prison and staffed by the same German and Ukrainian sentries, but the regime in the camp was relatively relaxed ...

We could hear firing outside the walls of our camp. It was growing weaker, however. The prisoners who came back from outside told us in outraged tones about what they had seen in the ghetto.

Two German sentries came in after lunch to get Krzysiek and me and lead us out of the camp, along with several other prisoners. Not far away, at the corner of Gęsia and Lubeckiego, stood a group of German officers in animated conversation. One of them wore a general's epaulets – this was probably Stroop, the commander of the pacification operation. Some artillery was set up in the middle of the street with a group of gunners scrambling around it. SS men with their rifles in the firing position ringed buildings in which there was no sign of life. Far down the street stood a column of utility vehicles and lorries. We were ordered to turn the gun around so that its barrel pointed towards ulica Stawka. After shifting the gun, we were herded back inside the camp. We had just reached the stairs when the building shook as the gun fired. Then it fired again and again.

We talked that evening about the tragedy of the ghetto. It was a warm night and there was no glass in our windows. There were longer and longer intervals of quiet. We were just falling asleep when we suddenly heard Germans shouting and cursing and giving orders. We also heard a child crying and the voices of women, and afterwards a volley of machine-gun fire followed by individual shots. Then we heard talking; this went on for some time and then fell silent.

The next morning, the prisoners with work assignments were led away after roll-call and only those who had recently been transferred from Pawiak remained in the camp. We were sent to the store room and given shovels, sledgehammers and spades. The German overseers led us to the corner of the camp yard near the gate in the wall that ran along ulica Gęsia. We saw to our horror that this was where the nocturnal execution had been held. The corpses had already been laid out. For twenty metres around lay various small objects – clothing, toys, rattles, bags of sweets, sacks. It all lay among puddles of clotted blood. Here and there were bits of human organs and brains. We were ordered to dig a pit a metre and a half deep and put everything that remained after the execution in it. The two sentries supervising the work gave us no chance to look at the documents lying about ...

One of the prisoners was walking towards the pit with a large bag containing several kilograms of sugar cubes. Another one stopped him before he could toss it in, suggesting that its contents might serve as food.

We were all famished after several months in Pawiak, but the trouble was that some of the sugar was pink with human blood. A discussion started up. Some prisoners favoured throwing the whole bag into the pit, while others wanted to save the part that was not stained. The Germans looked on ironically, and I had the impression that they knew what we were arguing about. The bag was left at the edge of the pit. Carrying a shovelful of sand to cover the bloodstains left by the execution, I 'accidentally' bumped my friend (although in fact it was deliberate) and he, trying to regain his balance, 'accidentally' tipped the bag into the pit. One of the other prisoners cursed us heartily, but that was the end of the matter and no one tried to retrieve the sugar from the pit ...

On Sunday, I saw a group of new Jewish prisoners for the first time. There were six of them. They were dressed the same way we were, except that they had no numbers on their backs. They were treated worse than those who had previously been murdered. No opportunity to beat and abuse them was missed.

After prayers one evening, we invited one of the new Jewish arrivals into our cell for a cigarette and a talk. Late into the night we listened to his account of what he, his family and friends had been through. He was a Polytechnic graduate. I cannot even recall the details of this unfortunate man's narration, but they must have been the same as thousands of other stories. On the other hand, I remember perfectly well a question I asked him, and the way he answered it. I asked why he had not run away. After all, he knew what had happened to hundreds of thousands of Jews in the camps. He also realized that neither his looks nor his accent would betray his origins. Why hadn't he taken the risk? It had not been impossible. More than a dozen of our 'Aryan' fellow prisoners, not threatened with extermination, had escaped in their prison uniforms. Yet not a single person from among the recently-murdered group of Jews had tried to get away, despite being guarded no more strictly and being dressed in their own clothes. Why? Clothing could always be found.

I listened to his melancholy reply. He did not know why others did not escape, but he supposed it was for the same reason that he did not do so. He was fully aware of his destiny, and knew that his looks and accent posed no danger. Furthermore, he had many 'Aryan' friends on whose help he could rely. But why should he want to put them at risk? His wife, children, parents and friends had been murdered, and he was only alive by accident. He was no more deserving of life than they had been. He was a walking corpse.

PART TWO

CRUELTY AND INDIFFERENCE

Introduction

These stories exemplify how close to the surface can be the violence in the human character and how readily it might emerge, given the circumstances and the opportunity for power. This was true not only for the Germans, but also, as is mentioned, for the Ukrainians and Poles, even towards their own neighbours. For an act of betrayal, as opposed to one of aggressive cruelty, there might also be a pecuniary motive. Cruelty could also take the form of indifference from bystanders, sometimes because they had to close down their compassionate feelings out of fear, perhaps, or because the situation was simply too painful to face. They, too, had to withstand the impossible circumstances of the German occupation. As Wieslaw Antochów writes (13): 'I did not shed a tear then, but I am weeping as I write this.' In the novel by Saul Bellow, *Mr Sammler's Planet* (1972) a survivor of the shooting pits in Poland says: 'I know now that humankind marks certain people for death. Against them shuts a door.'[1]

Wieslaw Antochów tells of a horrifyingly brutal attack by the son of the Ukrainian Latin teacher in Czortków on his Jewish school friend, a doctor's son, after the Germans had driven out the Soviets in 1941. Movingly, after returning with the Red Army, the doctor's elder son did not take revenge upon the Latin teacher who had remained in the town, whilst his son fled with the retreating German army.

In 'It could have been one of us' (20) the onlookers are horrified at the German's cruelty and apparent murder of a small boy, who manages, miraculously, to survive in the sewers. Marianna Adameczek (15) tells of how the casual cruelty and selfishness of the neighbours, who had been entrusted with all her family's possessions, comes out in their refusal after the war even to tell her uncle in Israel that she is the only survivor of the family. In Halina Drohocka's account (17), the Polish passengers on a tram passing by the ghetto wall in Warsaw witness the execrable murder of a Jewish boy with silence and hysteria. Józef Andrzej Kaja (18) remembers a German gendarme whistling jauntily as he returns to town after murdering two young Jews in a meadow. Maria Majewska (19) reflects a young girl's bewilderment at the bestial behaviour of an intensely handsome young German gendarme.

The violence in these stories is so inhuman and shocking, that were it not for the fact that these eyewitness accounts have been set down on paper, they would be dismissed as myths.

NOTE

1. Cited in Norman Geras, *The Contract of Mutual Indifference. Political Philosophy after the Holocaust* (London and New York: Verso. 1998), p.7.

13. In a Certain Little Town

Wiesław Antochów

My parents, my three siblings and I lived in the county town of Czortków in Tarnopol province, which belonged before the war to the Polish Republic. I was 12 years old in 1939 and had finished the fifth form in primary school. Although still a boy, I understood, and of course still remember, many things. Some events from those times have, however, grown hazy – especially people's names.

Three communities lived in Czortków and the surrounding country-side: Poles, Jews and Ruthenians (the term 'Ukrainians' was rather not used) coexisted, generally, in harmony and mutual respect ...

War! The Nazis had attacked Poland [1 September], and on Sunday, 17 September 1939, the 'liberating' Red Army of workers and peasants crossed the border. Soviet occupation had begun. Poles, Ruthenians (they began to be called Ukrainians) and especially the wealthy Jewish merchants had whatever they owned nationalized.

We had to leave our flat on ulica Zamkowa and move to 6 ulica Boczna, quite close to the City Courthouse (turned into barracks by the Soviets) and the prison. The days were uncertain and filled with anxiety and a terror no one had ever experienced before, and the nights were full of arrests and deportations to Siberia. There was no shortage of vodka or sunflower seeds, but it took a whole night of queuing to get a kilogram of sugar.

The very sight of amaranth-coloured NKVD [the Stalinist secret police] caps drove people out of their minds with fear. That fearful institution waited to snatch up anyone who dared to criticize the Soviet authorities, their alliance with the Nazi Germans or, God forbid, Stalin. The NKVD punished not only deeds, but also mere thoughts.

It was mostly Poles in varying conditions who were deported to Siberia in the most bitterly cold weather. The fact that a person was ill, feeble or had just been born, or that a woman was pregnant, concerned them not at all. The transports were waiting at the station. They regarded the Polish intelligentsia and Polish priests as their greatest enemies ...

On 22 June 1941, the Soviets were invaded by their greatest friends and allies, the Nazi Germans. The Soviets fled in panic, but on the night of 1 July 1941, before escaping from the city, the NKVD murdered dozens of priests and brothers at the Dominican friary. I shall return to that incident.

The Germans entered Czortków on July 6, 1941. The power of their mechanized war vehicles, the uniformed men riding them with their sleeves rolled up, and the joyous 'Heil!' on their lips all made me, a 14-year-old, wonder if there was a power anywhere that could defeat them.

The hatred of Ukrainian fascism for everything Polish or Jewish erupted immediately. Now the Jews were facing their Golgotha ...

The things I saw then often come back before my eyes at night.

That same day that the Germans arrived, people went straight to the prison to break down the locked doors in search of their relatives. They found the cells empty, but the cellars and dark spaces used for solitary confinement were packed to the ceilings with the corpses of murdered men and women, bound with barbed wire. Since it was the middle of the summer, everything had decayed and the stench was overwhelming. The NKVD had shot all their prisoners before escaping.

The Germans and Ukrainians rounded up a large group of Jewish men to remove the corpses the next day. There were macabre scenes. The Jews had to carry the corpses out with their bare hands and lay them by the wall in the prison courtyard. No one drove away the gawkers. The Jews were beaten with clubs, metal rods and anything else at hand until they passed out, and then they were splashed with buckets of water and it all started over again. No one had the courage to stand up for the victims.

There was a concrete rubbish tip in the prison yard. A dung-hill of the sort of raw sewage used for fertilizer was brought from a nearby estate and poured into the rubbish tip to the brim. The Jews were driven there and forced to jump in. The Nazis shot anyone who surfaced too soon. The 'Huns' and their lackeys had a jolly time.

The Soviets had erected a bronze statue of Stalin on a tall concrete plinth in the middle of town. The next day, the Germans herded about forty Jews there, gave them ropes and told them to pull Stalin down. The Jews put a noose around Stalin's neck and, after no small amount of work, managed to bring him crashing down. The ropes were then used to 'harness' the Jews. They had to drag 'their leader' through almost all the streets of the city, while being heaped with abuse and beaten. At the end of the day, they used rocks to reduce Stalin to a pile of rubble in the cemetery.

A Jewish physician lived with his wife and two children in his own villa near us on ulica Boczna. The older son, who was 20, had fled eastward with the Soviets. The younger son, 18, stayed at home with his parents. During the Soviet occupation and even before the war, this younger son had been great friends with a Ukrainian, the son of the Latin teacher at the Ukrainian secondary school, a respected and dignified gentleman. Now the fascist devil came out in the young Ukrainian. As some of my friends and I looked on, he began beating and kicking his Jewish friend in the middle of the street, calling him every dirty name in Ukrainian that he could think of. The Jewish boy tried to fend off the attack and asked for mercy in Polish and Ukrainian. His assailant was not yet finished: he ripped out a fence-post that had a nail sticking out of it and laid into his victim's legs. The blood spurted out. We could hear the boy's parents wailing in hopeless despair from their nearby home.

In this particular case, my memory jumps forward to March, 1944, when the Red Army marched back into Czortków.

The older of the two Jewish sons returned with the front. No trace remained of his parents and younger brother. No one knew where the Nazis had killed them – in Bełżec, Treblinka, Majdanek or Auschwitz, or during the liquidation of the Czortków ghetto by the Gestapo and their local collaborators. Knowing what would be in store for him now, the young Ukrainian had fled westward with the Nazis. His father, the Latin teacher – that respected and dignified gentleman – had remained in Czortków. The older of the Jewish boys never took revenge on him ...

A week or more had passed since the Nazis took Czortków, and the front line had moved far to the east.

I was sitting in the arbour of a nearby house with some friends when a terrifying sound shattered the quiet of a sunny day. It echoed down the streets, off the houses and into the garden. Birds took off and circled in the air. We ran into the street. We could see people running toward the prison wall, and we joined them. Ladders and crates had been propped against the wall. Onlookers stood atop the wall. While my friends made for the wall, I ducked into the courthouse and ran up the staircase two or three steps at a time to the landing on the second floor where a window overlooked the prison yard. My 14-year-old eyes saw the end of the world. A long, deep ditch had been dug in the left-hand corner of the yard. A tangled heap of bodies lay at the bottom of the ditch, and puddles of blood stained the earth.

About twenty young Germans stood in two ranks facing the ditch, rifles in their hands. To this day, I recall their dress. They wore fresh, green, well-tailored uniforms. Their high, polished boots gleamed and they wore small helmets. Behind them lay boxes of ammunition. An officer in black gloves, with a pistol in his belt, commanded this death detachment. Armed soldiers ringed the area.

More than a hundred Jewish men aged 18 to 40 stood against the wall across the courtyard, with their hands behind their heads.

The prison building blocked part of the courtyard from my vantage point, but the line continued where I could not see.

One Nazi counted off ten or more and led them to the edge of the ditch, facing the pit. The firing squad commander shrieked an order and the deadly volley rang out. It was all paralyzingly loud, in the Nazi manner.

Not all of the victims died, and not all of them fell into the ditch. Gripping his pistol, the 'execution' officer stepped carefully over the puddles and finished off the wounded right and left with gunshots.

Then an SS man counted off the next group, which marched to the edge of the ditch. The victims first had to throw the corpses in. Then it was their turn.

I watched three 'rounds' and could not take any more. It was the first time I had seen people being killed.

I ran home. What I told my parents shocked them. I fell ill.

People said that a special *Fliegendegestapo* unit (Gestapo flying squad) had come from Tarnopol for that execution. The Germans were doing everything they could to turn people against each other and foment hatred – in this case, against the Jews. They announced that the Jews had been executed for the murder of the Dominican friars by the NKVD.

It was also said that they shot more than 200 Jews that day. The county town of Czortków had a population of 22,000, of whom about 6,000 were Jewish ...

SPRING 1943

There was no longer any concealing the fact that the end was coming for the Jews. The Nazis made no secret of this. They mobilized the willing *Bahnschutz* (railway police) and kindred 'auxiliary' formations.

I remember a cold, cloudy day. I stood with other people on a balcony of the market building, watching. A big, old, covered lorry, painted a horrible shade of green, stood parked near ulica Mickiewicza and ulica Górny Koszar. Behind it, armed police, SS and Gestapo surrounded a smaller vehicle with a machine gun mounted on its roof.

Jews were hiding in the deep cellars of the buildings adjoining the ghetto, where barrels of beer and other goods requiring cold storage had been kept before the war and where leatherworkers and glaziers had had their shops. Gestapo men were trying to flush them out. Suddenly shots came from inside the cellars. The SS threw smoke- and tear-gas-grenades into the cellars. There were gunshots in the cellars, and then silence. I do not recall whether or not any of the Gestapo went inside.

In the meantime, a group of men and women of all ages was led out of the Jewish quarter with their hands clasped behind their heads. The Germans started loading them into the lorry – they had to keep their hands behind their heads all the time – pushing them so that they stood crowded tightly together.

To this day, I remember a handsome young Jewish woman with flaming hair, wearing only a dress, and the awful, piercing way she screamed and begged for her life in Polish and German: 'I haven't done anything wrong! I want to live! Don't kill me!' (Pardon this personal note: I did not shed a tear then, but I am weeping as I write this.) Not even the rifle butts could quiet her. Two SS men with rifles at the ready jumped onto the gate of the lorry and it drove off, escorted by the vehicle with the machine gun, to the place of annihilation.

During their occupation in 1939–41, the Soviets had begun building a military airfield far beyond the 'Upper Barracks' on the left side of the road to Jagielnica. They had excavated deep foundations for the hangars. Those foundations would be the graves of the Jews of Czortków. Our local Gestapo outdid themselves in perfidy: they made each Jew pay nine złoty at the *Judenrat* office for his or her own death – three bullets at three złoty apiece.

A lorry driver, who had promised the Gestapo not to 'see or hear anything', later reported that the whole 'operational terrain' was surrounded by gendarmes, SS men, *Bahnschutz*, German soldiers who had volunteered, 'Kripo' (criminal police) and their collaborators. The victims were shot on a makeshift wooden bridge placed across the ditch so that they would fall in. Seated on a stool, the Gestapo man Radke shot them with a Schmeisser. Our local Gestapo and gendarmes helped. They all took breaks to consume sandwiches and alcohol between 'deliveries' from the city.

Already accustomed to an atmosphere of terror, the city was paralyzed by the bestial liquidation of the residents of the Jewish quarter.

14. The Betrayed

Zyta Bachurska-Kruk

All this happened between 1943 and 1945 in a tiny hamlet between Włocławek and Choceń. Since I do not know the precise dates or the real names, I can only describe it in this simple way: the world of the Occupation, seen through the eyes of a little girl who was 8 in 1943.

She and I were rivals. Only three people knew. Or, really, two and a half. He, she and I. What he said to me backs this up. Not that he said much. But the things he came out with were sometimes sublime. They always went straight to my heart. My 8-year-old heart. I never forgot them. My mother and I had been deported to a 'colony' near a large village. My mother was a servant to the *'Bauer'* [farmer] woman who had taken over the big Gruszka estate as a farmer-'colonist'. Gruszka, his wife and three teenage sons had been kicked out of the house and lived in one of the outbuildings. They all worked as hired hands for that German woman from Bessarabia. As did my mother. Our little bungalow, one room with a kitchen, stood on the boundary of the farm. On the other side of the fence and beyond the orchard was another farm, run by a different *'Bauer'* woman. The Polish women called this woman on the other side of the property line 'Widow Rajfart'.

I was the only one who ever knew Widow Rajfart's first name. I knew it from him, from Józef. He told it to me one day when we were taking milk to the dairy in Śmiłowice. I mentioned 'that old Widow Rajfart'. He replied quickly and decisively, but still gently: 'Frau Lili isn't old at all'. And then he added hastily, 'But that's between the two of us, alright?' Why did he have to say that? He knew perfectly well that whatever passed between us was our secret. Like for instance the fact that he, Józef, was the love of my life.

He had arrived in our village in 1943, and the headman took him to the Rajfart woman, as a hired hand, because the Rajfart woman needed a good hand. Old Mr and Mrs Kubełkowskis were working at her place. As soon as Józef got there you could see the difference. The horses were brushed, the cows milked properly, and the farmyard was clean and looked bigger. 'All thanks to Józef', my mother said.

Józef was handsome. Tall, blue-eyed, with long legs and curly blond hair. He moved differently from the village boys his age. He had beautiful teeth, a wide smile, full lips. People used to look at those lips of his. I didn't know why then, but I do now, of course. Those lips were all that marked him as 'different'.

When Józef went to work for Frau Lili, she was already a widow. Her husband had died at the front. He was an officer. Everybody knew that, because before he died he used to visit sometimes for two or three days and then people would say, 'It's Christmas for the Rajfart woman because the captain's home'. They said this without malice, because Mrs Rajfart was a decent German. She said 'Gut Morgen' to people and never mistreated the old Kubełkowskis. She was different from the Bessarabian woman, who used to have Gruszka beaten regularly, once a month. An SS-man, a rugged blond with a neck like a bull, would make a special trip out from Choceń just for this purpose. After the SS-man's visits, Gruszka would wash himself in the trough by the well and the water turned red. The fat woman from Bessarabia looked down on Frau Lili. After all, Frau Lili was beautiful. She had red hair, green eyes and was as slender as a puff of smoke, as the peasant women used to say. For a German woman, she wasn't bad.

A month or so later, Józef came down from his loft in a lovely sapphire sweater. When I saw him in it, I fell in love. I ran circles around him all morning shouting for him to take me along when he went to Śmiłowice with the milk. And at last he said, 'Alright, hop on, little one!' I was sitting there beside him and I couldn't have been happier. I wolfed down the hunk of bread with butter that he gave me, and then I stared at him enraptured. That sweater! 'Is it from your mama, Józef?'

He looked at me sadly, didn't say anything for a moment, and then said, 'I haven't got a mama any more. I haven't got anybody close.' Looking at that sapphire sweater, I burst out crying. Józef let me cry. He didn't say anything but just sat there looking straight ahead.

From then on when Józef came out dressed in a new shirt or better trousers, I never asked if they were from his mama. I already knew I had a rival. Frau Lili only found out about me a little later. I think Józef told her about me, because I noticed that he started having nice things for me, too. An apple, some hard candy, a notebook for scribbling in, even a book with pictures to cut out. These were real treasures. But the greatest rarity of all were the pastries. As big as he was and as skimpy as I was, he always cut them in two even parts. I think he deliberately chewed his portion slowly.

As I grew, I noticed and understood more. I caught myself being jealous over Józef. He spent too much time in the house with Frau Lili. There was always something that needed doing inside! We had less time to spend together. That worried me. On the other hand, there was something to cheer me up – Józef wasn't so skinny anymore. His cheeks had stopped being sunken and his eyes were brighter. He smiled more. He would often talk to my mother. After these talks, Frau Lili paid my mother to look after her linen and clothes. My mother brought blouses, towels and sheets back from that work. In wartime, these were priceless gifts. The Rajfart woman really was a decent German.

When the January offensive started, the Germans organized the evacuation of their people. The Rajfart woman was all packed and sitting on her cart. My mother was cleaning up inside. Józef was doing something in the farmyard. He was watering the horses ... and then he finally took a big sheepskin over and wrapped it around Frau Lili's legs. At that moment, a motorcycle with a side-car drove through the gate. A soldier was on the motorcycle and an officer sat in the side-car. It was that red-faced SS-man. He started unhooking something from the side of his uniform as he got out. The Rajfart woman screamed and grabbed hold of my head, because I had been standing there watching jealously as Józef wrapped the sheepskin around her legs. When she pulled my head to her breast and cradled it there, a shot rang out. My mother ran out of the house like a madwoman. She pulled me away from the Rajfart woman and dragged me into the barn. Through a crack in the barn door we watched as the SS-man slapped Frau Lili across the face, snapped the whip at the horses and drove them out of the farmyard. The Rajfart woman sat like a pillar of salt next to that red-faced bull with the death's head on his cap. Józef lay in a puddle of blood by the well. People were starting to gather round. I didn't see how they carried Józef away. My mother wrapped a kerchief around my face and led me, crying, the opposite direction from the way the evacuees had gone. We were heading home.

Several days later, when Gruszka's farmyard was full of the Red Army, I saw my father coming down the road towards me. He was returning from a labour camp. Our whole family was together at last. Our war was over. People were going back to their homes and their farms, to their normal occupations.

We told father about Józef and the Rajfart woman. Father went to the village in the morning and didn't return until evening. He said that they hadn't been able to bury Józef in the cemetery. He was a Jew. There was no place to bury Jews in the village or the whole surrounding area. They were going to take him to Włocławek, where they were exhuming the bodies of other Jews who had been shot, and planning to bury them all together. Our Józef had been from Warsaw. His parents had been wealthy, educated people, and Józef had been a university student when the war broke out.

I do not know who it was that knew the secret of Józef's family. Nor do I know who had saved his life in Warsaw. Nor have I any idea what happened to Frau Lili. I don't know who informed on Józef. And I do not want to know. Will God, if he exists, forgive Judas?

15. What People did to People

Marianna Adameczek

Time heals all wounds. That may be true. It is nevertheless good that the time has come when all those things that were painful can be spoken about. The time of pain and silence has ended.

I was born in June 1930, in Charlejów, a village in Siedlce province. My parents, Herszko and Fajga Kurchand, had a lot of children. There were seven of us: five girls and two boys. I was the second youngest. My father worked at home as a cobbler and mother looked after us. We had nothing, but my parents tried to provide us with what we needed, especially in winter. Mother spent a little time selling fruit in the summer. I remember how she put up supplies for winter: flour, sugar, fruit.

My brothers and sisters were growing up. My oldest sister learned tailoring and went to work in Warsaw, where father had relatives. All the others graduated from the seven-form elementary school, except for one who dropped out in the fifth form and, of course, me.

I remember a few things from my childhood. I recall my father, for instance, admiringly. He had no schooling and could not even sign his own name, but he knew how to take measurements for a pair of shoes, to remember which piece of paper with the length and width on it belonged to whom, and how to make shoes that fit. Education was what he wanted most for us. He often talked about how hard it was for him without schooling.

When the war broke out, I was nine and ready to start the third form. I only went to school for a few more months. Jewish children were not allowed to attend anymore. My non-Jewish classmates kept going, and they graduated. This was hard for me to take, especially later. It was the Poles, I remember, who harassed us first. They prowled outside our house at night and broke our windows. There were four other Jewish families in our village. The Poles insulted us and even boycotted the Jewish shops. My parents knew things would get worse. My father had Polish friends. They made sure we had a place to hide from danger. That required a great sacrifice; a whole family had to put their lives on the line for us.

Before we hid with that family, the hoodlums prowling the village followed my three grown sisters around, looking for a chance to catch and rape them. I recall how the girls hid in the attic of some Poles they knew, and knitted sweaters. The situation kept deteriorating. Fearing the worst, my father decided to rent a flat near the police station in the town of Serokomla, so that he could call for help if need be. Father knew in his heart what lay ahead. He told mother to be careful and put what little we possessed in trustworthy hands. I helped my mother carry a bundle containing our blankets, pillows and sheets, along with some dresses and other clothes, to a neighbour's. I remember what she told them: 'If any of us survive, give it back. If not, it's yours.' That was the bitter truth.

We only spent about half a year in Serokomla, however. Life was harder and harder. A child, I had to look for work. I found a job in Hordzież, grazing cows. It didn't last long. Our first family tragedy occurred while I was there in Hordzież, grazing cows. It was like this. Two Germans were killed in Budziska. Revenge came quickly. The Germans decided to take the Jews from Serokomla as hostages. They surrounded the town. My mother, three of my sisters and one brother were at home. They were all caught and, together with the other Jews in town, shot near the ditches at the shooting range behind the (public) school building. (Polish eyewitnesses told me about the whole tragedy that had occurred in my absence.) They were all made to lie face down on the ground and had to wait about half an hour before being killed. They were killed with a volley of shots. Then the wounded were killed off and the corpses thrown into the ditches, where they were covered first with lime and then with soil.

What about the rest of the family? I survived because I was grazing cows a couple of kilometres away. My father was in Poznań, where he sewed shoes for a Pole, with my remaining brother and sister. I heard the terrible gunfire in the pasture where I was, and when some Polish children brought their livestock there, I asked if they knew what had happened. They replied truthfully, 'They're killing Jews'. I had no idea what to do next. Shortly afterwards, two little Jewish girls showed up. They had escaped by fleeing through the woods and across the fields. They told me exactly what had happened, and I knew that I had lost my mother and three of my sisters. My tears and sorrow were indescribable, but no greater than my terror for myself and the rest of the family. Was there anywhere left to go now? Terrified, weeping and helpless, the little Jewish girls told me how they had saved themselves. They had hidden in the priests' farmyard. The Germans came in and searched for them, but the girls were hidden under the straw beneath the cows' manger. When the shooting stopped, the girls came out and set off for Adamów, where they knew there were a lot of Jews. I decided to go with them.

A Jewish family took us in. We did not know their names. I stayed there for about two weeks. By the way, here is what happened to the other Jewish families from Charlejów. The local agronomist convened a village meeting at which it was decided to catch all the Jews from the four families there and take them to Serokomla in a rented cart for the purpose of killing them. This was done; some had to be lashed to the cart. Their arms and legs were tied, and my father witnessed this from a window; he was, as I have mentioned, in the village of Poznań. He was living near the road to Serokomla. As intended, all those taken to Serokomla died there. They were shot.

How did I find my father and the rest of the family? I decided to go back home. No one was there. I waited at night, hidden in the cellars or attics of Polish acquaintances. Some of them never knew I was there, and others gave me a slice of bread as I waited in terror for my father to come home. My father was doing the same thing. He would sneak out of the village of Poznań at night and look for me in the attics of Polish friends. He called my name in a hushed voice. And then one night, by a miracle, our two longing souls found each other. What joy – and what fear! Now what? Still, being under my father's care made me happy. It was hard for us to take the loss of my mother and sisters, but sometimes we just sat in silence for a long time, each mulling over what could happen any moment. Father went on sewing shoes to earn something to live on. So it was for half a year. He had various schemes. One day, he said, 'We're moving'. There was more fear as the four of us crept at night to the Adameczek family in Charlejów. At first, we hid under the straw in the barn. The family fed us. They sometimes brought our food in a dog dish, so that no one who happened to be passing by would suspect that anyone was hiding in their barn. There were days when we had more than enough bread, and others when we went both cold and hungry. Father did all he could. I have to admit that many Poles helped us. Somehow knowing that worse was to come, Father made shoes for many Poles without taking money. When things got bad he would go to these people at night. He always brought back something to eat and, sometimes, a change of clothes – there was no way for us to wash. It would be hard for anyone who did not live through it to imagine our life. This situation lasted for about a year.

It was fine summer weather. Father had found out where some other Jews were living and had contacted them. He decided that those other people would take all the children to the big forestry complex near Serokomla for a week or two so that we could get some fresh air. My father and brother spent a long time there. Then my sister and I went to a different hiding place in the forest. Our happiness lasted barely a week. The Germans descended on that forest from all sides. What a horrible sight – people fleeing, killed, moaning in agony. What was I, a lone child, to do? I will never forget the sight of my father, wounded, and begging for someone to finish him off as he held my dead sister's hand. Now what? How could I help? Where could I find help? Then there was a German and the terrifying shout, '*Halt!*' I ran, not looking back, as fast as my legs would carry me. In my fear I did not even feel it when I was wounded. I had run about six kilometres before I realized that no one was chasing me, and then I noticed the blood on my clothing and how badly my hand was torn up. It turned out that I was not far from death. When I reached the hiding place in Charlejów, my hand was all clotted with blood. They bandaged what was left of my hand, with the bones visible, and showed me a waiting dugout to hide in. It was terrible. There was no medicine and my hand would not heal. The stench cannot be described. I was not allowed to cry or moan, and the pain got worse by the day because of poisoning from the bullet. Every moment was precarious. What a thing for a child without a father or mother to live through! With the lack of food, the filth and the lack of medicines, the wound drew lice and insects, and I could not keep them off. Seeing the state I was in, the people taking care of me got hold of some grain alcohol to pour over the wound. I remember that as if it were yesterday.

The pain was easing when the day – or rather night – came when my one brother who had escaped from the roundup appeared before my eyes. Several days later, he returned with a Jewish girl named Dorka, about my age, who had also escaped. That was a year before liberation. At last, I had someone to talk to. My brother took the place of my father. He often visited us with food. I was happy to have at least a brother. He could sense that something bad was in the air. I will never forget how he told me: 'If it weren't for you, I would survive. But because of you, I'm going to die soon.' Why is fate so cruel? My one, last joy was soon snatched from me. Polish outlaws killed my 20-year-old brother. The pain and despair broke my heart. The necessity of keeping silent made it worse. I could cry only in my heart.

Time passed very slowly. My only goal in that later period was to find out how my brother had died. I spent a long time trying to find out who had killed him. Only many years later did I find out, and perhaps things will be better if I write about it now. Three of them had a hiding place in Serokomla. Someone must have informed on the farmer. The outlaws called themselves partisans. They went from house to house by day and by night, stealing whatever they could, livestock or grain. They must have got some sort of satisfaction out of killing people. When they heard shooting, my brother and his two companions tried to escape from their hiding place. One of them, a Jew from Suwałki, grabbed the hand of a child standing by the roadside, and the Polish outlaws decided not to shoot at him. He survived, and he is the eyewitness who told me the story when I finally located him. I could even give the names of those bandits today, but I will leave the judgement to God. All I will say is that some of them came from Krępa near Kock, and the others from Charlejów.

The people protecting us sometimes took us inside their house, where we played with their youngest child. There was a hiding place prepared for us in case anyone knocked unexpectedly at the door. Time passed very slowly. I can still hear the voice from the farmyard: 'Come out, girls. We're free.' I will never forget that moment. It was a beautiful sunny day. The sun blinded us. What a lovely world that was! With Dorka and several other Jews who had survived, I rode in a horse cart to Serokomla, in Siedlce province. There, we met another group of Jews. I saw the joyous outbursts of those reunited with a family member who had survived. I stood there like a fence-post. I had no one to run to, and no one was paying any attention to me. At that moment, I thought: 'What good is freedom to me?' The little groups soon departed, leaving Dorka and me standing there. We have no choice, I thought, and suggested that we go to my home village. Along the way, we stopped at the more prosperous farmers' and asked them if they needed farmhands. Two neighbours took us on to graze cows. My wealthy employer demanded that I work harder than I was able. It was a dawn-to-dusk job, but I had no choice. The work was too much for a frail girl, and it told on my health. I missed my family and it was hard to go on living. I had no one with whom to share experiences and worries beyond my years.

I lost my job in the late autumn for the simple reason that there would be nothing for me to do in the winter. My only friend Dorka had earlier been taken by her brother-in-law and since then I had not heard from her. (Someone told me that she is still alive, but I do not know where; I would very much like to get in touch with her.) I was left like a stray dog and had nothing to live on. Soon, however, I met good people. I went back to my own village and my own small and – worst of all – empty old home. I could not settle in there. A kindly old woman neighbour worried about me and took me in. She gave me food and shelter. I can even recall how she gave me a linen blouse. I did little odd jobs around her farm. That peasant woman became a mother to me. I had brought little from my own home; now she began teaching me to cook, do laundry, spin flax, knit and bake bread. These things were not easy for me, but I did them eagerly because I knew they would be useful later. It is hard to believe, but that is the way it was. Her son, ten years older than me, decided to take care of me and asked me to become his wife. I agreed, because I did not want to keep wandering alone through the world. With my family gone, I longed for someone to be close to.

People kept showing their desire to kill Jews until the end. A man from Lipiny near Wola Gułowska came to my husband before we were married and said, 'If you want, I'll take care of her and you'll be free'. Not until several years after the wedding did I learn about this.

The woman who had lovingly protected me became my mother. She helped every way she could. I was very grateful. I had barely turned 17 when I had my first child, a daughter. A child in the role of mother! I could never have made it without my mother-in-law. We were a poor family, and we needed more and more. I had neither clothing nor bedding. And now I had a child! I remembered where my mother had taken our clothing and bedding for safekeeping. Only now did I go there to ask them to give it back. They stated that they had nothing, but that if I insisted, there was a barrel outside with a little duck down in it, which I could use to make bedding for my baby. I did not take it, because the pain in my heart prevented me from speaking. I thought: If God has allowed me to survive after going through so much, then perhaps I can live without this. I felt all the more sorrowful when I saw their daughters in my sisters' dresses.

There was one more reason that I felt resentment towards that family for a long time. My father's brother had escaped to Israel during the war. Soon afterwards, he wrote one letter and then another to that family, asking if any of us had survived. I can only imagine what led them to reply that none of us was left alive. I was practically next door, and they did not tell me for ten years! I do not know how they can live with that feeling, especially since they knew well that I had no one. Their conscience must have bothered them only as they approached death. I was given my uncle's address right before the farmer died. What joy! We wrote back and forth many times! My uncle also sent me clothing and, from time to time, some money. This was a great joy, and also a great help. My uncle knew how badly off I was, and he also asked his relatives in France to help me from time to time.

I had such a strong desire to see my one surviving relative that I decided to go to Israel. I had taken out a loan and reserved an airline ticket when the Polish authorities refused me permission at the last moment. This was a real blow. Now we no longer even correspond. I believe that my uncle is dead, and his children cannot write in Polish.

Time went by, and there were children – seven of them, of whom three boys and three girls are still alive. I do not think I could have made it without my mother-in-law. My husband was also a good man and helped me a great deal. My mother-in-law was bedridden for many years and I took care of her until the end. She died when she was 84. Our marriage had many joyous moments and, as in all unions, some sad ones. The children grew up and needed to be educated. All of our income came from our seven-and-a-half-acre farm. Things were not easy when the children were in school. Thanks to the help of God, they all graduated from either secondary or vocational school. We have teachers, a forester, a cobbler-shoemaker, a machinist and a bricklayer in the family. They all have families of their own. I am alone again, my husband having died several years ago. 'Alone' does not mean lonely. I have a room of my own, an invalid's pension, and I am independent.

Now, with the children having flown the nest and my husband gone, the everyday burdens have been lifted and I could at last feel free. It would be wonderful if not for my illnesses. My childhood experiences not only left indelible memories, but they also ruined my health. The two years I spent in a hole in a cellar, the backbreaking work, the undernourishment and all the wrongs I suffered at the hands of other people took their toll. I have had two serious operations and a difficult course of cancer treatment. I also have a nervous disorder of the digestive system and bad rheumatism. I am constantly under a doctor's care and on a strict diet.

Aside from my parents, I lost my seven brothers and sisters during the war. I had seven children of my own and raised six of them. Today, my family has grown by fourteen grandchildren. I am not alone. I have someone to visit and someone to talk to.

When I saw your letter and the title, *Events That I Cannot Forget*, I thought: it is indeed impossible to forget. I would prefer, however, to return to those tragic memories as little as possible. Writing this has felt like opening an old wound. It is bad for my health, but I have done so thinking of my children and grandchildren. May such a history never repeat itself. How could people do such things to each other?

16. The Gravestone

Wanda Rylska

I can remember one night from 1942 or 1943. We happened then to find out about the presence of a crowd of Jews in the village square. They were waiting to leave for Bełżec. My mother carried bread and milk to them, and I went along to help her distribute it.

A black throng loomed in the darkness of the square, and those in the first ranks held out trembling hands for bread and tin cups of milk. There must have been more than a thousand of them. A German sentry cried, 'What's the use? *Das sind doch Juden!*' [They are, after all, Jews!].

We saw the endless procession of those miserable people on the road near the manor house the next morning. In the ditches, numerous corpses – those who had been unable to keep up – marked the route. I will never forget the sight.

Nor will I forget Chajka's children. I would like them to remain alive in this account, at least, even if they could not survive in reality. Let this be a tiny gravestone for them.

They looked like two lovely Jewish children from a painting by Murillo. They must have been around five and seven. They had escaped from the Bełżec death camp, after being transported there along with their grandmother and their infant brother from their village of Uhrynów. They had travelled alone, on foot, with no provisions, for about forty kilometres. They were on their way back to their mother. Chajka was a young, pretty Jewish woman from the lowest and poorest class of village Jews. Her husband looked like an old man, unshaven and dirty, in a long ragged coat. I have no idea how they made a living. Those beautiful children were her treasure.

One summer day at the height of the Holocaust killing, she came to us. After all, we were the owners of the village. Wasn't there something we could do to help? Did we have any advice? I will never forget her or her children. They had made it back from Bełżec on foot, and now what was she to do? If you can imagine, we only shrugged our shoulders and uttered a few words of sympathy. Today, such indifference is incomprehensible. Yet it is a sample of the mentality and realities of the borderlands in those times. In the days before our own catastrophe, the slaughter by Ukrainian bands and the exodus of all Polish families under

German escort, those poor children of Chajka's were only a small element of the great Apocalypse. Yet, at the ages of 5 and 7, they had covered those forty kilometres from one place of mortal danger to another. And then, somewhere, they surely died.

17. The Tram

Halina Drohocka

I can no longer remember exactly when it happened. It must have been the autumn of 1942. The tram was passing near the ghetto wall in Warsaw. I was sitting at a window and the wall was so close that it seemed I could have touched it if the window had been open. As the tram began to slow for a stop, I was looking at the wall and the gendarmes who stood every few metres. There were openings in the wall at ground level and I do not know what they were for, although they may have served to let water out when it rained. The tram stopped opposite one of those openings. And then I saw a black, fuzzy shape moving in the hole. A moment later a small boy, perhaps 5 years old, emerged holding an empty sack. Standing up and preparing to set off, he did not notice in his haste that he was right next to a gendarme, and he practically tripped over the gendarme's feet. The German grabbed him by the back of the neck, threw him to the ground, and began stamping on him. I could see his hobnailed boot crushing the boy's head. He was literally trampling the boy into the ground. I heard no scream, and since the window was closed I do not even know if the boy managed to scream. All was silent in the tramcar. No one made a sound. Suddenly, the woman sitting next to me, one of those simple peasant women with a basket full of food that she must have been carrying to market, began screaming and cursing hysterically. Someone tried to calm her down. The tram moved away from the stop.

18. The Scream that goes On and On

Józef Andrzej Kaja

Turobin, which had once been a city and had declined before the war into a township, numbered about 2,000 inhabitants during the Nazi occupation. At least half were Jewish. They had lived in Turobin for centuries. They were concentrated in the centre of town; all the streets around the market place were Jewish ...

During the early years of the occupation, their situation was tolerable. They were forbidden to move or travel, and high taxes were imposed on craftsmen and merchants. This soon changed. In 1940, the Germans began introducing a whole system of measures that grew increasingly oppressive. Next to the Polish 'blue police' station, they set up a gendarmerie station commanded by *Wachmeister* Ulmann, a fanatical Nazi henchman with the deaths of many Jews and many Poles on his conscience. He took particular delight in humiliating people. One day, for instance, he got his boots muddy while crossing the road. He beckoned to two Jews with his finger. He commanded one of them to get down on all fours. He put his feet on this man's back while making the second one shine them with his cap. Ulmann 'paid' each of them with a hard kick and hearty laughter. I saw similar scenes often. Ulmann also demanded that everyone bow to him and stay out of his way. Every passer-by, Jewish or Polish, had to remove his hat and say, '*Guten Tag*' [Good Morning]. Anyone who failed to do so got a whipping with Ulmann's riding crop, or a slap across the face (Ulmann always wore gloves). There was a whole masquerade: he would call the 'impolite' passer-by to him, shout '*Mütze ab!*' [Tip your hat!] and make the transgressor walk past and perform the proper greeting three times. Then came the slap or the whipping and a kick in the pants. This was Commandant Ulmann's way of amusing himself. He was the terror of the whole township.

The first harsh measure against the Jews was the rounding up of healthy young men, and women as well, for special local work brigades. Later, such details were also sent elsewhere, including Izbica ...

I saw the following scene: I was sitting on the bank of the River Por with a fishing rod when two young Jews came running across the meadow. A German gendarme was chasing them, firing his automatic pistol on the run. I hid in the reeds on the bank. The gendarme shot one of the young men dead as he ran, and wounded the other. The latter fell to the ground, writhing in pain. The gendarme stood over him and shot him at point-blank range to finish him off. The gendarme walked back towards town, whistling as if he had had a pleasant morning stroll.

I also recall a fine day in May of 1942. This was the weekly market day, when the streets around the market place were always packed with Jewish traders. Suddenly, shots rang out from several spots around the square from SS men in black uniforms, with Ulmann and his gendarmes joining in. I also saw a civilian firing near me as I stood in front of a big white house on a corner of the square. The Nazis were shooting with pistols at close range and only at the Jews, who were easy to identify because of their dress and yarmulkes. The Germans calmly picked them off, one by one, as if it were a shooting gallery. There was panic and shouting mixed with the groans of the victims. People were running in all directions, bumping into each other and falling down. The Germans kept on shooting. When the square and the adjacent streets were empty, they began 'pacifying' the Jewish quarter. They dragged men, women and children, old people and infants, out of the houses. They shoved the people into ground-floor rooms or closed gateways, and then lobbed in bundles of hand grenades which blew the victims to bits. The town shook with the explosions. By then I was sitting at home, listening in fear and unable to tell what it all meant. Clouds of smoke rose over the centre of town. The Germans had set several homes alight. They plundered and profaned the landmark synagogue, killing all those who had sheltered inside. The bloody pacification continued late into the afternoon. As evening fell, the SS and Gestapo drove off to Krasnystaw, having ordered the local authorities to bury the dead and clean up the town during the night, so that by the next morning there would be no sign of what had transpired.

Now came the second part of the tragedy. The Jews who had survived the pogrom came out into the square and the nearby streets. There was a great, blood-curdling groan, a piercing collective scream of despair, which echoed throughout the town. None of the residents of Turobin could help hearing it, and they froze in dread and heart-breaking sympathy. The cacophony of groans was broken by penetrating screams in Yiddish: '*Ay vay gevalt! Ay vay tatele, mamele! Ay vay gevalt!*' [Help, father, mother, help!] I shall never forget that scream of despair as long as I live. I cannot forget it, because it goes on and on.

19. Apollo the Beast

Maria Majewska

The scene which I shall describe here took place in a small town called Łosice in Podlasie. I lived there on ulica Bialska with my parents and brother from 1932 to 1945. My father, a professional soldier, had been seconded from the garrison in Siedlce to Łosice, where he ran the Riflemen youth organization.

We spent the whole Occupation in Łosice. I was 10 when the war started. Several thousand of the inhabitants of Łosice were of Jewish origin. I remember hearing the figure of five thousand bandied about in my childhood (out of a total population of seven thousand). There was grinding poverty. In order to provide us with milk, my father kept a couple of goats. I grazed them on the common near the pre-war fire brigade building. Nearby, 200 or 250 metres away, stood the Jewish cemetery. The common that I have mentioned was the site for the execution of partisans. One very hot day, as I recall it, in what must have been the summer of 1942 (the macabre liquidation of the Łosice ghetto had already occurred), a one-horse cart escorted by Łosice gendarmes on motorcycles drove onto the common. The cart driver was ordered to throw down his load. I was standing quite near. It was a girl, so badly beaten that she could not stand on her own two feet. She was Jewish. One of the gendarmes, a very handsome young man, proceeded to torment that still-living girl by stamping on her with his army boots and beating her with a whip. Blood flowed from her nose and mouth. When the gendarme (whose name I recall to this day) had had enough of brutalizing this defenceless creature, he shot her dead. How did the gendarme react to my presence? At first, he might not have noticed me. I was grazing the goat on a knoll and the scene that I cannot forget was being played out on the flat ground below. I can see that flat ground, I can see the knoll, I remember the vegetation. I remember that bloody, helpless shred of a human body. I saw it all because I was petrified with fear. I could not move, either to walk away or to flee. I could not go looking for the goat that nourished us. With that scene in my mind, I became acutely conscious of what it means to be petrified with fear. There were many other moments of danger, but I do not think of them so often. Perhaps I cannot forget that scene on the common because the murder was committed by a youth as beautiful as Apollo. He trampled the body of the girl, or young woman, with his hobnailed boot and then shot her as she lay tormented and abused. I was petrified with fear and terror and, as a child, could not understand – Why? Why did that young, beautiful boy do it? Now I know why.

20. It Could Have Been Any of Us

Zdzisław Morawski

I was walking along ulica Nowy Świat in Warsaw in the spring of 1942. We were living in the country and I had come to town for one day on a lorry full of apples. I was 15 years old. As always, the bustling street fascinated me. There was heavy pedestrian traffic on the pavements and rickshaws – the taxis of the period – pedalled through the warm afternoon sunshine. From time to time, a German car passed.

A miserable-looking boy of about 7 years old tramped along beside me. He was wearing cut-off trousers, a dirty checked flannel shirt and canvas shoes on his bare, stick-like legs. As he passed me I noticed that the feverish, shiny eyes sunken deep in his pale face were full of such fear that he could only be a Jewish child. Blades of grass or straw clung to his tousled black hair and he was carrying a cloth mottled with greasy stains.

Now and then one of the pedestrians tried to stop him. An old lady in a straw hat with a bouquet of artificial flowers even grabbed at his hand, trying to see if there was money in his sack. The boy looked at her in terror. His face became a mask of pain and he jerked his hand away from her.

He trotted ahead.

Fifty paces in front of me, almost at the intersection with Chmielna, stood three well-fed German military gendarmes in helmets and brand-new green uniforms. They seemed to have materialized out of thin air. They wore automatic pistols at an angle on yellow leather straps.

The boy stopped before them, paralyzed. As if it could protect him, he held up his filthy sack at chest height, with his hands clenched in little fists. His back heaved as he gasped for breath.

'*Sind Sie Jude?*' [Are you a Jew?], asked one of the gendarmes with relish.

The boy said nothing.

A second gendarme caught hold of the boy's chin, twisted his face upward, and gazed at it in satisfaction.

'*Ja, ja, verfluchte Jude*' [Yes, yes, damned Jew], he said in a booming voice.

The old lady in the straw hat ran to the child, who had begun to shake. She took him by the hand. 'Say that you're a Pole. Cross yourself and recite the Our Father.'

The boy crossed himself awkwardly and began mumbling something that sounded vaguely like a prayer.

The gendarme pushed the old lady away and proclaimed again, '*Das ist ein Jude, nicht wahr?*' [He's a Jew, isn't he?]. The other two nodded in agreement.

They stood conferring for a moment. One of them took the little boy's hand. The one in the middle suddenly chuckled in obvious pleasure at an idea that had just come into his head. He stepped into the street and started flagging down passing rickshaws. He gestured to one of the rickshaw drivers and pointed at the round iron manhole cover. 'Come on, move! Open it up!' he said in comprehensible Polish.

The rickshaw driver tugged at the heavy cover and then said sheepishly that he could not budge it.

'Can't, can't', mocked the gendarme and aimed a powerful kick at the rickshaw driver. The driver crouched low and pulled at the cover with hands that were already filthy. He finally succeeded in shifting it a bit to one side. Then he dragged it clear and the black opening yawned in the street.

The gendarme who had been holding the boy by the hand now grabbed the scruff of his neck, or rather the collar of his flannel shirt, and lifted him off the ground. The child hung limply, as if he were already a corpse. The gendarme approached the opening, peered in as if checking to see that it was deep enough, and then dropped the little boy in. He drew his pistol, stuck the barrel into the manhole, and pulled the trigger. One shot rang out.

The gendarme gestured to the petrified rickshaw drivers, pointing at one of them, and at the manhole cover. The driver quickly dragged it back into place.

Then the three gendarmes looked around at the bystanders and began roaring, as only they could, '*Ruhe, ruhe*' [quiet, quiet] – Move along! They were still shouting as they strode into the crowd, in step, shoulder to shoulder.

The people scattered like a flock of pigeons when someone throws a stone among them.

The old lady in the straw hat cried half to herself and half to those around her, as the tears ran down her face, 'It could have been any of us, any of us, but not that child!'

A man passing me said to the woman on his arm, 'We're all abject, all of us! Because we couldn't do anything as we watched that happen, completely helpless.'

P.S. The boy who had been thrown down the manhole survived. After the Germans left, someone climbed down another manhole on ulica Foksal. The bullet had missed and the boy was alive. Someone took him home. Could he have survived the war? Could he still be alive?

21. A Game

Ryszard Sobol

A beautiful and sunny but cold November day dawned in 1942, another grim day of the occupation. The unseasonably early frost troubled the grown-ups, but for our band of 10-to-12-year-olds it represented a delightful occasion for playing on the ice. I set out with several playmates for a pond about 100 metres from the farm buildings. We intended to slide on its frozen surface.

Unfortunately, the ice was too thin for sliding. It bowed and shook dangerously under our weight. We decided not to risk getting wet or facing the consequences with our parents. On our way home, we noticed three figures approaching our village of Grabniak out of the woods, from the direction of Sobolew.

We went close enough to see that they were Jews from the Sobolew ghetto. There was such famine there that the inhabitants frequently sneaked out to seek food at farmhouses. We could tell from the way they acted that these were three poor Jews. They went begging from farmhouse to farmhouse. The Poles offered them what they could – a few potatoes here, a little bread or lard there. It seemed to be a family, with a father about 50, a daughter about 13, and a son about my age, 10. They had the misfortune, as they reached the third farmhouse, to encounter a group of Germans coming back from a visit to the German owner, Mrs Berger. These were gendarmes from the police station in Sobolew, and had come in a cart with a Polish driver. The four Germans had, of course, an Alsatian dog. They ordered the driver to stop the horses. Then they got out and walked up to the Jews, who were petrified with dread. The drama began. The Germans were a little drunk. They unshouldered their rifles and ordered the Jews to walk straight ahead. I was standing nearby; the presence of an observer must not have bothered them because they did not order me away. I thought that the worst possible thing was going to happen: the Jews were going to be shot on the spot. However, this did not happen. The Germans had noticed the unfortunate pond where we had intended to go sliding, and they marched the Jews towards it. They ordered the three of them to walk out onto the ice. The ice could not bear their weight. It broke and they fell through into the water that came up above their waists. The Germans stood around the pond doubled over with laughter at the sight of the Jews in the water. It was a small pond, about ten metres by fifteen. The Jews wanted to get out of the freezing water, but every time they approached the bank, the Germans lashed them with their leather whips across their wet backs, or turned the dog on them. This game went on for about fifteen minutes. Then they ordered the Jews out of the pond and, keeping their rifles levelled, walked them to the edge of the woods about 100 metres from the village. On emerging from the pond, the Jews had thrown themselves at their tormenters' feet and begged for their lives. The Germans kicked them away, shouting '*Weg! Weg!*' [Away! Away!] and pointing in the direction of the woods. As they walked, the Jews kept turning around to beg for mercy. It seemed they would be shot any second. However, this did not happen. The closer the Jews got to the woods, the slower the Germans walked. As soon as they reached the trees, the Jews ducked into the underbrush. The Germans never fired. The drama was over. The Germans went back to their cart, satisfied at having inflicted the misery of immersion in the water with the temperature at five degrees below zero. They returned to their gendarmerie station in Sobolew.

22. They Were Handsome

Barbara Swinarska

The *Tygodnik Żydowski* [Jewish Weekly] carries information in its issue dated 18 December 1931 about the opening of a new photographic firm in Tarnów. 'Have your photographs taken at the new Rembrandt Photographers, 2 Sobieskiego Square (across from town hall). Open daily from nine until seven in the evening. Attention: Photographs taken in the evening by electric light.'

When Rembrandt opened his doors in 1931, he did not know that ten years, nine months and two days of his life remained, or that his life would end in the courtyard of the house at 2 Sobieskiego Square at two o'clock in the afternoon on 30 September 1942.

How do I know all this? Because I had an identification-card picture taken there on 28 September 1942. I had just got my second job of the occupation and needed a new *Ausweis* ...

I still have that photograph today, with the date written on the back: 30 September 1942. A provincial girl in a white jacket.

The second great *Aktion* against the Jews of Tarnów had begun on 10 September. The *Bekanntmachung* [notices] had been posted several days earlier. In two languages, of course.

Point Three of the *Bekanntmachung* read: 'Every Pole who takes in or shelters a Jew during the *Aktion* will be shot.'

Suitcases, bundles, bags, baskets and people were left lying on the street after each *Aktion*.

I was supposed to pick up my photograph at Rembrandt on 30 September. My friend Wanda Dąbrowska came with me. She also had also had her photograph taken, since she had become a trunk-call telephone operator at the Post Office (very useful to the Resistance later). The Rembrandt firm was in a courtyard annex, at the end of a long passage through the building. We found the door open. Photographs lay on the counter and the drawers were open. It looked as if Rembrandt had stepped outside for a moment. We waited. A woman leaned out of a window overlooking the courtyard and said, 'He's over there'. She pointed around the corner of the annex. Rembrandt was lying on the cobblestones with which the courtyard was paved. But it was half of Rembrandt. Because he had only half his head. It was the first time I had ever seen human brains so close-up. The brains were stretched out over two metres of the cobblestones. Pinkish-yellow, they reminded me of a dog's tapeworm. Rembrandt had only a mouth and nostrils. One ear lay nearby. It was homeless, but also autonomous. I looked at that ear and those brains. And then a fly suddenly entered Rembrandt's open mouth. The fat, meaty fly, with its silvery rainbow colours, looked around, choosing a path to walk across the brains. It stopped and picked with its feelers at that pulpy mass, moved backwards, then returned. It had taken a taste, and liked it.

I suddenly ran. Wanda was right behind me. Why? After all, I had already seen so many corpses. I stopped at the end of the passage and pressed myself against the wall. It was sweltering outside, and yet here it was so cool. That coolness suddenly became something palpable, coalescing into one great chill, one object. It was somewhere behind my back. It was an automatic pistol, and it was very cold. A *Rottenführer* [low rank SS officer] from the *Einsatzkommando* had taken hold of me, and he was saying, '*Nicht weinen, Kind*' – Don't cry, child.

I still spoke German badly, but managed to dredge up out of my memory the phrase, '*Ich weine nicht, ich staune*' – I'm not crying, I'm just surprised. It was true. I was not crying, just horrifyingly bewildered ....

'My' *Rottenführer* was a boy of 21 or 22. Very handsome. But there was nothing strange about his being handsome. They were all handsome. That was part of the psychological warfare. Tall, handsome, sometimes even beautiful, they walked around the 'Aryan' part of town (the 'non-Aryan' part was sealed off during each *Aktion*). They were at ease and even, as people say today, 'laid back', idle and indifferent and, one might even say, polite. But they were also unapproachable. Their objective was to fill us with respect, fear, admiration, a sense of something beyond the material, of an unbridgeable distance. We were supposed to feel respect and admiration for the mission, the task, the work that had been entrusted to them. The Sacred Task. They were supposed to instil in the 'Aryans' a feeling of superiority to the people now kneeling in the town square with their hands raised over their heads. Superior for now, but awaiting their obvious fate.

PART THREE

CHILDREN OF THE SHOAH

Introduction

The stories of the suffering of children are particularly poignant as are those of the intensity of childhood friendships which endure through difficult circumstances and mark individuals for the rest of their lives. Many Jewish children were saved by non-Jewish Poles, despite the threat to the families of the latter. One also sees the instinctive sense of humanity which is present in many of the Polish children, which is unsullied by prejudices of ideology, race or religion. Children became significant smugglers of food into the ghetto, mainly because it was easier for them to slip through the barriers.

In account 26, the simple curiosity of the Polish children, who were able to approach the ghetto wall and view the sorry state of the Jewish children on the other side, led to compassion. Given the opportunity, they would throw sweets and biscuits towards the ghetto, and the Jewish children would crawl through the barbed wire to pick them up. A poignant image here is that in their brief moments of communication, the Jewish children taught Yiddish songs to the Polish ones.

Łucja Kreszczyńska recounts how the pain of the loss of Fajga, her childhood friend who had 'such tact, practical wisdom, gentility and intelligence', and who taught her so much, continues to haunt her (27). Jerzy (Jehuda-Ber) Flajszman (23), like many others, prematurely worldly because of his precarious experience in the Łódź Ghetto, describes how a strong Jewish mother determinedly keeps her family together as long as possible.

As a boy, Zdzisław Rozbicki (31) experienced the horrors of the German torture and murder of the Jews in his town, Sokołów Podlaski, which traumatized him. One memorable event, which seared itself on his memory, was of incidental violence, the casual slaughter of a Jewish girl by a German soldier working at a field hospital for wounded soldiers, accompanied by a nurse. After the murder, the 'pair of smiling lovers ... chatted pleasantly as they walked back towards the hospital'.

A Jewish boy, perhaps 8 or 9 years old, Bronisław Tzur-Cyngiser (32) witnesses not only German Police, but also Polish 'blue police', and firemen participating in the destruction of the Przysucha ghetto, but also experiences the generosity of Poles. For the 9-year-old Hanna Wojciechowska (33) the trickle of blood from a lorry transporting Jews away from the town, conveys to her the full horror of what is happening.

Anna Maria Leska (29) reflects that because she had fair hair, blue eyes and Polish parents, she was allowed to live while others were murdered. 'Is there anything I can do about that?', she asks, the helpless guilt of the survivor.

23. From Łódź to Auschwitz

Jerzy (Jehuda-Ber) Flajszman

In March 1940, not yet 13, I saw people being killed for the first time in my life. I saw how they were beaten and kicked, with the use of wooden clubs and hobnailed boots, as they lay on the cobblestones of ulica Franciszkańska in Łódź, trying to get away. It was a band of Germans in brown uniforms with swastikas on their arms (or perhaps they were freshly-minted *Volksdeutsche* from Łódź) who carried out the assault. They beat and kicked the people who lay where they had fallen. In the belly, over the head, with clubs across their legs, on their heads …

I was standing at a third-floor window in Nachman Strykowski's flat. Next to me stood his son, Szmulek, my dear friend from the courtyard and from school. The windows of that gloomy house overlooked the intersection of ulica Franciszka, ulica Smugowa and ulica Jerozolimska. A crude gate separating the newly-established Łódź ghetto from the rest of the city stood at that intersection. One of the trams that was still running had just arrived there, crowded with Jews expelled from the city to the ghetto. The screaming gang of Nazis had appeared suddenly. '*Juden raus, schnell, schnell, raus, raus!*' [Jews, get out, quick, quick, out, out!] They dragged the Jews off the tram and began assaulting them. They beat and kicked them wherever they found an opportunity, attacking everyone who did not manage to run to the gate. The victims shielded their heads with their arms or lay in puddles of blood. Their assailants beat them, kicked them and smashed them with clubs.

We stood frozen and terrified at the window. At one point, Szmulek's father stroked my head and said softly, 'Your father did the wise thing by escaping to Russia while there was still time. It's a shame I didn't go with him. All the men are going to die here.'

'The Germans are a civilized nation. There's a war on, so it's natural for them to intern all the men. But they will not do anything to the women and old people. So what if they're Jews? That's only propaganda.' This is the sort of thing our neighbours in that building told each other. This is the sort of thing people told each other everywhere.

My mother, Chawa Flajszman *née* Diament, was an energetic woman. She had worked at Pan Profesorski's hosiery factory on ulica Pomorska since she was a young girl. She never imposed her opinions on anyone, but if asked, she advised following the dictates of common sense. Many people, mostly her female co-workers, came to ask her advice in women's matters. Now she grew stubborn. I had never before seen her so obstinate and uncompromising. 'Symcha', she told my father, 'today I'm going to pack your suitcase, and tomorrow you leave for Siedlce' – we had an aunt and her family living there – 'and from there, you go to Białystok and then on to Russia. When you're in Russia, just keep going. When things quiet down here, I'll come to you with the children.' And so my father's wisdom was my mother's wisdom. It consisted of the fact that he listened to her. But my mother was wrong. Things didn't quiet down here.

BEYOND THE WIRE

We referred to the fence that kept us shut up in the ghetto as 'the wire'. People said 'beyond the wire' (in other words, on the 'Aryan side') or 'on the wire' (someone was killed 'on the wire'), and so on. The wire ran along the left side of the street from ulica Północna, along ulica Franciszkańska and down the pavement to Smugowa, where it turned the corner and extended as far as number 14, closing off our route to the fields and meadows that smelled so beautiful in the springtime. My house stood about twenty metres from the wire on the corner. Armed sentries kept watch day and night at the gate of the ghetto, which no longer served any purpose since it was permanently locked. They often used their rifles. Mostly it was children playing in ulica Jerozolimska and ulica Franciszkańska who were killed. The hunting stopped after a while, but people were afraid to be seen by a German even at a distance. I worked at 12 ulica Smugowa. I never went to work or came home along the wire, even though it was just a few steps that way. Instead, I took the round-about way through the courtyard of the Mariavite Sisters' convent on Franciszkańska (the building had housed a school when the ghetto was being set up) and the courtyard to Świętego Jakuba, or sometimes Wolborska, before arriving at the gate of 8 Jerozolimska, which faced 9 Jerozolimska. It took half a minute to cross the street. Coming home from the night shift at six in the morning was horrifying. There on the corner stood a thug with a rifle, and the fact that my life depended on his whim made me numb with fear. So I stood in the entrance of 8 Jerozolimska waiting for the German to turn around, go off to the side or perhaps go into the guard post (a cheerful pre-war dive that now served these criminals). But he would not move. He stood staring, as if he was waiting for me. He stood there contented, no doubt absorbed in thoughts of how good he had it here instead of at the front, as long as he had to watch out for me, the deadly enemy of Germany and German culture. I was full of dread because I had seen children's bodies riddled with bullets. My mother wondered why I didn't come straight home from work. But she never asked about anything. I once saw her across the street, in the entrance to our building. She was waiting there to give me courage by means of her presence. She waited with me until the German moved, so that I could dash across the street. She was ten or fifteen metres away, but it seemed like a whole world.

THE LIQUIDATION OF THE GHETTO

They are liquidating the Łódź ghetto. They lead us to a train siding in Marysin. Hurry up – 'Schnell, schnell, schnell!!' They load us into the cattle trucks. Everybody gets bread for the journey. My sister and I immediately hand our portions to our mother. That was what we always did in the ghetto. Then she rations it out to us in small amounts so that it lasts longer. By now, this habit has become natural to us. Perhaps it has saved us from degenerating into the sort of wildness we have seen in our neighbours, who fall into rages over a slice of bread, a spoonful of soup, a bit of potato peel. Even at our hungriest, we never imagined that things could be otherwise. Mother gave us our minimal portions, full stop. The fact that she did not consume all of her own starvation ration, but instead pared off some extra bread for me or sometimes for my sister, also seemed totally natural. I never thought about it. That was the way things were. We are crowded onto the wooden floors of the trucks. After many hours, the train finally moves. We are going. We do not know where. I am thirsty. The train thumps along all night. It is cold. It stinks horribly. People are dead on their feet. It is quiet. No one even moans. There is nowhere to urinate or defecate no matter how badly one wants to. The train thumps along the tracks all night. It is my first train ride. I will never like trains. I will avoid them whenever I can. Even today, I have never been able to get used to trains.

They chase us out of the cars in diabolical haste and separate us. Women and children, of whom there were very few in this transport from Łódź, to the left. A man swollen from hunger stands beside me. There are Germans and all sorts of capos, and 'Canadians' [the 'Kanada' work unit sorted the looted Jewish possessions for use by the Germans]. They inform us succinctly, 'And you gentlemen will all go to heaven through that chimney', pointing at the smoking camp chimney. 'Give us what you've got hidden. Nothing will ever be of any use to you any more.' In the meantime, the Germans are directing some people to the right and others to the left. The swollen man tells me, 'You, son, are young. If God grants that you live, remember what you've seen here. This is the face of fascism. This is fascism. Remember.' I remember.

24. 'My Little Lamb ...'

Gizela Fudem

This is supposed to be about a scene I cannot forget. And what if it isn't a scene, but only a sound? A voice and two words repeated over and over. How can I describe it so as to convey even a part of what cannot be forgotten after so many years?

There was no visible scene to accompany the sound. The broken-hearted, wailing calls came from the street. Along with a hundred other people, I was walled up in a dark, tiny cellar under a bakery. The bakery was open. It was on ulica Folwarczna in the Tarnów ghetto. We were in total darkness because no one had an electric torch. There were candles, but matches went out instantly from the lack of oxygen. That voice rang out at dawn, or perhaps it was already morning: the voice of a mother grieving for the child taken from her in that 'action'.

We had gone into the cellar when it became known that an 'action' was imminent. Almost all the tenants of that crowded house – two or three families to each flat – were there, and others as well, relatives or friends of tenants. A few people, who at that moment happened to have the 'right to live' granted by stamps that might be invalid the next day, had stayed outside. Before leaving for work that morning, one of them had walled up the lone remaining hole through which we had crawled into the cellar and then heaped coal against the fresh brickwork. Most of us wore two or three layers of clothing; we wore whatever we had, since the end of the summer of 1942 was approaching and if they deported us they would not permit us to carry anything.

How long had it lasted? Twenty hours? More? People had begun fainting after the first hour. We soon lost track of time. We were suffocating. I crouched in the corner next to my sister. The wall was hot from the bakery oven. Some people had had the foresight to bring water, but how could they give it to those who needed it, in that darkness where no one could cry out? Pan Werner was of some help. He was a German Jew who had been expelled to Poland before the war. His forebears came from there, and his 'Aryan' wife, a plump blond, was with us. Their son Horst, tall and fair with the ideal Nordic handsomeness of a matinee idol, was somewhere outside the ghetto (later, he managed to get his mother out). Finding himself in the middle of the cellar, Pan Werner had shown that sense of order peculiar to Germans and divided the space into sectors with numbers that he ordered us to remember. When someone fainted, those nearby whispered the number and the water bottle was passed in the right direction.

Twice, we had heard the footsteps of hobnailed boots and conversations in German. They had been above us once and in the neighbouring cellar the second time. The children, having been tranquilized with Luminal, did not cry.

Then there was a commotion in the street, some sort of loud noises, until at last an endless silence fell. Then finally, somewhere around dawn, there was that wailing voice right nearby, but outside. Two words repeated over and over. The voice moved off, then came closer again, as if the woman were circling the house: '*Mayn shayfele, mayn shayfele* ...' [Yiddish – my little lamb].

No one had ever called me that. On those rare occasions when my parents spoke tenderly to me, they used my nickname, perhaps adding 'dear'. That woman might not have spoken in such a way to her child either, if she had still had her child.

When we got out of the cellar the daylight blinded us, our clothing reeked of sweat and we staggered around from the surfeit of air. My mother and little brother, who had found themselves by accident in a different shelter, had also survived this time.

I remember the voice of that woman to this day.

Is it worth telling about such things? How many mothers were crying for their children then? How many thousands had lost them and would go on missing them for those fifty years that have passed since then?

PANI RAPAPORT

When we had to move again as the area of the ghetto was reduced, the five of us, my parents and we three children, got the second room in a walk-through row on the second floor of a house on ulica Folwarczna, facing the *Judenrat*. There were two families in the first room: the Franks with their son and, on the other side of the wardrobe, Pani [Mrs] Rapaport with her two daughters and her granddaughter. Yes, she was one of the Rapaports from Bielsko [textile factories' owners]. A very distinguished lady and two thriving, grown daughters. The younger was 17 but looked older. The three year old daughter was the child of Pani Rapaport's son, who had found himself on the Soviet side along with his wife. They had been in Lwów first, then they had supposedly been seen in Vilna, and then the trail had grown cold. It seemed to us that the daughters knew something which they were keeping from their mother.

The little girl's grandmother and two aunts adored her. She brought some joy into the life we were forced to share. I can still remember her comic songs: 'And now, ladies and gentlemen, Funia Neuman from Pińczew will recite and sing ...'

Although she was a veteran of wandering through several cities, Pani R. struck us as a wealthy woman who looked after herself. She still had fashionable clothes and lingerie, and seemed proud and aloof. She carried herself with graciousness and gave the impression of benefiting from certain connections in the *Judenrat*.

In August 1942 there was another 'action', euphemistically referred to as a deportation. How it was that Pani R. found herself with us in a bunker packed full of people while both her daughters were outside on the square, I cannot recall. There were still those who believed that the people who assembled on the square would be sent off to work. On the other hand, hiding in a bunker with a small child was next to impossible. The others would never agree; the child might burst out crying and betray the hiding place. The Luminal that children were given in small doses had only a short-term effect. Larger doses could cause death, as had happened nearby.

I remember that Pani R., of course unaware of the possible consequences, had originally insisted that the younger of her daughters take her granddaughter. The girl had balked: no one would believe that it was her child. As if that would make any difference. The older daughter reported to the square later.

When we came out of the nightmare of the cellar, temporarily 'safe' again, some of the people who had been assembled at the square were still being held at the Kapłonówka school, outside the ghetto. The first transport had been unable to accommodate all of them.

In despair, Pani R. tried pulling every possible string to win the release of one of her daughters, who was still there.

I do not remember if anyone ever succeeded in doing such a thing. In any case, Pani R.'s intervention was fruitless. One or two days later the school stood empty.

Realizing that she had sent her own children to their deaths, Pani R. stopped speaking to anyone. The atmosphere in the flat was unbearable. The Franks had also lost their son; he had said that he was young and strong and not afraid of work. Pani R. paced the room. She would pause at one or the other of the windows, and then go on pacing. My sister and I tried to stay out of her sight, since we were more or less the same age as her daughters. We felt guilty at being alive.

At a certain moment, Pani R. saw our *Judenälteste* [The Elder of the Jews] Volkmann from the window. Briefcase in hand, he was on his way to the *Judenrat* building. That was when Pani R. scrambled onto the window-sill and jumped. She landed on the cobblestones at his feet and lay there beside the black briefcase that he had dropped.

Stunned by what I had seen from our window, I realized in terror that a feeling of relief overwhelmed my shock.

ON THE 'ARYAN SIDE'

Gedenk az du bist a yidish kind. [Yiddish] Remember that you are a Jewish child – that is literally what he said, although I was no child. I was to remember not to stray from the faith of my ancestors. That was all. My father did not kiss me or send me on my way with his blessing. I was going over to the 'Aryan side' against his will. 'I cannot forbid it', he said, 'because I know that you will not obey, so I would only burden you with the sin of disobedience' (Honor thy Father and thy Mother). But we should not seek a fate different from the one God has marked out for us. Let what happens to all the Jews happen to us.

Ela and I had been in the same class at the Queen Jadwiga School in Tarnów, but only from the fifth grade on. She had transferred from the Ursuline Convent school then because her father had died and they had been unable to afford the tuition fees. She lived in a different neighbourhood, beyond the Shooting Gardens. We had not been particularly close at school. Half the form were Jewish girls from my neighbourhood, and we stuck together.

I saw her years later when we were sent in groups of five to work outside the ghetto. It turned out that she worked several doors down and on the other side of ulica Lwowska from the Madritch garment factory where my sister Tosia and I were employed. She managed to visit me there several times. Such contacts gave those working outside the ghetto a chance to sell something from home and buy some food.

The first 'action' had already taken place. Thousands of Jews had been murdered on the spot or sent off to their death. I was feverishly seeking a way to get out of the ghetto. I had already found a contact who would sell me a counterfeit *kennkarte*, [Identity Card] but I did not yet have the money for it. I had bleached my hair to 'improve my appearance', but the effect had been the opposite. My hair had come out too harshly blond and made the effect of my dark eyes more noticeable than ever.

The first thing I needed was an authentic birth certificate on the basis of which I would acquire additional, fake documents. Documents alone were not enough, but they helped. It turned out that Ela had been christened outside Tarnów and could not get a duplicate birth certificate without drawing attention to herself. 'But Mama says that if anything happens you can hide with us', Ela told me.

At the time this seemed unimportant. I already had a fake identity card in her name, which would be useless if I were staying with her. What I really wanted, anyway, was to get out of Tarnów. I had lived there all my life and would therefore always be in grave danger when I moved about the streets.

I heard one Saturday that another 'action' was coming in a day or two. There was not a moment to lose.

Earlier, during the great August roundup, I had indeed managed to survive in a bunker, but I had lost my 'right to life'. [Because a certificate was to be given to every employed person] a representative of the Madritch company had come to the ghetto several days later to put a new stamp in the *ausweis* [permit] of each employee. Tosia had got her stamp but then could not find me until it was already too late, for the German had left.

That November Saturday, I had a hard time calling children from the other side to the ghetto fence and getting them to take a message to Ela in exchange for a promise of payment.

On Sunday, as we had arranged, I went to work with the group of legal Madritch employees. The Jewish *Ordnungsdienst* police did not pay any attention to me. My face must have seemed familiar. Let them worry if the numbers don't tally later. Work stopped at noon on Sundays, and it would get dark around five. I was to spend those hours in the toilet. More precisely, at a sewer opening in the floor, one of two (the right-hand one) on the long wooden balcony running around the rectangular courtyard on the first floor. Ela was to come for me at dusk.

The five hours in that stinking compartment are a chapter unto themselves. There was nowhere to sit. I was dressed in my best clothes and set my bag, containing a few pieces of clothing and a change of underwear, on the floor. The hours dragged interminably. I was petrified the whole time that she wouldn't come. The building was totally silent.

The caretaker lived across the courtyard on the ground floor, up a couple of steps. As it turned out later, he was sound asleep, perhaps having drunk something with Sunday dinner. I peered out the heart-shaped cut-out in the wooden door and watched it get dark. It seemed black, and still no sign of Ela.

The one thing finally happened that we had not foreseen in our hasty plan. Ela found the gate locked.

The first words I heard after all those hours were, 'Jesus! Mary! Now what do we do?' I was overjoyed that she had come! When her repeated hammering finally roused the caretaker, she told him that she needed to use the toilet. Nothing better came into her head. Half-asleep and half-dressed, he pointed towards the toilets on the ground floor, but she pretended not to understand and ran upstairs.

I followed her back downstairs. The impatient caretaker was ready to lock the gate behind her when he lay his astonished eyes on me. I jammed a fistful of coins into his palm and before he could look around we were turning the corner.

What do I recall from those first hours? Stammering 'Praise be' (to Jesus Christ) in greeting, as I had been instructed.

Ela's two brothers who lived with her were not supposed to know who I was, but they soon figured things out. The third brother, married and living elsewhere, was never fully informed. A fourth brother was in the Auschwitz concentration camp, where he had been sent with the first transport from the Tarnów prison. The one who in fact supported the whole family was a butcher; we had bread with lard for breakfast. Every mouthful of that doubly *treyf* breakfast (lard and following that milk, without a six-hour break) stuck in my throat.

Soap was produced from the large quantities of animal fat that the butcher brought from work. I had to be constantly prepared to hide in the bathroom whenever a client knocked.

'What beautiful black eyes. Don't be offended, Pani, but you look just like a little Jewess.' That was what I heard when I didn't manage to hide in time and had to be presented as a friend who had come from the country to visit the dentist.

Ela's mother: the personification of righteousness and benevolence. 'Oh, look, there goes one of yours on a bicycle', she called to me once. When I recoiled from the window in fear, she could not understand why I would be afraid of the Jewish *Ordnungsdienst*. 'If they come, I hope they take only me. I'm old, I haven't got much time left, just so nothing happens to the children.' She hadn't yet turned 60.

The rosary and the Apostles' Creed, which Ela taught me. And the medallion with the Virgin Mary which was hung around my neck.

I answered help-wanted advertisements. No replies came.

An 'action' took place a week later. Ela, who carried notes to Tosia from me, returned with her head hanging down: 'Tosia's there ...' was all she said.

I sat with my eyes swollen from crying. 'She's got a toothache', Ela's family informed a railroad worker of their acquaintance the next day, as he told us how he had been ordered to uncouple the goods wagons near Bełżec [one of the death camps].

Then Tosia's pleading letter came: she couldn't stand the loneliness. I went back to the ghetto the way I had left. This time, Ela's brother held my hand.

At home, our parents' beds were still unmade and the impressions of their bodies were still visible on the mattresses. The things belonging to my little brother, who had begged me to take him with me, were still strewn around.

They had hidden in the same cellar where Ela and I had been several months earlier. At the very end of the 'action' they had been turned in by a Jew whom we knew by name. That had been the price he paid to get out of the transport as he stood at the door of the goods wagon. Of course, he too died later.

No, I never tried and never wanted to forget that I am Jewish. I never could. What if I had wanted to? I have not the slightest doubt that somebody would always have turned up to remind me.

THE CHILDREN FROM PŁASZÓW

Now I regret not having tried to write down what I remembered right after the war, as I was urged to do. It was not because I was trying to escape from my memories. On the contrary, I had a need to talk about it. Perhaps that talking took the place of writing. I talked about it vividly and in detail. The more sensitive people couldn't listen for long. I also read a lot about the occupation, everything that was available then. Memoirs, diaries: Borowski, Szmaglewska, Rudnicki, Andrzejewski, Szczucka [famous Polish writers]. Perhaps that is why I did not try to write.

Later I grew less and less certain about dates, numbers, names.

I cannot remember, for example, where the *Kinderheim*, the children's barrack, stood in the Płaszów camp, or how many children there were. The experiences of any one of them would have sufficed for a whole adult life. As a result, they were wise with that instinctive wisdom of a mortally threatened animal. Those were Cracow children, smuggled out by their parents during the liquidation of the Cracow ghetto and later legalized. After every 'action', as they were called, people appeared who should have been dead, and they stayed on. Until the next time.

None of our Tarnów children were in the children's barrack. They had been taken from us during the loading of our transport in the late summer of 1943. Olga had carried her little Jurek (5 or 6, freckles, a turned-up nose) in a sack. He had sat silently the whole way from the Bus Station Square, where we had knelt since the previous day, through the city, right to the freight carriages. That was where they took him away from her. Earlier, she had had a chance to give him to her 'Aryan' friends for safekeeping. But, at a certain moment, she had yielded to parental urging and, despite her convictions, allowed him to be circumcised.

And so I cannot remember where the *Kinderheim* stood. I can, however, recall the exact location and layout of the barrack called the *Waschraum*, our latrine and washroom in the women's part of the camp. This long barrack stood on pilings and was divided along its axis by a wall that did not reach to the ceiling. On either side of that wall ran a sort of long box with a row of holes on it. The latrine ditch was below. Near the outside walls was a washing trough with taps. At either end of the building were wide doors through which one could enter either the left- or right-hand half. And at one end, the witch of a latrine warden had her own room where she stood guard. If someone happened, for instance, to walk on the floor when it was freshly mopped, or if she was simply in an ill humour, she would smear them with a mop dipped in excrement to the accompaniment of exotic curses shouted in her hoarse voice.

Below the women's part of the camp and across the road stretched the vast *Appelplatz*, the roll-call square.

That was where all the prisoners, men and women separately, were driven early on a sunny May morning in 1944 (I think it was the fourteenth). They stood us in rows of five, by barracks.

I was in Płaszów with my sister, who was four years older. We had stayed in the same group of five, which also included three girls her age, since we were in the Tarnów ghetto. I was 19. But little Edzia, the sister of one of my sister's friends, was also with us. She had made it from Tarnów by miracle, since she was so small for her 12 years. She had shiny black eyes and hair, a lot of resourcefulness and, like all children in that situation, a great deal of practical wisdom. In 'better' times she went to work sewing work clothes with us. She was adept at sewing buttons on. When things got more dangerous, for instance when they were rounding people up to donate blood for transfusions (for the master race, the ones with the pure blood), which was more or less equal to a death sentence in the light of our nutritional situation, we would hide her between the ceiling and the roof of the barrack and she would sit there hunched up for hours.

Now, on the *Appellplatz*, we put her in the middle of our rank and trembled in fear that she would be noticed.

A selection was underway, the first of its kind in Płaszów. Until recently, we had been an *Arbeitslager*, a work camp. Now (perhaps on that very day, I cannot recall), it became a concentration camp.

Victims were being picked out of the ranks. The children from the *Kinderheim* stood somewhere far off to the left. The sun beat down mercilessly. The hours dragged slowly by. Music blared from the loudspeakers. Yes, there was music. As a result of the sense of humour peculiar to the Germans, it was always appropriate. Once they had caught an escapee and led him before his assembled fellow-prisoners wearing a sort of sandwich-board with *Ich bin wieder da* ('I'm back') written on it. That spectacle had been accompanied by the song *Komm zurück* ('Come Back') over the loudspeakers.

The camp hit was *Es geht alles vorüber* ('Everything Passes'). The lyrics went on to say that after every December comes a new May. I have been able to hum that melody at any moment ever since, although I am not particularly musical.

We were fainting from the heat and thirst when, after so many hours, there was a commotion behind us and to our left. Although no one was allowed to move, the news soon came through: they were taking the children away. We could hear screams and the sobbing of the mothers. The loudspeakers played *Weine nicht, du Mutti weine nicht* ('Don't Cry, Mommy, Don't Cry').

They finally dismissed us.

Tormented by the long hours of standing, thirst and holding back our physiological functions, but most of all terrified by the selection, we returned to the barracks. Edzia was still with us (she was taken from us several months later on the ramp at Auschwitz).

The inmates of our barrack had happened to be standing close to the road. I was therefore among the first score of women who hurried into the latrine. Suddenly, when the first ones were sitting down at the holes, a child's voice called from underneath: 'Please be careful, because I'm here.' Then there were voices from several other holes. We almost fainted. There were children down there in the latrine ditch!

Olga was the first to collect her wits. She rolled up her sleeves, pressed herself against the seat board and, with an effort, pulled the first child up out of the depths and through the hole. I do not remember how many there were. A dozen? Fewer, I think. They were rinsed under cold water in the washing trough. The children, boys and girls, were 5 or 6 years old. The oldest was a boy of about 7. As far as I recall, his name was Spira. He was the one who had shouted, as the children were being led near the hill where the latrine stood, 'Run for it!' That was when those little children carried out a manoeuvre that any hardened fugitive would have been proud of. They did not run straight ahead, away from the SS men – of whom in any case there were not many, because who keeps children under such close guard? Instead, the children scattered in every direction around the latrine. The dumfounded SS-men were unable to catch them all at once. They obviously wanted to avoid opening fire. Some of the children ran inside the latrine building which, as I have mentioned, had doors at either end and was divided down the middle. Conscious of the danger, the braver ones dove into the stinking black abyss. Those who did not make it or who hesitated were caught. Did the SS-men notice that some were missing? I do not know. What was the further fate of those who saved themselves? I do not know this, either.

At first, as usual, they remained in the camp semi-legally. I have not encountered their story in the literature. Someone mentioned that the boy who was the ringleader had survived.

Three months later, in August, the first mass transport to Auschwitz took place. Two or three months after that, there was a second transport and the Płaszów camp was liquidated. I was in the first transport, which afterwards was sent almost in its entirety to Stutthof and drowned in the sea. How I avoided that is another story. I doubt if many of those who were present at the rescue of the children in Płaszów are still alive. Olga survived, but she and her husband left Poland after the death of her second, post-war child, a golden-haired girl who had some sort of birth defect.

So let me at least recall those children sunk in excrement and fighting for their lives.

THE WHEELBARROW

It was four days after the liberation of the camp in Bergen-Belsen by the British Army. The war was still on. I was coming back from the ward, a sort of hospital, where my sister was dying. Tosia was 24 and looked 14. I, the stronger of us, was a typical '*Mussulmann*' [in the camps' slang: a starved person on the brink of death], barely able to shuffle my feet. Later, after being fed for two months, I weighed thirty-seven kilograms.

I had spent almost the whole day trying to do the impossible: baking the potato pancakes that Tosia had been dreaming of. After a lot of difficult scrounging I managed to find a nail and a piece of tin sheet. Using a stone, I laboriously punched several holes in it. I grated the potato and collected trash for a fire.

Tosia tore off a bit of the pancake, held it in her mouth for a moment, and pushed my effort away. She could hardly eat anything by then.

British soldiers were wandering around the camp. Their incredulous, shocked gazes took in what was left. The SS men who had not managed to escape or who had nowhere to escape to were digging enormous mass graves. Beside the barracks rose a sort of second barracks made of meticulously laid-out, as they put it, corpses. One row lengthwise, and on top of it a row sideways, and so on to a height of two or three meters. Loose corpses were also lying around everywhere. More than ten thousand all told, with hundreds or a thousand more each day. By the time the last grave was covered over, the number of corpses had doubled.

I walked past the corpses, barely seeing them. In general I noticed and felt little. I was not happy when the British Army arrived; I did not know how to be happy. I listened in astonishment to 'real' English. Once, five years earlier, I had studied that language, but it somehow sounded different. In fact, I understood little of what was happening around me. I did not know how to put my thoughts together, just as I did not know how to get up off the ground without first crawling to something I could use to support myself with.

And yet I remember one image precisely.

Along the path where I was returning from Tosia stood a wheelbarrow. It was more of a box with a short handle and one wheel underneath, square and fairly deep. In the box were the corpses of two women. But they really weren't corpses. They were two skeletons with yellowish skin stretched over them. Yet the faces were almost normal. The hair had just started to grow back from being shaved; it was even shorter than mine. They must have been from a later transport. Their cheeks were sunken, of course, like everybody's.

Somebody had left the wheelbarrow in the middle of the road, leaning on the short handle. Those two women, intertwined, one taller, stood leaning against the bottom of the box which was tipped up into an almost vertical position. They stood with their eyes open and grimaces of suffering on their lips. Two macabre mannequins waiting to be dressed in a macabre window display.

Is that what I thought then?

Only two British soldiers with a camera who had been strolling nearby and paused, looking on for a long time, before taking a picture. Maybe it still exists somewhere.

But in my memory, as time passed, one of those women took on the shrunken and emaciated face of my sister Tosia, who died three days later on the eve of her 24th birthday.

25. A Lesson in Loving One's Neighbour

Zygmunt Gemel

Life under occupation was hard, especially in winter. Then the frost and blizzards compounded the problems with food shortages and fear. We lived on potatoes, rye bread and milk. The quail that hid in the deep snow and hares were poached, and trees that had been marked for shipment to the Reich were stolen from the forests. Life was easier in summer, when fruits and vegetables made up for dietary shortcomings. I remember how a clandestine, iron grain mill was passed from house to house in the village. It had to be concealed, for the penalty for possessing a mill was deportation to a concentration camp. The mill was clamped to a table or board at night and the family cranked it by lamplight to produce flour for whole-grain bread. Whole-wheat bread was delicious, for it was sweet and not mouldy. Whole-rye bread was a rarity, for the Germans limited the legal milling of rye to a minimum, too little to make bread for a family. I only mention these facts to show how hard life under occupation was, even in what seemed like a peaceful village. People thought only of surviving, and it was hard to ask sacrifices of them because the instinct for self-preservation was mobilized in the fight for life.

The winter of 1943 was approaching. Jews were still wandering the villages in secret, although there were fewer and fewer of them. The frosts started in October. The fields were empty. A crust of ice covered puddles and the edges of the ponds. One day in late October or at the beginning of November, I was walking home from the village. It was late afternoon. As I turned into our farmyard, I saw a child crouching near the door of the house. He was dressed in rough-hewn sandals and ragged clothes. I watched, or even stared in wonder as the child gnawed a frozen swede. As the child bent low to pick up another fragment from the ground, he noticed that I was watching. We looked at each other for several seconds – a hungry pauper child and a stupid village boy. Suddenly my father appeared out of nowhere and said in a sharp, decisive tone, 'What are you gaping at? Can't you see that he's hungry? Go inside and tell your mother to give him something to eat.'

I cannot recall what other food was in the kitchen, but there was certainly bread. The poor child gobbled it down, and then disappeared along the road through the fields with a bag containing bread and some potatoes.

Now, decades after the event, I remember. How grateful I am to my father for that lesson in loving one's neighbour.

26. Through the Barbed Wire

Elżbieta Jeziorska

I was 3 when the war broke out in 1939. My parents, my older brother and I lived at 50 ulica Twarda [in Warsaw]. A few doors away, at 40 Twarda, across from where the barbed wire around the ghetto closed off ulica Śliska, my mother ran a small sweet shop called 'The Sweet Nook'. There were three tiny tables where customers could drink kvass, soda water from a spritzer, and lemonade. The shop sold tart candy drops out of a big jar, red lollipops, sugar bananas, caramels, biscuits, *ersatz* cocoa, and loose sunflower and pumpkin seeds by weight.

Aside from regular clients, the shop was a contact point for young people from the PAL [the communist underground 'People's Army' (*Armia Ludowa*) which was later merged into the Polish People's Army (LWP)] and Home Army resistance movements. I can remember Włodek Majchrzak from the Home Army who sometimes held me on his knee, Mr Rabanowski and Gieniek Lewandowski. The *volksdeutsch* Leszek N. would also come in. Mother forbade us to talk to him aside from saying 'hello' and 'thank you'.

'The Sweet Nook' was open every day from 9 a.m. until 6 p.m. I spent whole days there, across the street from the barbed wire of the ghetto, with my brother and the neighbourhood kids. On the odd-numbered side of ulica Twarda, the way into ulica Śliska was blocked. The ghetto lay behind that wire. A German soldier armed with a pistol and a rubber truncheon strolled along the 'Aryan' side. At times, a Polish 'blue' policeman stood watch over the ghetto. Adults were forbidden to approach the wire, but we children were notorious for running up close and looking from short range at the kids our age on the other side: skinny, ragged, dressed in grown-ups' old jackets and worn-out felt boots with no shoestrings, sad and hungry.

Hunger forced the Jewish children to venture outside the ghetto in search of food. Before our eyes, the drama of children tangled up in the wire on ulica Śliska was played out every day. Returning with scraps of food they had begged or found in dustbins, the children had to wait for the right moment to throw themselves into the wire and wriggle through to the other side. They didn't always make it. They would get snagged, cut themselves, tear their hair out on the barbs, and rip their clothing while the guards beat them mercilessly with truncheons. All that could be heard were screams, crying, laments and cursing in German. Dried bread, peelings, onions and potatoes spilled onto the cobblestones of ulica Twarda from their bags and from pockets with drawstrings at the bottom. The Jewish kids were beaten until their clothing fell off them, or they managed to free themselves of their rags and leave them hanging on the wire. I will never forget the sight. To this day I associate the word 'ghetto' with the figures of those children, as emaciated as Pinocchio, struggling on the barbed wire.

My friends and I ran near the wire, and when the soldier on guard was looking the other way or watching another group of Polish children, we threw candies, biscuits and whatever else we had towards the ghetto. There were some children that we knew. They taught us a Jewish song. I did not know what the words meant, but to this day I can remember the melody and several verses.

Since our shop was right on the edge of the ghetto, Jewish children would wait in our doorway for the best moment to cross the wire. The shop had a passage from the back room to the doorway. That was our aid station. With Mother's permission, we fed those children. What a treat a sugar banana or a giant lollipop was for them. I remember that we often made our own sandwiches – bread with water and sugar, with marmalade or with margarine. We squatted on the landing of the staircase and watched how they ate. Afterwards, we stood lookout and gave them a signal when they could make a run for the wire.

When a high wall was built down ulica Twarda all the way to Żelazna, 'The Sweet Nook' was cut off (until the Warsaw Uprising) and we could no longer see what was going on in the ghetto.

27. Fajga

Łucja Kreszczyńska

Fajga was the name of a friend I once had, a Jewish girl. Among the many girls I knew, she is one I will remember forever. She lived near my parents' house. Her parents were grain merchants. She had two sisters, Chaja, a seamstress, and Bliminia, a university student. Chaja sewed dresses for me, which is why she was such a frequent visitor in our home. Fajga, on the other hand, helped her mother around the house. She did everything: the laundry, the cooking, the darning and the cleaning, and she did it without a murmur. She weeded the garden and watered and sometimes grazed the goat on the boundaries, where I would join her. She was 15 when the war broke out in 1939, and I was two years younger. She impressed me with her knowledge and breadth of reading in those times when books were practically the only source of information. I wanted to know as much, and know how to do as much as she did. Fajga, I would ask her, tell me why this is the way it is or why that is what it is.

'What can I tell you?' Fajga would answer in her melodious Yiddish accent. 'I'll bring you a book, you'll read it, and then you'll know.' And she would bring the book. I would read and then go back to revise what I had read, because Fajga would discreetly and delicately check my comprehension by drawing me into discussions.

It would have shamed me to cheat Fajga in any way, because she was forthright and fair. She knew how to reward truthfulness, reliability, magnanimity and goodness with a smile or a glance. Her bright brown eyes would smile gently as she looked at you then, and her reddish-gold hair formed a particular sort of halo around her beaming face. I loved Fajga. I could confide in her and trust her with any secret. She never let me down, never went behind my back, never laughed at me, never gossiped ...

We lived among the fields and meadows on the outskirts of a small city, far from the hubbub of the streets. Fajga taught me to see the corn flowers among the grain, to see the marigolds and the frogs in the meadow, the grasshoppers, ladybirds and the dew on the grass. We loved walking in the rain. Fajga used to hold her face up to the raindrops and say that the rain washed everything away, cleaned and refreshed everything. To this day, I like it when it rains. Fajga was true to her word, dutiful and punctual. When we agreed to meet at a certain time and place, Fajga was never late.

She once showed me a little notebook with a line down the middle of each page. In it, she recorded her good deeds and her bad deeds. Each day. She called that notebook her 'confessor'. She was highly self-critical. When something bad happened to her, she tended to blame it on herself. If she talked back to someone, overlooked something, or spoiled something she was working on, she gave herself a dressing down; she would confess and make a hundred apologies to whomever she thought she had wronged. Sometimes it was hard for me to watch how Fajga allowed herself to be slighted or taken advantage of, and sometimes I laughed at how often she repeated the words 'please', 'I'm sorry' and 'thank you'. I thought then that she wore these words out by overusing them. But what a lack there is today of people who overuse the words 'please', 'I'm sorry' and 'thank you'.

Who taught a simple Jewish girl like Fajga such tact, practical wisdom and intelligence? Was it her parents, those Jewish grain merchants? Was it her sister Chaja the seamstress, or Bliminia the student, or was it all those books she read?

Then came 1941. The German occupation authorities established the ghetto and shut people of Jewish origin inside.

Fajga came to me one day. I will never forget that day, never ever. She looked at me with love and sadness. Her reddish-gold hair that had always formed a beautiful halo was limp and tied at the back with some sort of string, and her eyes had lost their fire. She held a necklace made of tiny blue corals, threaded in the shape of a forget-me-not. She handed it to me. 'It's for you', she said, 'because we might not ever go walking in the meadows again. It's to remember me by.'

She had come to say goodbye. She could not say much because her voice kept breaking. She held a small bundle under her arm. I did not understand then where Fajga was going or for how long. I did not understand the tragedy of those times. I did not realize that I was seeing her for the last time, that she would never grasp my hand in her hot palm when I committed some gaffe or tactlessness in her presence.

She went away in her dreadful sadness, and I did not even say much of a goodbye because it all seemed so temporary to me, as if it would last but a moment. Only when the months passed and I could not see Fajga would I walk past her abandoned home overgrown with nettles, that home in the shadow of which we had frolicked, played tricks and told each other everything from the times when we were small children until we achieved the maturity of 15-year-olds. Now there was emptiness. How I missed Fajga.

I thought even then that it would end, that we would meet and tell each other everything. I vowed in my heart never to tease Fajga again, never to laugh at her worn-out, frumpy dresses and her down-at-heel sandals tied up with string. I would apologize for everything. So I thought. But Fajga was burned in a crematorium in the autumn of 1942. My Fajga.

'Fajga, is there a God?' I used to ask her sometimes.

'Oy vey, how can you talk that way?' she answered. 'He hears everything.'

Fajga my darling, did He hear how you cried, how you prayed, how you wanted to live? I lost my faith. Your death was the answer to my question.

Today, there are showy memorials at the cemetery with flowers on them. Where is Fajga's grave? Where is her immaculate, humble soul, so great in its value?

28. The Captain's Daughter

Barbara Kronicz

'You rotten little Jewess!'

I regarded the schoolroom slander as absurd, a schoolmate's awkward outburst.

I was in my fifth year at the public primary school in Nieśwież. This little town with the grand palace of the Radziwiłł princes was, like dozens of other 'Anatevkas' in the Polish eastern marches, an aggregation of many nationalities. Poles, Byelorussians, Jews and Tatars lived cheek-by-jowl without sharing affection. Speaking their own languages, they had their own history and their own customs. Religion determined national identity. I was a Pole and a Catholic. I had received first communion and confirmation with my form and got good marks in religion.

I went to church one afternoon with my mother's sister. An unfamiliar woman blocked our way. 'What are you looking for in church, Fryda?' she snorted.

'Excuse me, but this is my Aunt Fela', I protested.

'She's Fryda the Jewess', the Daughter of the Church snarled.

I had never before noticed what 'Semitic' facial features my aunt had. Now I began inspecting myself in the mirror, the drawn-in face, big, heavily-lidded blue eyes, a straight nose, full lips, light chestnut-coloured hair. 'What a pretty girl', ran the compliments I heard. Could I be Jewish? Uncertainty and anxiety took the fun out of courtyard games.

The year 1939 came. Anti-Semitic wrangling spilled into the street. The ditty:

> Marshall Śmigły-Rydz, our leader true,
> Says that it's alright to beat a Jew ...

was even sung at school. 'Get out of the way, Jew', shouted a drunken corporal as he pushed an old man off the kerb and into the cobblestone street.

Father learned about the outbreak of war through the earphones of his radio. The Red Army took Nieśwież on 17 September 1939 and Mother, who knew Russian, got a job as a teacher in a Belorussian village. The NKVD arrested Father several months later. He never returned. Threatened with deportation to Siberia or Kazakhstan, we moved to the village of Paniutycze near Snowo. Mother continued teaching small children and sent my sister and me to an elementary school. There were many Jews in my form. Rywa got the best grades. I envied Iga's glorious hair. When she sat on the school bench her thick, dusky braids touched the floor. Icek's silly remarks got on my nerves and we hit each other with our wooden pencil-cases during breaks. The Belorussian girl Lida dragged me through mud and snow on the way home after school. The gaze of our teacher, from the depths of Russia, imposed a cease-fire on our nationalistic wars over pencil-cases and rulers. We were allowed to speak only Russian during lessons.

Nazi occupation descended on us like lightning in June 1941. And then Mother had to tell her daughters the truth. Yes. I was Jewish after all! My father, a Pole serving as an officer in the Border Defence Corps, had married a young Russian immigrant of Jewish origins. Sonia had become Zosia. She was baptized in the Catholic Church. She raised her two daughters as Poles and Catholics. Mother's origins were never mentioned in the family – or at least not in front of the children. Still, there were people around who recalled the captain's *mésalliance*. We started being afraid of these people.

The Germans closed the school. Mother hired herself out as an agricultural labourer and I learned how to beg.

'*To doczka naszej uczitelnicy*' – That's our teacher's daughter – said the Belorussian women warmly. I always got a little milk, bread, some potatoes. When the Germans appeared in Paniutycze I fled to the attic, behind a partition I had built out of straw with my own hands.

'Will somebody inform? Have they already done so?' I cried, and prayed to the Blessed Virgin.

We ran out of everything at home. It was worst with salt and lamp oil. I went to Snowo and queued in front of the shop. 'What a pretty Jewess', I heard from a Belorussian boy. It was a compliment. There were Germans standing nearby. I slipped away from the queue unseen and ran home, to Mother.

Then I went back through the meadows to the village. Perhaps I was looking for oil. Near my old school, I saw Germans. They were hurrying a Jewish work unit along – boys and girls from my form at school, carrying shovels. From behind a tree I peered into their faces. I should have been among them. The yellow star of David had been sewn for me.

I cannot remember the date, but it must have been 1943, when the village shook with gunfire. The Jews of Snowo had been herded to their deaths in the woods one kilometre away. I can see today those woods, that ditch, the yellow sand thrown into the pit. I can hear the screams, cut off by a salvo. I threw myself to the grass, stopped my ears and cried for them, for myself, for the fate of those I loved best. Villagers said that the ground was still stirring at the site of the crime a day later.

Mother decided that we would escape from Paniutycze. The Germans came there too often, tracking partisans.

One night, our neighbour had knocked at the window. '*Uczitielnica*', [Teacher] he whispered to Mother, 'the Germans are to shoot you, and the girls, and your sister. They've ordered a grave dug. Make a run for it.' He did not say whether the sentence had been passed against a Polish or a Jewish family.

In the morning, Mother put on her burgundy-coloured dress that fastened with a buckle. It was the last dress that she had not bartered for bread. She took along the photograph of Father in his Polish officer's uniform. And documents: her church marriage license, the children's baptismal certificates, and souvenirs of our first communions. She went to the gendarmerie headquarters and the translator led her to the commandant. He was drunk and busy with some woman. Mother's determination, or rather her madness, staved off death – for days, or a week. We did not know. A gendarme's whim on that horrible morning, I think today.

The Germans were already in retreat. Allied planes flew at very high altitude over Belorussia in the night. We listened to the roar as if it were miraculous music.

We moved to Kleck at the beginning of 1944. This was the last small eastern town of my childhood and adolescence.

The Red Army entered Kleck on 4 July 1944. The routed Nazi forces had passed through twice. Now it's their turn to be afraid, I thought joyously. There was another skirmish and we hid in the wood-shed. I heard a shout: *Partisanen! Banditen!* A series from an automatic rifle, aimed at the women and children, filled the shed with smoke. As I hugged Mother, I felt her shift sideways. I looked up. On the left side of her bright blouse was a vivid red bloodstain. The bullet had gone in between her heart and lung. The shed was on fire, bombs were falling, the artillery boomed constantly. Before nightfall we were left alone in the burned-out structure that everyone else abandoned. My sister and I lay Mother, who was unconscious, on a piece of mattress under a big maple tree. My sister went off in search of iodine, bandages and help ... I did not leave even for a moment. I wanted to be there when she died. I leaned a picture of the Blessed Virgin [in Ostra Brama, Vilnius] against the tree and begged, prayed, blasphemed. The face of the icon took on a lifelike appearance in the dark.

'How like me you look, Mary, you Jewess!'

29. The Shadow

Anna Maria Leska

'You didn't survive the war. You didn't survive anything', the woman next door told me recently. She was 12 when the Gestapo took her away in the night. Nobody took me away, although I was also 12. I had fair hair, blue eyes and Polish parents.

Is there anything I can do about that? Or is there anything I can do about the fact that 11-year-old Lilka Adelman perished without a trace in the ghetto, while I am alive and a grandmother?

People who regard their own lives as uniquely tempestuous or dramatic are badly informed. But today I will tell you about Lilka Adelman.

This is how it was. Lilka Adelman and I lived in the same block of flats in Warsaw (we were both nine then). We followed the same route to school each morning, with book-bags on our backs. Lilka had crinkly, wavy black hair, eyes like coals and pink cheeks. When she laughed, cute dimples appeared in her cheeks. She was generally quite merry. We both laughed, our copybooks shook in our book-bags and our pencil-cases rattled. Before long, the Germans closed the school.

We held dolls' parties in Lilka's flat. Her mother allowed us to cook custards that we ate from tiny cups with tiny spoons. I remember the wonderful taste of that water-based (there was a war on) custard. My friend's Mama was a seamstress and her father a tailor. They spoke Polish a little different than other people, and conversed between themselves in some foreign language. Mrs Adelman sewed a lovely blouse for my mother. I marvelled at the way it tied with elegant ribbons that ended in balls stuffed with fabric. Those ribbons were truly lovely. And then one day the Adelmans were gone from our building. They had had to go to the ghetto. I heard nothing more about Lilka for fifty years ...

After fifty years I ran into an acquaintance, Dr M., a physician, who had been a playmate in our courtyard. M. said, 'I was in love with Lilka Adelman ...'

I have so many different woman friends. Dark-haired Shulamith, saved as an infant by Poles, lives in Israel and speaks Hebrew and Polish. Fair-haired Annerose speaks only German, since she is a German. She was born after the war. One friend, a Jewish child, spent the war in a camp. Another one spent it the opposite way, as the fifth daughter of a high-ranking German naval officer.

I have such different friends. I have my family, children and grand-children. And I still walk to school with Lilka Adelman.

30. A Boy and the Cherries

Teresa Łosiewicz

I witnessed this tragedy as a child, since I had not yet turned 10 when the war began. We lived in Warsaw then, at 59 ulica Piotra Skargi. We had a room with a kitchen on the first floor and the Firgencwajgs, a Jewish family, were below us on the ground floor. There were six of us, and six of them. Our family contained two older brothers and two younger sisters, and so did theirs. Their premises were larger, because they also had a cobbler's shop with its own entrance from the street. This was a fairly large room and they must have changed part of it into sleeping quarters at night.

The boys Motek and Icek were probably just the same age as my brothers who died in Mauthausen, and the girls Hania and Bronia were the same age as my younger sister and I. We therefore played together at times. I remember the boys playing catch and a game called 'pikuty' while we played hopscotch and other childhood games. The boys sometimes played ball-in-the-hole and hide-and-seek with us.

Both my father and Mr Firgencwajg were the sole wage-earners in their families. My father worked on the railroad. We apparently had similar standards of living, but they must have been a little better off because Icek took singing lessons and had to drink eggs, which we could never have afforded. Hania said that he went to 10 ulica Inżynierska. Some lessons from Polish Primary School number 48 were later held there, since the school's building on ulica Kowelska was taken over by the Germans at the beginning of the war.

We never saw our friends' father on the street, only running to the toilet in the courtyard, always dressed in his work apron. He repaired shoes from morning to night. Good-natured, perpetually smiling, he obviously loved children.

When people began saying that the Germans were preparing a ghetto for the Jews, the average child could hardly have understood what the word meant. Our aunt who lived at 56 ulica Chłodna (where I had been born, in my grandmother's flat) came first and reported anxiously that Poles were being evicted from Wola, and thus also from Chłodna above the intersection with ulica Żelazna. She did not know what to do. People were being evicted all the way to ulica Wrona. Our aunt was not evicted then, but that whole part of the street was burned down during the Warsaw Uprising and her family went through the concentration camps. We said, 'How fortunate our old grandmother did not live to see this', for she died just before the Uprising.

And then one day a cart was standing before our building, and the Firgencwajgs were loading their belongings on it. Somebody said, 'They're going to their death'. They disappeared without trace. Later, we could see smoke in the distance and we knew that the ghetto was burning.

We wondered what was happening to our neighbours. It was easy to make suppositions on the basis of the crumbs of information we received about the ghetto. Taking the tram to visit our aunt on ulica Chłodna, we crossed the Kierbedż bridge over the Vistula, passed Hala Mirowska, and then rode without stopping through the ghetto on Elektoralna and Chłodna. The ghetto was surrounded by a high red brick wall with pieces of glass sticking up on top of it. At pavement level the wall contained openings to let rain water out. From the tram I saw a child hurriedly pushing what could have been potatoes or apples through one of these holes. The tram went past too quickly to see what happened to him. I did observe the emaciated, terrified people walking furtively around in the ghetto.

My father told of seeing trains full of Jews crossing eastward over the Gdańsk Bridge. Cattle carriages with small windows screened over. Tin cups were sometimes held out through these windows in hope of catching a drop of rain water. Famished people were transported with nothing to eat or drink. Railroad crews were forbidden to delay these transports. The workers saw everything but could not help because a German worked at every station along with the Poles.

The hunger problem was becoming more acute for the average residents of Warsaw. What could we say about the closed ghetto? At the age of 10 I made my first visit to the countryside, to a village near Siedlce. I went there several times during the war because, in exchange for hard work, I could eat my fill of potatoes and milk there. At times there was something better, like fruit in the summer. I was standing under a cherry tree once trying to spot the ripest fruit. The trees were quite full. Suddenly and noiselessly a Jewish boy a little older than me was standing there demonstrating a trick that would prevent anyone guessing that the cherries had been eaten by people rather than birds. He put a bunch of ripe cherries in his mouth but left the stems sticking out. He held the stems so that they stayed together. I tried it myself, and when I turned around he was gone. He appeared just before dusk the next day offering me a leaf full of blueberries from the forest. I understood that he went out to the woods very early in the morning to graze the cows belonging to the farmer who was sheltering him. At this period, the Germans were conducting searches and roundups in the village at night. I could not at first comprehend why he was dressed in an overcoat whenever I saw him, even on the hottest days. Then I understood that he was always prepared to flee and kept all his belongings on his person. My brother, who sometimes visited from Warsaw, told me that my acquaintance was named Abram. I also learned that he had often watched me and listened when I talked to other people before coming to trust me enough to show himself. He craved contact with people. Unfortunately, I cannot say whether, by some miracle, he survived. I fear that he did not.

31. Near Treblinka

Zdzisław Rozbicki

Sokołów Podlaski is a small town in eastern Poland. Most of its inhabitants were farmers and craftsmen. There were also a few workers from the railroad and the sugar refinery. Most of the shops and workshops in the centre of the town belonged to Jews. My parents' contacts with Jewish families and the atmosphere of the Polish-Jewish town had a great influence on my attitudes: I treated young Jewish people normally, like everyone else.

My family was a large one and had lived in those parts from time immemorial. My great-grandfather had been a landowner, but nothing of the estate remained for my father. However, my mother had inherited three *morgs* of land from her father. Our farm lay near the railroad along which transports of Jews would be taken to nearby Treblinka ...

The hostility and hatred that the Germans felt for the Jews were evident from the first months of the occupation. For me, the first blow was learning that I could no longer have contacts with my Jewish friends. The Sokołów ghetto had just been set up. Several streets had been blocked by high walls and barbed wire. I did not yet understand why my classmates from the first form of elementary school had been evicted from their homes and forcibly resettled behind the barbed wire, with several families in each flat.

With several boys from my street, including Zdzisław Kamiński and his cousin Tadeusz, we went to the ghetto wall. We chose a place far from the sentries. We tried to look inside. It was not easy, for the wall was high. Tadeusz knelt down and I climbed on his back to try to see how the people inside were living. Several boys on the other side immediately ran up to talk to us. Their ravaged faces and ragged clothing shocked us. The people walking the streets of the ghetto seemed like somnambulists, especially the older ones, who dragged themselves along with great effort. We went there from time to time to throw some food, usually potatoes but sometimes a hunk of bread, over the wall. It so happened that Mr Kosiorek's bakery was near our home (we could get there by jumping a fence). My parents made an arrangement to purchase loaves of stolen bread from Kosiorek's apprentice. I could therefore deliver some bread to my Jewish friends every so often. Initially, I tried to hide such actions from my parents. The bread was given out in appropriate portions once or twice a day. On one occasion I was wrapping a piece of bread in a cloth when my mother came in. I feared a whipping. However, she looked at me tenderly and said, 'Just be careful, son, or the gendarmes will shoot you'.

We were not the only ones risking the danger that threatened us for rendering even the slightest aid to Jews. Many residents of my city, adults and children, did the same. I was already old enough to remember specific incidents, and I do not recall any that indicated indifference by the inhabitants of Sokołów Podlaski to the fate of their Jewish neighbours. There may have been distasteful events, but I cannot remember them.

It was an evening in the late autumn. Heavy rain drummed against the window pane. The wind was howling. We were eating supper. The whole family sat around the big kitchen table. Mother was giving us beans with milk. Father was saying something about how the pigs had not yet been fed; he was upset. The potato peels were cooking in a big pot. Mother tried to soothe him by saying, 'You can't go out in that rain anyway'. Then the door suddenly opened (we never locked it when anyone was home). Someone walked in – a frightening spectre. She was a Jewish woman; rainwater was dripping from her profusely. Without saying a word, she began devouring the boiling potato peels like an animal. She swallowed them without minding how hot they were. None of us reacted for several moments. We were stunned. Then my mother, as usual, spoke first. It turned out that the woman was an acquaintance. She had trusted us to give her something to eat. Mother pulled her away from the pigs' food and sat her on the sofa near the kitchen window, which was covered with black paper as the German authorities required. She gave her a bowl of beans, while my father got up and locked the door. How did she eat? She gulped it down. Every so often, she looked at us with her terrified eyes. When she had finished, she stammered that she had not had anything to eat for several days and that back there, behind the barbed wire, her family was starving. We gave her a few potatoes, some beans and some of the flour we had ground for ourselves in the hand-mill after drying it on a metal sheet in the chimney. It was not really flour, but rather crushed grain. My older brother Józef agreed to meet her at a certain point along the wall several days later in order to give her more food that he would acquire in the meantime. That shadow of a woman left after less than twenty minutes; my father led her out. The next day, we started trying to acquire food by barter.

News about the Treblinka camp and the smoke pouring from the chimneys there had spread by word of mouth. Farmers from the nearby villages told their acquaintances about it when they came to town on market days. They said that transports full of people arrived every day, and shipments of clothing, hair and other personal effects departed. There were even rumours that the residents of the Sokołów ghetto would be sent to Treblinka in a few days. This information was later said to have come from soldiers in the German auxiliary battalion made up of former Red Army POWs. At night, many people fled from the ghetto to the forest five kilometres away. When the Germans realized that this was happening, they took immediate steps. They strung loudspeakers along the edge of the forest and transmitted several hours of propaganda and psychological warfare urging the fugitives to come out. They promised them security and good jobs. They explained that it was communists and Bolsheviks who were spreading tales about supposed camps for Jews. Unfortunately, many of the people in the woods fell for these German lies and returned to the ghetto.

I was an underage witness to the mass murder of people for no other reason except that they were Jewish. There were terrible, macabre scenes. I could not understand why these people were dying. I saw tears in the eyes of my mother and our neighbours. My siblings and I were not allowed to wander away from home. Yet even great danger fails to deter the curiosity of the young. What I saw is inscribed forever in my memory. Nothing can ever efface these macabre images. I feel and express revulsion these days when I hear the voices calling 'Down with the Jews' or when I see ugly slogans written on walls and fences. They must be written by people who never saw what the Jewish people went through. The anti-Semites must be treated as abject and morally depraved.

Two streets, Lipowa and Węgrowska, led from town to the railway station. I lived on Lipowa. I therefore saw columns of Jewish people walking past our house to the station, where goods wagons with windows covered with barbed wire stood waiting for them. This was one step on the road to legalized mass murder down which madmen were leading them. I watched that shocking procession for several days from a hiding place against the wall or behind the bushes in the garden. Young people and old people walked past, and mothers carried infants in their arms. Unable to walk, those babes who had never asked to be born were dependent on adults. Now they were dependent on murderers. Once or twice I was brave enough to stand beside my mother just inside the gate. I saw the faces of people on their way to their death. Several waved farewell to my mother. I heard someone say, 'Goodbye, Mrs Rozbicka. We won't be seeing each other any more.' Horribly, they already knew what lay in store for them. The expression in their eyes is difficult to describe.

The sporadic sound of machine guns accompanied that death march. The Germans did not spare their ammunition to shorten the way for some. Bodies lay all over the street. Many still fought for life. These were hellish scenes enacted on earth. Some of those who knew what was to come, especially the young, tried to escape. They ran from the column towards the gates of houses. The numerous and vigilant escorts gave no one a chance. A young woman carrying an infant was ripped by gunfire as she tried to open a gate. She hung on the low fence in agony for several hours. Her child only fell silent long afterwards. I saw this with my own eyes. This is the way it was. The threat of death gripped our street and the people sitting at home. Everyone, children and parents, shared the fear. Many of those who had been shot called in vain for aid. The threat of death for anyone who approached them intimidated even the bravest. Only in the evening were the wounded killed off and their bodies collected for burial in the mass graves.

The deathly procession of Jewish people down our street ceased after several days. Later, I heard grenades exploding in the ghetto less than 500 metres from where we lived. Those still hiding there were being liquidated, and then the Jewish police were ordered to carry away the remains of their brothers. The injured were killed on the spot. Gunfire and the explosions of grenades could be heard in the town. A Jewish girl aged somewhere between 14 and 16 was killed before my eyes. That afternoon, when the liquidation of the ghetto had been completed, I went out to graze the cow. Evening was falling. To her misfortune, the girl was walking along the road between the fields instead of cutting across them. She was plainly lost and disoriented. She must have known what had happened to her family. The nearest woods were to the east, but she was walking west. Tall grass grew near the road. Two figures suddenly emerged from this grass: a woman wearing the uniform of a German nurse, and a man in an army uniform. They both worked at the field hospital that had been set up in the building of the order of St Francis de Sales to treat soldiers wounded on the eastern front. Before the girl realized what was happening, the German man was beside her with his pistol drawn. She wanted to defend herself or flee but she was too exhausted to do anything but fall to her knees and beg for mercy. On the narrow farm road, I saw it all. The German loaded his pistol as the girl grasped his boots and said something. He kicked her in the chest. She fell to the ground. He fired. She was still alive. She had enough strength to roll onto her side and beg the nurse for mercy, taking hold of her ankles. There were two more shots. The pair of smiling lovers chatted pleasantly as they walked back towards the hospital. I could hear them, but I could not understand a word of their conversation and their infernal chuckling. Every time I walked that road until I moved away in 1951, I relived that horrible scene.

My family and neighbours could attest that I was unable to eat or drink for weeks, because of the human bloodletting I had seen. I groaned for mercy and woke up screaming at night. For a time, my parents relieved me of the chore of grazing the cows. I feared going into our fields. I was terrified of the transports carrying victims to Treblinka: the faces, on which there still flickered the hope that someone would help them avoid their fate, looking out of the small windows through the barbed wire. This was a daily sight for all of us who worked in the fields. Some tried to escape by tearing through the barbed wire or smashing holes in the floors of the wagons. Most of these, however, were killed by the machine guns mounted on the train. Many nameless graves were dug on both sides of the track – in our fields, as well.

Two Jewish people hid in our home for some time – it must have been a couple of months. They were the tailors who had made clothes for us. One hid in the barn loft where we kept hay, next to the sty that held a couple of fattening pigs. To avoid suspicion, my parents had me carry the food out in a bucket, inside of which was bread and a pan with something hot. I pretended to be carrying a heavy bucket full of slop for the pigs. One day, I was terrified by the appearance of a clerk from the tax office, who asked if my parents were home. I was afraid that he would come near and see what was in the bucket. I said 'yes' and hurried along, just to get away from him. The second fugitive was in the house, in a nook covered by a blanket. Whenever anyone called, we signalled to him to duck behind the blanket. It was an insecure hiding place. Anyone who pulled back the blanket would know that he was there. Both fugitives knew that they were unsafe. The Gestapo and the gendarmes had posts nearby, as did the town administration. We could be under observation. One morning, I was carrying food to the barn as usual. I put the bucket on a pitchfork and was passing the bucket into the loft. I whispered something, but this time there was no answer. At first I wondered if our guest was asleep or ill. The loft could be reached by ladder through an outside door. I climbed up. It was empty. He had left in the night. He had been afraid that, if the Germans found him, not only he but also our whole family would die. He had told me this several times when I went to the loft. When I went there, I often found him praying. I would wait until he finished. He regretted not being able to help our family: 'Your parents have six children to feed, and I'm also eating off your table', he would say. I answered that my parents could get by. We had our fields and some things that we could sell. When he learned that there was someone else hidden in the house, he decided that he would sneak off to the forests one night. He told us that he would try to get in touch with the partisans, for he had acquaintances there. My parents did not try to talk him out of it.

32. Friendship at the Cost of Life

Bronisław Tzur-Cyngiser

I do not know my exact date of birth. Yet I must have been born in some year. On the basis of what older people – acquaintances and my remaining relatives – said, I have chosen for myself [what would appear] the appropriate date. Accordingly, I am now 61 years old, and my date of birth is 1 April 1933.

I remember little of the past and take no enjoyment from looking back. Often, however, I dream of the town where I was born: Szydłowiec. I can recall the house with its old walls. What I remember best is the gloomy day when the war broke out. I can still see the long cannon rolling into town, and my mother's sad, tearful face. I remember a few other things as well, but best of all that day when my mother woke us up in the early morning and surprised me by dressing me in my best clothes, although it was a weekday. This was extraordinary, for we used to wear our good clothes only on holidays. The big table, which was usually pushed back into a nook, stood in the middle of the room. It was covered with a white tablecloth and set. Mama was serving something, and the rest of the family sat there in the company of a tall gentleman. We were all ill at ease, and unable to behave naturally.

That was the last meal I ever ate with my whole family, and the last day we all spent together. I left Szydłowiec in the late afternoon with my father and that tall man. Five years would pass before I came back to find no one there.

That was how I found myself staying with the Polish Jagiełło family, good friends of my father's, in the village of Krzczęcin. My father came to visit me from time to time. This had a dual purpose. He could see me, and at the same time get some food for the rest of the family, who were in the ghetto. So it was until the liquidation of the Szydłowiec ghetto. When the 'resettlement' began, my father and my older brother, Janek, managed to flee to the village where I was staying. Mother and the others were transported to Treblinka, from which they never returned.

We spent only a short time with the Jagiełło family, in order to avoid putting them at risk. We learned that there was a ghetto in the nearby town of Przysucha, and we went there. We remained in that ghetto until its liquidation. Father used some method to get out that only he knew, so that he could go to Krzczęcin and get hold of the food that kept us alive.

One evening, German gendarmes, Polish 'blue police' and firemen surrounded the town of Przysucha. Fortunately, Father had returned the previous day with a supply of food. He had an excellent sense of orientation and always knew when trouble was approaching. He understood that, this time, it was the end, and our last journey lay ahead of us. We therefore decided to escape regardless of the cost. We went to the assembly point in the evening, and Father rapidly took up a collection to bribe the sentries. While he was handing a bundle of fifty-złoty banknotes to the chief of the resettlement operation, we broke through the cordon and ran. A whole crowd of people followed us. The money that had been handed over obviously meant nothing, since a terrifying fusillade erupted all around us. Almost everyone died on the spot. However, my father kept his cool and his excellent sense of orientation enabled us to reach the village of Krzczęcin and the Jagiełło family. The farmer built us a 'hideout' in the barn, where the three of us, my father, my brother and I, stayed for a time. In February 1943, malevolent neighbours informed on the Jagiełłos for harbouring Jews. The gendarmerie surrounded the village and my father died in the subsequent *Aktion*. My brother and I escaped. We saw with our own eyes how our father ran towards the rifle barrels. We heard the shots and watched him fall and die.

Jagiełło, who had done so much to help us, was taken to Auschwitz. He did not return.

A new phase of our wandering from village to village ensued. Now we could rely only on our own resources. We depended on the help of good peasants, and especially the Jagiełło family who, continuing to risk their own lives, helped us right up to the moment of liberation. Our homeless life lasted until the end of the war.

Here is what I went through on one of many days:

My life depends on the help of the local people and, even more, on what I manage to find in the fields. But here comes a blizzard, when I am badly weakened by illness and hunger. I have no way of getting any food, because all the nearby villages are full of German soldiers who are digging in hereabouts. Practically half-naked and barefoot, I try to make my way at nightfall, along the side-roads, to Mrs Jagiełło's. It is a long way. Thick layers of snow stick to the rags wrapped around my feet. Then the rags fall to shreds. My feet are totally bare. The snow causes a jabbing pain in my feet. I sit down exhausted in the snow and rip up the empty cloth bag in which I usually carry any food I manage to collect. I wrap my feet in the rags. It is dark when I reach my destination. As I approach Mrs Jagiełło's farmyard, I see that it is full of German soldiers from the garrison. Regardless of the danger, I creep into the barn and fall into a deep, sound sleep. Some time later, the barn door opens with a horrendous screech. I wake up and see that German soldiers are sleeping all around me. Fear of the cold night and everything that is happening immobilizes me. Ready to pass out from the frost and the terror, I stand up with the last of my strength and sneak out. No one notices. These were soldiers just back from the front. I am out of breath and have no strength to go on. I walk a few more metres and stop in the next barn, on the edge of the village, until morning.

I am awakened by the roar of military vehicles. But I have enough experience by now to keep moving, until liberation comes. From village to village, from barn to barn.

Finally, it was 1945. The war ended. Both of us – my brother Janek and I – stayed with peasant families until 1947, when the Jewish community took us. They placed us in the orphanage at Helenówek, near Łódź. A new life began.

33. What Did You See?

Hanna Wojciechowska

Our family was deported from the Poznań region. My mother, my aunt, my 15-year-old brother and I, a 9-year-old graduate of the first form of elementary school, travelled together to Stanisławów [Eastern Poland, now in Ukraine]. We had neither a roof over our heads nor anything to eat. We left a village ravaged by hunger, where we were becoming too much of a burden on our distant relatives. We had an uncle here in Stanisławów. He had himself escaped from his hometown of Postołówek in the Zaleszczyki region just ahead of the Red Army. Leaving behind the mill and house he owned, he went into hiding in Stanisławów. He admitted neither the mill nor his university diploma to the Russian authorities. When the Germans arrived, he got his diploma out.

There in Stanisławów, we felt as if we had struck gold. Arriving from a village in the Sub-Carpathians where no one had seen sausage for years, we found rings of it hanging from nails to dry, just waiting for us. There was flour, there was buckwheat, and there were jars of liquid golden honey in the sideboard. No one was hungry any more. For the time being.

It did not last long. In the snowy winter of 1941, when we rode on the sledges of the Hucul highlanders, we might not have been eating sausage, but we were not hungry. The spring of 1942, however, was a time of famine.

People looked for potato peels in the rubbish. The lady neighbour had a funny way of speaking: whenever she opened her mouth, she clenched her teeth together. My devout aunt flew into a holy rage when we children tried to talk the same way: 'Don't you dare mock her, or else the Lord God will punish you with such scurvy that your teeth will fall out.'

That was when I first saw Jews begging in the streets of Stanisławów. Their legs were swollen and must have been covered with sores, for they were wrapped in cotton wool tied with string. I took a close look at the face of one such woman. Her skin was gray, and a mossy mat of hair was growing on her cheek – just like our neighbour, Pani [Mrs] Brzes-zlakowska.

We weren't getting anything at all for breakfast any more except for half a glass of that liquid honey. Only we children. Mother and my aunt were saving it for us. They ate applesauce that they made by boiling and grating the apples that fell at the beginning of June. This gave them agonizing diarrhoea, but at least it kept them from feeling hungry. I went often to the office where my uncle worked to find out when he was expected back from the village. He did not come back, but Pani Jadzia gave us a bag of buckwheat. Other people we knew were eating nettle soup.

When my uncle returned, we had cornmeal. Nothing else. We ate it as cornmeal porridge in the morning, and we ate cornmeal pancakes for dinner.

We ran outside to hear what all the noise was about. Anita was chasing two small boys out of her yard, calling them Jews. The pair of small redheads fled in panic. Since I was standing at our gate, they ran into our yard. They said that they were from Zosina Wola and were very hungry. I took fright. Not long before, I had heard the adults talking about having seen children playing: they were all chasing one child, shouting 'Jew! Jew!' A German was walking past. He drew his revolver and took a shot at the child who was being chased. He missed, but hit the child's brother and killed him. I told the two small redheads to go into a wagon in the yard. It was a closed wagon used for carrying pigs and had belonged to the pre-war butcher, Apostoluk. The three young Apostoluks, Michał, Romko and Dańko, were indeed Ukrainians, but they were my dear friends. So I felt as if the wagon was mine. I went out into the street. Everything was peaceful. Old Apostoluk's parents lived on the ground floor of our house. Since no one knew anything about them, you needed to watch yourself with them. Across from the Apostoluks lived the Sokołowski family. They were Poles, but the father was a railroad inspector and worked together with the Germans confiscating what people tried to smuggle in from the countryside. At the worst of times they not only had something to eat, but also made sure that everyone knew they had it. It was therefore a good idea to watch what you did in front of them, just as with the old Apostoluks. But none of them had a window with a view of the yard. So I led the two boys from the wagon to our kitchen. Mother gave them our cornmeal pancakes with honey. They ate so greedily that she gave each of them three more pancakes. She told them to come back again, but to make sure no one saw them.

I heard my aunt complaining that evening that my mother was taking pancakes 'out of the mouths' of her own children.

'If you share with somebody, then somebody will share with you,' my mother retorted. 'Besides, who knows when those children last ate?'

Zosina Wola was on the outskirts of Stanisławów, or it might have been a nearby village. Hungry people from there started coming to us.

A boy turned up in the yard. He was even older than the oldest Apostoluk boy, with whom I had more fun playing, but with whom I also got into worse fights than with my own brother. This boy was tall, skinny and had freckles. He also had a mirror with a picture on the back, which he promised to give me in return for something to eat. I checked to make sure that Anita and her mother, or others of their ilk, were not around, and then took the boy in to my mother. He had a milk canister, which she filled with barley-and-potato soup. I sat next to him on the kitchen stairs. He was so hungry that he gulped the first half-canister of that soup – that awful wartime soup that we ate almost every day and which I have not been able to bring myself to prepare even once in the subsequent half-century – right down, before taking his time to savour the second half.

'Do you want to take some back for anybody?' my mother asked. 'Finish that and I'll refill it so you can take some with you.'

He had a younger sister. She was in the Jewish orphanage because their parents were dead, and he was her only living relative. He was living in the ghetto, but those were the days when Jews were still allowed to come and go. So he went out looking for food for himself and his sister. After that first day, he came back two or three times more. He said that a peasant woman had promised him farm work. If she took him on in the spring, he could have his sister live with him. Then he came back and told us that he no longer had a sister. The Germans had blown up the orphanage. He had seen a scrap of his sister's dress hanging in a tree. That was the last time. He never came back.

Bloodcurdling stories circulated about the Jewish cemetery, called the 'okopisko'. The people who lived nearby could not sleep at night for the shooting. Lorries kept shuttling back and forth to the cemetery. Every such story ended with: 'When they finish with the Jews, it's our turn.' In their evening conversations, my mother, aunt, uncle and their friends also told about the particular appearance of the lorries on their way to the cemetery: the canvas flaps were drawn shut, and gendarmes sat outside at the back, aiming their rifles inside.

I was walking to school one day along ulica Matejki, where I lived. Somewhere nearby, a newspaper seller was crying, in Polish, Ukrainian and German, 'Gazeta Lwowska, Lwiwski Wisti, Lemberger Zeit-u-u-ung!', when I saw one of those lorries I had only heard about: the flaps drawn shut and the two gendarmes on the back aiming inside with their rifles. I stared at it, hoping that it would turn out to be a normal lorry full of coal or sacks. Perhaps my fears were groundless – I heard no screams, and the gendarmes were not shooting anyone. However, when the lorry stopped near where I was standing, at the intersection with ulica Gołu-chowskiego, I saw that blood was dripping from it onto the snow. I managed to drag myself to school. The lesson had already started. I did not, as was the custom, either say 'Good morning' or excuse myself for being late. I walked past the teacher and past my bench, and sat in the last row with my head in my hands. The teacher's pets grumbled threat-eningly. 'Leave her alone. Let her sit there', the teacher said.

All lesson long, no one spoke to me. As soon as the bell rang, our sweet gray-haired 'Pani' came over and asked me matter-of-factly, 'What did you see?'

Then I understood that she was used to such situations.

PART FOUR

THE RIGHTEOUS AMONG US

Introduction

What makes a person act in an ethical manner in extreme circumstances is not always predictable. Just as the bestial in man can lurk beneath the surface of an apparently balanced individual, so too can an essential goodness reside in the most ordinary one. Such acts of goodness offer redemption in a despairing world.

The motive for many of the protectors of Jews was money, but in many of these eyewitness accounts, the simple instinct is to save another human being in danger of losing their life for no justified reason. Jerzy Kucharski (43) simply states, 'Rescuing people gave me satisfaction'. Despite the extent of anti-Semitism in Poland, particularly in the 1930s, and the traditional Christian view of the Jews as 'Christ killers', many Polish Catholics risked their lives and that of their families, and whatever limited resources they might have possessed, in order to save Jews. Władysława Bednarek (35) and her father, having lost the horses and cows on their farm, were nevertheless prepared to share their meagre rations of bread and barley soup with the Jewish woman hiding in the barn. She mentions that the inhabitants of a village nearby had been murdered for helping Jews, and yet she asks of her father, 'Could he have been present, watched, and then left her there?' It is still a rhetorical question, as though there was no other possible response.

From the stories we can appreciate that it was easier for Polish people to identify with Jews with whom they had more in common, for example, if they had received a Polish education or identified with Polish culture or, particularly in the case of the middle classes, if they had a similar profession. Cecylia B. Federman was saved by her former teachers in Cracow Teachers' College 'without hesitation or discussion' (39). The urge to help was clearly stronger when neighbours were concerned. Regina Wojcieszuk's family helped their Jewish neighbours in Wołomin with food when they were transported to the ghetto (51). Irena Daniszewska-Froelich's family, instead of being transported to the Warsaw Ghetto, were hidden by neighbours in the Warsaw Officers' Settlement (38). Elżbieta Cielecka (36) brought a one-and-a-half year old girl to her family, when the Jews were being deported from her village. The girl was later taken to Warsaw by a relative of Elżbieta when the risks in the village became too great. As Kazimierz Kisielewski (40) comments: 'it was easier to shelter a fugitive in a large city ... than in a small town where everyone knows everyone else'. In Warsaw, the relative feared blackmail by a Polish policeman, and placed the child in an orphanage. In an assertion of Polish Solidarity, Bolesław Kulczycki (44) describes how a railway worker exerts his authority and saves the life of a Jewish girl, Gina Lanceter, who is later helped by a Catholic priest.

The risks taken were often immense, but for some the risks were irrelevant – that there was no question of how to act is clear from many of these accounts.

34. She Tried to Warm Me Up

Róża Aleksander

The night of Saturday 28 February 1942 was freezing cold in Krośniewice, Kutno county, Łódź province. Two women with little girls came out of the ghetto, which was located on ulica Kutnowska. One woman was my mother, who was with me. I was 11. The other woman was Helena Strykowska, with her daughter. It was the night before the liquidation of the Krośniewice ghetto, when all the Jews there would be transported to the death camp at Chełmno.

We went to the house on the town square where a chemist, B., lived with his family. They did not take us in. Helena Strykowska and her daughter returned to the ghetto. They would die at the camp. My mother and I went to the Dziwirski's on the town square. Mr Dziwirski owned a horse-wagon, and we wanted to get away from that dangerous place as quickly as we could. However, Mr Dziwirski was not at home. His wife took us under her roof, nevertheless, and gave us a place to spend that horrifying, freezing and hazardous night. I remember that we were taken to Mr Dziwirski's bedridden mother, who spent the whole night trying to warm me up because I was so cold and frightened. She prayed for us to be rescued. The next day, after the Germans had deported all the Jews from Krośniewice, we fled in the afternoon to a small town nearby. I must add that the Dziwirskis helped us in a completely disinterested way, and that we could not have survived without that help.

Later came the ghetto in that small town and in Piotrków Trybunalski. Then, from October 1942 until the end of the Warsaw Uprising on 2 October 1944, we lived in Warsaw on 'Aryan' papers, as Poles. We lived in the Marymont district, and our neighbours did not know who we were. I do not think they were very interested. There was only one dangerous incident. Someone must have suspected us, because a 'Blue', [a Polish] policeman, was sent and spent two hours interviewing our neighbours. Then we were transported to Kielce province after the Warsaw Uprising and stayed there until the end of the war. Our nerves were ruined but we survived; we believe that this would not have been possible without the help of Poles. Mother kept in touch with the Dziwirskis after the war, and even helped Mr Dziwirski when he fell ill. I can say only one thing to the Dziwirski family: be proud of your parents and grandparents – I am sincerely thankful to them.

35. The Fear

Władysława Bednarek

I can remember only the fear. I am not sure of the date: was it 1942 or
1943? Something tells me it was autumn, or perhaps December. I was
12 years old. I was afraid of everything then, even of a gentle tapping
at the window in the evening. When my father went out, I was afraid
that he would never return and that I would be left alone with the four
younger children (my mother had died of typhus in 1941). I was afraid
that there would be no barley to make soup with the next day and that
we would all go hungry, that the Germans would find the flour mill
and kill us, that the five chickens would be gone from the henhouse in
the morning, just as one morning I had found the cows missing from
the shed – they vanished in the winter of 1941. Afterwards, there had
been no milk for the children for years. I was afraid of my father's de-
spondency. He often sat by the stove with his head in his hands, sighing and not wanting to talk with me, only whispering from time to
time, 'My God, my God ...'. I was afraid that we wouldn't get the field
ploughed or sown because we had no horse. The army had taken it in
1939. I was tortured by constant fear over my youngest brother who
should already have started walking, but neither walked nor talked.

But that autumn, which after all must have been 1942, I experienced
the greatest fear of my life. From hushed exchanges among neighbours,
my aunt and my father, I knew that the Germans were deporting the
Jews from Parczewo and that it was forbidden to help, that the whole
village could be wiped out for helping. They whispered fearfully about
how a nearby village (its name escapes me) had been burned and
twenty-three people killed. A girl who had escaped by some miracle
was staying with her cousins in our village; her parents and brothers
and sisters had been shot.

To me, Jews meant the shopkeepers in Parczewo, the cobbler Ela
who went around the village mending shoes, the tinker who cried 'Pots
to solder!' or the junk dealer on his old wagon shouting 'Rags!' We children waited for him because his cart was full of wonders like rubber
balls, badges, hair clips and pans that he would sometimes
exchange for rags if Mother allowed, and even if she didn't allow, we

could still look. Jews had children who spoke differently from us village children, were wary of cows, didn't know how to play hopscotch and turned up their noses at the most delicious thing in the world – kielbasa.

I cannot even recall if my father went to Parczewo (he sometimes walked the seven kilometres through the forest to buy salt) and brought her back at twilight, or if she came to our house at the edge of the woods in Czeberaki settlement, Milanów township (in the Radzyń Podlaski district) and knocked at the window. In any case, my father told me right after the war how the Germans had flushed the Jews out of their homes in Parczewo, beating them and shoving them onto the lorries, separating small children from their mothers, turning ferocious dogs on them. He told me that they took two boys from her, aged 7 and 3 (that stuck in my memory). He had got her out and led her seven kilometres through Jasiennik forest. Could he have been present, watched, and then left her there?

On that cold, drizzly autumn evening, he ordered me to put the children to bed early and to stay inside. He spent a long time doing something in the shed or the barn. When he came back in, he asked me angrily why I wasn't sleeping and whether we had any barley soup – always food! – and when I replied that there was some in the kitchen, he ordered me to bed. Putting out the carbide lamp, he carried the barley soup to the shed or the barn. I either saw that or sensed it. He was frightened and I was catching his fear although I did not know what was going on. He went out at night and may not have slept. As I prepared the barley soup for breakfast, he sat by the stove sighing, 'My God, my God...' Then he went to Aunt Barbara's to fetch the litre of milk for my youngest brother that she gave us in exchange for grazing her cows. He did not touch his soup and ordered me to save it for supper. He was at home all day, chopping a little wood in the shed, and he left at dusk for the village. He instructed me to watch the children all the time and stay inside.

The next day, in the hallway, he quietly said, 'You're big, you're the woman of the house now. Don't be afraid, but there's a Jewish woman hidden in the hay in the barn. I'm going to Radzyń today. Take some barley soup to the barn every evening until I return, but first put the children to sleep so they don't see anything. Leave that soup on the chaff-cutter. If anybody asks where I am, say I took a dog to the flayer in Radzyń because we can't afford to pay the Germans' dog tax. I'm taking Aza because she's old. 'Remember', he said, 'not to let the children in the barn see and not to tell anybody what's in there.'

The sun was coming up when he caught a ride on a wagon to the Milanów station. He was carrying a sack with our dog Aza in it.

I looked after the children, gave them their barley soup, combed their hair and picked their lice, fed the chickens with offal, and was afraid. We sat in the cottage watching out the window for our father. When it was almost dark I heard a rustling at the door. It was Aza, but Father wasn't there.

After giving some barley soup to the dog and some to the children, I lay down, wondering all the time whether the Jewish woman was smothering in the straw, and whether she ventured outside. If anyone saw her and the gendarmes found out, they would shoot the children and burn down the farm. When the children fell asleep I put the rest of the soup in an old pan and carried it to the barn as Father had commanded. I felt my way in the silent darkness.

Father came back when I was in bed. He was surprised to see the dog, explaining that he hadn't had the heart to give her to the flayer, but had turned her loose at Radzyń station and then gone to the dog office to register her as lost. If she was smart enough to find her way home, he said, he wouldn't take her back there. Perhaps the Germans wouldn't find out. Then he asked me if there had been any trouble, if anyone had been around.

He called me into the room the next day to impart a secret. 'You don't have to worry anymore. She's going to get Polish papers and she'll be leaving in a few days. She's got fair hair like us. She might make it. She speaks beautiful Polish and knows German. Go find your grandmother's old scapular and I'll give it to her to wear.' But I could tell he was frightened. When he went out to the shed to chop wood after breakfast, he kept watching us, and the barn, and the road to the village.

I can't remember how long she stayed with us. I only know that when I baked bread, which I did twice a week using rye flour ground in the hand mill, I gave some to Father to take to the barn along with the barley soup. I know that he managed to get her to the village and turn her over to someone with a horse, who took her to Radzyń. She supposedly survived in Warsaw and even found work as a translator. So Father said after the war. He also said that she had been an acquaintance of his from Parczewo, the owner or the daughter of the owner of an iron-goods shop. There was never a sign of life from her after the war.

Father did not regard himself as a hero. He may have helped the woman, or been the first to help her. Later, in the barn, she had told him who else could help (in our village nobody boasted about rescuing Jews), and he contacted those people in Radzyń and the village. Rescuing Jews or escaped prisoners or wounded partisans was no great deed, just an everyday task: a hole in the straw, barley soup, a slice of rye bread, an old coat, showing the right road, leading them to the forest or to the next village. And fear about loved ones, about one's own survival.

It hurts very, very much when people say now that Poles are responsible for the destruction of the Jews, when after all we too were doomed to destruction – when our turn came.

36. In the Lion's Den

Elżbieta Cielecka

I am writing this account to supplement the one written by my sister, Janina Okęcka (see No. 47, 'The Rescued Little Girl'). When I was 11 years old, I went to the school in the village of Mordy. Since the population of the village was predominantly Jewish, I had a lot of Jewish schoolmates. We found each other interesting and were friends. I even remember being invited to the wedding of the sister of my dear friend Idka Kuc. This was a great honour. Unfortunately, I was too young to remember anything but the bride's lovely dress and the wedding songs, which were completely different to ours. Adam Brukarz, Icek Josek, so many of them. Now every trace of them has been blown away by the wind, so I shall write a few words about them. In our school we had two female Jewish teachers, as well as the husband of one of them. I cannot recall anyone ever treating them differently from the rest of our teachers. We all lived in perfect harmony, except for petty gibes and the great differences in customs. I spent seventeen years among them and cannot recall any significant misunderstandings. So it is hardly surprising that when the Germans closed the ghetto in 1942 and were preparing to deport them somewhere, we could not imagine, even at that terrible moment, what they intended to do with them. Only after that nightmarish day when they forced them all to Siedlce on foot, killing many – mostly women and children – along the route in a ghastly way, did we understand and feel that nothing could save them.

On the evening before the deportation of the whole Jewish population of Mordy, which was 20 July 1942, my friend Dziunia Maj, the daughter of one of our teachers, came running to see me. She whispered that I should go with her at once because Mrs Róża Kafebaum was calling for me. All the Jews were to assemble in the town square by morning. The Kafebaums begged me to save their daughter. Hania was their first child. She was a year and a half old. They would go with the others, for they had no strength left to hide, but they pleaded with me to save their daughter. They said that they would not take her to be slaughtered. Crying, the mother packed the girl's clothes and a few toys in a bag. I did not hesitate even for a moment about taking her. A little sleeping powder in her mouth, a few last kisses, and I had Hania in my arms. We ran out of the cottage on the edge of town. I could not bear watching any more of those farewells. I held her, wrapped in a thick black shawl. Dziunia followed with the bag. We passed the town square where wagons already stood, loaded with baggage belonging to the victims. People were wandering around everywhere and it was a dangerous place. Dusk was slowly falling. Secret agents sent by the Germans must have been watching everything. We passed the school and had to run past the church, because that part of the way was clearly visible from the square. We passed the community hall and the dairy and paused in front of St John. On a high pedestal across from our gate stood a large statue of St John Nepomuk. How grateful I was for his presence. The bushes around him provided more cover. At that moment a group of drunken peasants staggered down the road. We crouched with our bundle. Today, as an old woman, I believe that we had little idea of the situation we were in. But an instinctive fear made our hair stand on end. I could not risk anyone asking what I was carrying, and I did not know how I would be received at home.

The German staff occupied the first floor of our home. Officers, adjutants and aides were constantly milling around. Our parents had no way of concealing anyone who would be recognized. They were responsible for the fifty or so persons and refugees from all over Poland who were staying with us. My father had bargained with the Germans to have a group of Jews assigned to work in the forest. When things got dangerous, he ordered them to flee. They fled, and we never heard from them. Perhaps none of them had survived! All of this made things risky enough, and now I was bringing home this baby because of whom – as everyone who lived through the Occupation knows – the whole household could be murdered.

We ducked into the yard and a moment later I was standing before my mother, admitting what was in my arms. She told me to wait there, and went to confer with my father. A moment later she returned and told me to take the child and her things to the garden and not to move from there until it was completely dark, late in the evening. Dziunia ran home and, as I had been ordered to do, I stayed there, where I knew every nook, with the crying, tired child to whom I had already managed to become attached. It was very warm. I only went inside at night. There was no way to be sure that no one would inform. I must have spent two or three days (I cannot recall exactly) with her, feeding her and changing her in the hot August sun. On the lawn nearby, one of the officers spent hours exercising his mare, which was about to foal, while a giant boxer ran around in mad circles. Perhaps being in the very lion's den is what saved me. I only had to be careful that she did not cry and draw attention to us. My parents organized everything splendidly. My mother's niece arrived after a few days and took the child to Warsaw as her own child. She kept her at home for a while, but after paying off a policeman who attempted to blackmail her, she had to place her in the well-known orphanage run by Mrs Strzałecka (a great friend of our family) who has been written about with such gratitude and admiration by all who had the good fortune to know her. At a dangerous moment when the Germans wanted to take her away as a Jewish child, she was adopted and thus survived. Is she alive today? I would very much like to know, but have never attempted to trace her for fear of upsetting her life.

I cannot help weeping today when I recall those awful times. Those who experienced them but were unable to help because they were threatened with the death penalty can never erase or forget those days. Much of the hurt, regret and bitterness of that nation is justified. But no one can explain it these days. You had to see it with your own eyes. The world has a short memory for those who were not the victors.

If anyone of Jewish origin who survived the pogrom at Mordy near Siedlce is out there in the world and happens to read my words, I would very much appreciate their contacting me.

37. You Must Remember

Halina Cychol

I was a little girl then, when my father came home terribly upset one spring afternoon, took me by the hand, and said, 'Come with me! I want to show you how they massacred the Jews at Gruchałowa's a few minutes ago.'

'Let her be', said my mother. 'She's still a child. She's too young to look at such horrible things.'

'She has to remember this all her life', he said, and turned to me. 'Come on, Ina.'

I was terrified. My father led me to our neighbour's. Mrs Gruchałowa had sheltered a Jewish family for several months, then someone had denounced her to the Gestapo. The Germans came, went to the attic, chased everyone out into the courtyard, and ordered the two men to dig a hole. One of them managed to jump the fence and escape into a nearby alder grove but the rest of the people were shot. We got to the scene right after the execution. I remember the horrible sight of their emaciated faces, with their eyes bulging, their clothes splashed with blood, their matted hair ... no! That was not something that a 5-year old child should ever have seen. I hid my face in my father's coat and clutched his hand spasmodically as I screamed. Years later I would learn that Mrs Gruchałowa's old mother had been shot that same day, and Mrs Gruchałowa taken to Auschwitz. Only her children, Zosia and Julek, survived. They had been visiting relatives in the country that day.

Now I can no longer recall the date of that terrifying spectacle. My father, Józef Kozaczek, had earlier saved two Jewish girls, Hilda and Fejda Winheit, from the Holocaust. He still lives in Dąbrowa Tarnowska. With the help of his colleagues from the Home Army resistance movement, Franciszek Fijał and Karol Minor, he arranged 'Aryan papers' for the girls. A priest supplied them with false baptismal certificates and the two girls went to Germany legally, under Polish names, to work taking care of small children.

Only after the war did my father receive letters from the girls. They were in America, had married, and were doing well. We still have that letter at our home at 57 ulica Szkolna in Dąbrowa Tarnowska. My father also has a book called *Żydzi polscy* (Polish Jews), which describes the cooperation of resistance organizations with the Jewish community. There was a ghetto in Dąbrowa, but I cannot remember it and know it only from what my parents told me. Only four people managed to survive that hell. My mother, the poet Maria Kozaczkowa, wrote a beautiful poem called 'Stara Bożnica' (The Old Prayer House) about them, which has been translated into Hebrew and is known to wide audiences of Polish Jews.

> The old prayer house stands abandoned
> Across from the small-town cemetery:
> The sight of it is dreadful and sad.
> It has watched like a mother for years
> That its sleeping children would not be disturbed
> Although they will never return to the living.
>
> The facade is supported on four columns
> Like Christ, Man of Sorrows, holding his head
> Sorrowful as a father beside a coffin
> Who cannot afford the funeral
> And remembers in turn each detail
> Of the last moments of his children of Judea.

I have quoted only the first two stanzas, of which there are nine altogether, and the poem has been published in Polish.

38. Blackmailers and Saviours

Irena Daniszewska-Froelich

The Rajgrodzki family lived near us on ulica Okrężna [in Warsaw], in the Officers' Settlement. My sister Lili made friends at secondary school with their daughter Wisia. Contacts between our parents were rather close. One day, Mr Jan Rajgrodzki told my parents, Maria and Paweł Daniszewski, that his whole family was preparing to move to the ghetto within a few days. My father was thunderstruck. 'Don't go!' he shouted. 'It's the worst decision you could make. Anything but that. It's certain death!' They debated stormily all night until Rajgrodzki changed his 'irreversible' decision.

They began carrying small, valuable objects to our house in a way prying eyes would not notice. My father, my sister and Mr Rajgrodzki bustled about finding hiding places for the family (scattered, unfortunately) with trustworthy acquaintances of ours. Then a big flatbed lorry drew up in front of their house and they loaded it with their worst possessions and large items of furniture, amid loud proclamations that they were all moving to the ghetto. People in the small neighbourhood in the Officers' Settlement knew each other, and for most of them this was the best explanation for the disappearance of the Jews.

With a walrus moustache that made him look like a respectable Polish aristocrat, Mr Rajgrodzki moved freely around town looking after his family's affairs. Among other things, he met my father to receive the valuables he had deposited with us. Wisia graduated from the clandestine Kochanowski Second Municipal Secondary School, married and became the happy mother of a son. After the war she would work as a journalist for *Życie Warszawy*. Unfortunately, her older sister Danusia and Mrs Rajgrodzka spent the whole time until the Warsaw Uprising 'closed up' in hiding together. Danusia paid for this with heart trouble and would die giving birth three years after the war. And dear, unforgettable Mr Jan Rajgrodzki died in the turmoil of the Warsaw Uprising.

* * *

Mr Rajgrodzki's brother lived with his wife and two sons in Konstancin. Misfortune came without warning! When they were all out for a walk, the mother stepped into a shop to make a small purchase while the men went on ahead. The men passed two 'blue' policemen and a gendarme, and a moment later heard a shot behind them.

They heard one of the thugs snarl, 'She's a Jewess!' Turning around, they saw a woman lying on the pavement – their wife and mother! The sons started instinctively to run to her, but their father was brave and self-controlled enough to restrain them even though his heart was breaking. Anything else would have meant certain death. The boys came straight to our house afterwards. We did not even try to comfort them; our hearts were breaking, too.

My father travelled to Konstancin to locate the boys' father and find out about further developments. When he returned, he said nothing. Several days later, Lili brought new identity cards for our friends. They moved to one of her acquaintances' for safety's sake. Their father visited us after the tragedy. I never found out their new names or their subsequent fates.

*   *   *

My mother's brother, Stefan Jeżycki, came to us and asked us to put up temporarily a married Jewish couple who were in a difficult situation.

My mother hesitated. 'There are the girls, you know. And how will I feed them?' But my father waved his hand and said, 'Send them to us!'

They appeared and slipped through the foyer. My parents spoke freely with them, explaining something. Eavesdropping at the closed door to the room, Lili and I strained to overhear the couple's timorous responses. Less than two weeks later, a pair of ruffians called at ten in the evening, after curfew: young, vulgar men dressed in black leather coats (so they seemed to me as I looked over Father's shoulder). They demanded an enormous sum of money; otherwise they would inform the Germans that we were harbouring Jews. Father cursed them roundly and denied that there were any strangers in our home. But 'bounty hunters' were no laughing matter, and we did not sleep all night.

Mother cried. After the end of curfew but before dawn (it was March), the unfortunates left our home. Father told them where to wait for a signal from my uncle, who apparently found them a safe place in a village. The bounty-hunters never came back. They already had a reputation. Our friends took care of them. The Polish Underground sentenced them to death, and the sentence was carried out by Andrzej Kirszenstajn and Geniek Wesołowski (who were later caught and shot in the street) and Heniek Cypel, who survived the war.

* * *

Basia stayed with us as our first cousin, the illegitimate child of Mother's sister, Weronika Jeżycka. Mama had a 'document', a birth certificate, to this effect. This was the version we spread among our neighbours, friends and the many visitors to our home. Weronika, who was close to us and who had her own interests in the matter, approved of this version.

Basia was about 5 years old. She had blonde locks that combed beautifully. Mother rinsed a reddish hue out of them with hydrogen peroxide. She was sweet-tempered, energetic and careful of what she said. Basia must have been well prepared for staying among strangers. She never cried or made faces. Nor did she ever say anything about her family or use the words 'father' or 'mother', even with us, her 'sisters'. Her only authentic relative was an aunt, whom I met on walks at a safe distance from home (but never at home).

We took Basia to the church in Wilanów so that she could learn the religious symbols and the names of the furnishings. We taught her to pray: 'Guardian Angel', 'Hail Mary', Our Father'. On Sundays, she went with us to the mass for young people at the church in Czerniaków. We did not know how long she would be staying with us, but it was imperative that she blend in perfectly. Father told us that she was the child of his pre-war acquaintances who had owned the Bro-Ro hosiery factory (we remembered them). Her parents had died in the ghetto; only she and her aunt escaped from that hell. Father never told us how he came into contact with the survivors, but I suppose that it was indirectly, through Zugajewicz's plumbing firm, whose shop on ulica Królewska he managed.

Our home life followed the usual wartime routine. We all had things to do and Basia 'became part of the family'. She spent most of her time with Mother, the soul of the home. Then Basia's aunt appeared unexpectedly and said that there was an opportunity for the two of them to go the United States. We tried unsuccessfully to persuade her to leave Basia with us, but she was firmly convinced that money sent by American Jewish organizations had been used to bribe the Germans. The Germans announced that all Jews concealed in Warsaw should come out of hiding. Those who did so would be able to leave the General Government; transport across the Atlantic had already been arranged. All those interested were to assemble at the former Hotel Polski on ulica Długa on a given day.

My sister and I protested fervently against letting Basia go. Up to her ears in Resistance work as a medical student at the clandestine Warsaw

University, Lili was convinced it was all a German trick to lure the Jews out of their hiding places. My parents decided, however, that they had no right to make the child their own and keep her from her only relative. Basia's aunt, unfortunately, had the final say.

The whole family escorted Basia to ulica Długa on the appointed day. Her aunt, who had been waiting in great anxiety in the hotel courtyard since early morning, was clinging to the bars of the gate. Anyone could enter, but it was forbidden to leave no matter what documents one had. German gendarmes were keeping order. This fact made us all the more anxious about the fate of the gullible people. Through the bars of the gate, we begged the aunt one last time to leave Basia with us, promising to guard her like a treasure. It was no use; her faith in this one hope of saving Basia and herself went beyond all reason. We all cried and even Basia, understanding that once again her life had been altered in a way she could not comprehend, sobbed as she clung to Mommy. Then she slipped through the opening in the gate.

Perhaps being torn away from us, from the warmth of the home and the care we had given her was a shock; perhaps she connected the sight of her aunt at the bars of the gate with her earlier tragic experiences. There was no time to explain. We had to get out of there! Father hurried us along, so that we would not be suspected of maintaining close contacts with Jews. The modest parcel we had packed for our Basia was probably never of any use to her. Perhaps the small bag of sandwiches and sweets kept her from going hungry in her last hours.

Over the following days, rumours circulated that instead of permitting those people to leave (with transportation supposedly waiting), the Germans had executed them in the terrain of the former ghetto, which had already been razed to the ground. We never managed to find out for sure. Perhaps Basia is alive somewhere, and perhaps she remembered our family. We lived for a long time with the hope that the little girl had survived.

39. The Righteous

Cecylia B. Federman

In the summer of 1942, my life in the Warsaw ghetto became unbearable. While others went to work, I had to hide with my recently born baby in a dark cellar surrounded by old, foul-smelling bedding and clothing. I was hungry, with a starving child who could barely get a drop of milk from my breast. The danger to our lives was constant. All day long I could hear the sound of steps, heavy boots and barking dogs hunting for hidden people.

At night the family would come 'home', if you can call home a place from which the tenants had already been taken to their death and where the new ones would come only to spend the night, before rushing off to the factory that afforded them protection.

My desperation reached the point that I decided to seek help among the Poles – on the other side of the high, barbed-wire-topped wall surrounding the ghetto.

Without tears but with strong determination, I left my family and went to face the German guard, who had already been bribed, and then the Polish-speaking individuals who called themselves '*Volksdeutschen*' or of German descent, and who hunted for victims.

They cleaned me out of all my money and my few possessions. But then I was lucky to find the address of a woman who let us in. My plan to go to the partisans in the woods was unrealistic. 'They would not take you with a child', she said. After a night-time air raid, which we spent in the basement, the woman felt the danger. Someone asked her, 'Who is that woman with the child?' She said that she had no right to risk the lives of her own two children.

For several days, I looked for the house where my two teachers used to live. I knew only the name of the suburb, but not their address. I was ready to return to the ghetto, but it was a Sunday and no traffic to or from the ghetto was allowed. For the last time, I went to the Sadyba suburb and a young girl led me to the house I was seeking.

Without hesitation or discussion, my two teachers greeted me and admitted me into their home and into their lives. It was wonderful to hear the words 'We are so glad to have you here.'

'Glad?' I asked. 'Do you remember who I am?'

Yes, they did remember, because twelve years earlier I had been the only Jewish student in the Cracow Teachers' College, where Maria was the director and Sophia a teacher. Jews were not admitted to this school.

'What a fine, sweet child you have. And pretty, too', said Sophia's 17-year-old daughter. My child was only sixteen months old, and, in the nightmarish life in the ghetto, nobody had paid any attention to him.

For the two weeks that we stayed there, the teachers watched the street and observed the neighbours, who peered curiously into the garden trying to find out who the strangers were. Meantime, the ladies were busy looking for work for me, and for a home to place the child in. At that point, they had to share the dangerous secret with others.

Maria consulted their priest about baptizing the child, not only to save his soul by making him a Christian, but also in order to get him good, legal papers which could save his life in time of need. But the priest advised against it. 'The child is too old', he said. 'These days, people baptize children just after they are born. Now, it would only awaken suspicion from the authorities.' So my son remained unbaptized.

Sophia was successful in her search. She found a family with three children, poor, but willing to take care of my child. But there was one condition. I would not be able to see my son. I would get no address – I would not even know what part of the city he was in. This was for their protection. 'Do you agree?' she asked. I agreed, consoled by the promise that, once every few weeks, they would bring the child to an appointed place to which I could come.

Soon, the child was taken away and I was living in the city, in somebody's empty flat. I had hardly anything to eat but my breasts got fuller and fuller of milk. In exchange for this good food the caretaker of the house, who had small twins and not enough milk to feed them, offered me dinners. But this lasted only a few days. Next, I did the same thing at the nearby children's hospital, run by nuns. They fed me with leftovers; I remember the thin soup and heaps of potatoes or old bread rolls. This, too, came to an end when a nun who was friendly to me said, 'Don't come here anymore. People are asking who you are.' She knew who I was, warned me, and remained silent.

At my first meeting with my son, he did not recognize me and would not come to me, but just held on to Sophia. There was trouble. Money was needed to take the sick child to a doctor, to buy medication and special food for him. My only money was in my mouth – eight golden crowns had to be taken off my teeth, and it was done by a discreet dentist who said, 'We are supposed to build health, not destroy it.' The gold was sold and the money delivered to the good people. This helped for a month and then, in addition to the previous problems, new ones arose. The woman got sick and asked Sophia to take my child back.

Now the teachers undertook the job of finding work for me with a family who would permit the child to be with its mother.

When a new employer was found and asked if I was Jewish, Maria answered, 'No Jewish students were admitted to our school.'

For about three years, my teachers' house was the only place where, on fine Sundays, we would go to visit and feel welcome.

Years later, my son and I found out that the two ladies had died. Sophia's daughter, who had married after the war, had a child, divorced and lived alone in Poland, had also died. Her daughter, Kasia, had come to the United States. We located her about ten years ago. She had a family, was living well and was anxious to meet us. A warm relationship developed between us.

I reported Maria's and Sophia's names to the 'Yad Vashem' Institute in Jerusalem and the two women are now among those called 'The Righteous Among the Nations'. Trees were planted in their names and a plaque was placed in the wall with the names of those who, at risk to their own lives, saved others.

Kasia and her family proudly received the honorary diploma for their grandmother and great-grandmother.

40. Difficult Decision

Kazimierz Kisielewski

During the years of the Nazi Occupation I worked as a clerk in the Crafts Chamber in Cracow – under the supervision, I hardly need add, of a German commissar. It turned out, through a fortunate happenstance, that we were in possession of several pre-war Master Craftsman's diplomas, complete with the original signatures and stamps of the Chamber officials. My colleagues and I decided to make use of these diplomas as a way of aiding persons concealing themselves under assumed names and occupations. One such person was Robert Armer, the son of a well-known Jewish baker and a reserve officer in the Polish Army, who was in hiding outside the ghetto. Although he worked under an assumed name, Armer was unfortunately arrested by the Gestapo some time later in one of the bakeries. I am not familiar with the circumstances of the arrest.

One day, the Gestapo conveyed Armer to the offices of the Crafts Chamber in order for him to point out the clerk who had allegedly issued the false diploma. While admitting to its possession, Armer had stated that he did not remember the clerk involved and had obtained the document through other channels. Under interrogation, he had invented a fictitious description of the person who had provided him with the diploma. Through an unhappy twist of fate, this description fitted one of my co-workers exactly. As luck would have it, this man was my fellow Army officer and had returned only a few days earlier from the Oflag in Murnau. His release had been obtained by our commissar, since he spoke German. This was in 1942. The circumstances of his recent release from the prisoner-of-war camp saved us from another Polish tragedy. Unfortunately, I am unfamiliar with the subsequent fate of Robert Armer. I must add, however, that we came near to having all our activities given away. One of the female clerks, evidently infatuated with our co-worker who had fallen under suspicion, lost her nerve. While we waited in anxious suspense for the result of the confrontation between Robert Armer and our co-worker, which was taking place in the presence of the Gestapo behind the closed doors of the commissar's office, she underwent an attack of hysteria from fear about his fate. She was ready to sacrifice one of us to save him. We managed, however, to calm her down and lead her out of the office, averting a hazard of incalculable consequences.

Another unforgettable occurrence concerned a member of the Crafts Chamber Council, apparently a Lutheran, who had at some point converted to Judaism after marrying a Jewish woman. In order to protect his family during the Occupation (he had two small children) he claimed German nationality: his surname and fluency in the language afforded such a possibility. Unfortunately, although he managed to save his family from the Germans, he was nevertheless arrested in 1945 by the NKVD or perhaps the Polish Security (UB) and sent to a camp, in Jaworzno near Chrzanów if I am not mistaken, as a traitor to Poland. The only strange thing is that no professional organization came to his defence, despite knowing him, the circumstances of his tragedy, and the fact that he did no harm to anyone.

* * *

Looking back on that period in our history, I recall the many different ways in which it was possible to help even those members of the Jewish population who were confined to the ghetto. My sister provides an example of this. In order to augment our family budget (wages were at starvation level), she ran a shop selling household items, established through our common efforts and resources on Wolnica Square in Cracow. The shop stood in the Kazimierz district, not far from the ghetto. Before entering the ghetto, the former Jewish merchants of Kazimierz left much of their merchandise with neighbours, or even concealed whole warehouses full. The larger caches were of course discovered and looted. Similarly, many neighbours arrogated this property to themselves. According to my sister's reports, however, many neighbours did indeed hold such merchandise and return it piecemeal, as required, to its original owners who were in need.

She proceeded in a similar way in her shop, and not for financial gain. This made it possible to protect the Jews from death by starvation, up to a certain time. My sister's shop was a contact point. There, Jewish merchants deposited considerable quantities of merchandise, which they were unable to sell at once. They made transactions there with buyers they had met. My sister not only advised them as to current prices, but also found buyers for them so that they would not have to endanger themselves by going to the centre of the city – they wore the Star of David on their arms. They also availed themselves of the opportunity to purchase provisions from the farmers who came to the Square to offer for legal or illegal sale the foodstuffs that were distributed in small quantities to the Polish population on the basis of 'ration cards'. As is known, many Poles extended aid to the unfortunate Jewish people in just such a way, not to mention those who, at grave risk to their own lives and those of their families, sheltered and concealed the endangered Jews.

* * *

When the Jewish population was resettled in the Cracow ghetto that was created under the German Occupation in 1942, I was employed in the Crafts Chamber under German administration. At this time, a former employee, a Jewish woman (I do not recall her surname), came to our office. I believe that her first name was Iza. She was the daughter of a well-known painter and varnish maker. She was slender and young with delicate white skin and black hair, a typical Jewish beauty. While telling her former colleagues about the ghetto and the conditions under which she was forced to exist, she asked shyly about the chances of anyone sheltering her young daughter. These were the last days before the closing of the ghetto, and many parents were seeking ways of saving their children by placing them in private homes or convents. We perhaps failed to realize at that time that it was easier to shelter a fugitive in a large city like Cracow than in a small town where everyone knows everyone else. I can still remember Iza's large, frightened, dark eyes. She did not ask, but only discreetly requested her co-workers' advice. I listened in horror to the discussions about the fate of these people ... It somehow did not occur to me that I could help her. My family had just been evicted from the quarter taken over by the Germans. We were living on the sixth floor in the centre of town, among new neighbours. Nevertheless, my wife and I talked for a long time about how to help Iza. We indeed had a year-old son, but we were prevented from making a decision not only by the death penalty for concealing Jews, but also by our family situation: we were living with my mother, sister and brothers. And yet the conditions were not suitable. I do not know what advice her female co-workers gave her. The whole subject had of necessity to be kept a secret. I was myself long tormented by pangs of conscience over why I had not made the decision to save that child. Later, indeed, it turned out that there was a chemical firm working for the Germans in the building where we were living, which would have offered some sort of cover. But at the same time, the Regional Staff of the [clandestine] Peasant Battalion resistance movement was there, which made things dangerous. I long remembered Iza's sad face and was tormented by that refusal to help. To this day, when talking with my grandchildren, I recall that fact which it is impossible to forget.

41. A Pseudo-Turk

Magdalena Knoll

It was the end of 1943 or the beginning of 1944. We were living in Cracow. The German housing board requisitioned one room in the flat belonging to my parents' friends, the Tomaszewskis, and assigned it to a young woman and her two children. The woman introduced herself to her hosts as a Turkish citizen. Her name was Tamara. Her sons were 10-year-old Achmed and 5-year-old Ali. This tenant imposed by the Germans soon got on close terms with the owners of the flat. As they made friends, the Tomaszewskis began to see through the smokescreen and guessed that Tamara was Jewish. A visit from the Gestapo soon confirmed this.

Fortunately, the visit occurred at a moment when Tamara and the children were out. Once the Gestapo had left, one of the Tomaszewskis ran to the Cracow 'Planty' [garden] where Tamara usually went for walks with her boys, to warn her of the danger. The situation obviously ruled out her returning to the flat. Tamara and the children took shelter at our flat on ulica Dietla. We realized that it was imperative to get them out of Cracow as soon as possible. We decided that I (then 17 years old) would take them to Pionki, near Radom, where we owned a flat. This was in fact a mad idea, since that flat was a partisan safe house, but nothing better came to mind then and we had no other options.

We left Cracow several days later. We were fortunate to reach our destination despite various hair-raising incidents along the way. Tamara was a strikingly beautiful young woman, but her peroxide blonde hair could not conceal the fact that she had distinctly Semitic features.

Our flat in Pionki was hardly the safest place in the world, and so we tried to find a hiding place for them in one of the nearby villages. This turned out to be more difficult than expected. The people we approached recognized them as Jews and refused.

Tamara's stay prolonged itself. The situation became increasingly nerve-wracking. Both my brothers belonged to the Home Army resistance movement and weapons were kept in the flat. Almost all the neighbours suspected us of harbouring Jews. Despite their catastrophic predicament on the front lines, the Germans were not relaxing their repressive measures.

We never let on to Tamara that we knew about her true origins. We stuck to the version about her Turkish background. This was safer for all concerned. She said little about herself. There were times, however, when the need to confide in someone got the better of her deliberate self-control. From fragmentary remarks about her experiences I pieced together her story.

They had lived before the war in Częstochowa, where they had run what they called the 'Turkish Bakery'. That name must have given rise to the idea of claiming Turkish origin when the Germans arrived. Whether the Germans really believed them or only allowed them to go on running the bakery in exchange for bribes, I cannot say. Nor do I know when or how Tamara and her sons were deported to Majdanek. I suppose that they bought their release from the death camp for some enormous sum, and acquired Turkish citizenship. There were cases of Jews avoiding death in this manner. As it turned out, however, the guarantee of safety was far from permanent.

I shall never forget the expression on Tamara's face when she talked about Majdanek. There was so much terror, pain and despair. We still lived together. The expected imminent Soviet Army offensive kept up our hopes of surviving, for it was the end of 1944. Tamara's sister visited us from time to time. She was beautiful and looked like an authentic Turk. She came with a small daughter who had her leg in a plaster cast. We did not know her name or how she had avoided the fate of other Jews.

Days full of anxiety passed, yet by some miracle we evaded the worst. Only on the eve of the Soviet offensive of January 1945 did we place Tamara and her children with a certain farmer in a village near Garbatka.

When the Bolsheviks arrived, my brothers and I fled to Cracow, fearing the persecution being meted out to Home Army veterans.

I never saw Tamara again.

I must admit to feeling a certain sadness over the fact that she never attempted to contact me despite all the hard times we had lived through together. Finally, however, the fact that she and her children had managed to survive through everything was the most important. I learned from the Tomaszewskis that she had visited them to retrieve her belongings and had then set out for Belgium, and from there for Canada.

I never knew their surname, and Tamara, Achmed and Ali were certainly assumed first names. When I look back, I wonder about the further fate of that family.

Perhaps there is a list somewhere of those who managed to survive the Holocaust. Perhaps it would be possible to trace the former owners of the Turkish Bakery in Częstochowa, or their children.

42. A Handful of Sweets

Jerzy Kobielski

It was the end of the winter of 1943. I was 12 years old. I retain only vague, fragmentary memories of that period. Such will be this account – without any attempt at reconstruction.

We were then living in the most benighted backwater of Galicia, near the town of Opatowice facing the place where the Dunajec river flows into the Vistula. My father administered a large landed estate. We occupied a manor house on one of the demesne farms, with buildings that included several large agricultural structures as well as three or four cottages housing employees of the estate.

There was no German outpost in the vicinity. The closest one must have been in Kazimierza Wielka, about twenty kilometres from us, and the nearest 'blue police' post in Korczyń, a small town approximately ten kilometres away. There were no Occupation authorities in the nearest small town, Opatowice (about three kilometres distant). Completely devoid of paved roads (the only kind of transport was provided by the Vistula river boats running between Cracow and Sandomierz, and they did not operate in winter), the territory was full of partisan units of the Home Army resistance movement. Increasingly numerous and troublesome, the bandits who came out at night also invariably claimed to be part of 'the organization'.

I cannot remember the details of the liquidation of the Jews in Opatowice. In any case, there were not many of them; that locality was more of a village than a town. It seems that they were transported away in horse-drawn carts brought for that purpose by the 'blue police', certainly under German command. I can, however, remember how a group of Jews – several families – evaded deportation by fleeing from the town. They wandered around, in the fields and woods, sleeping in hay ricks and trying to stay out of sight. Some peasants secretly sold them food in exchange for clothes and valuables. As far as I recall, it was a relatively mild winter.

Those living rough included a relatively wealthy merchant by the name of Preis, with his family and small children. My father had previously had business dealings with him (Preis must have been a grain dealer), and liked and respected him. He was a serious, intelligent, middle-aged man whom my parents regarded as someone who stood out among the small-town Jewish community. They also knew his wife and children who, it seems, liked my mother.

From among the group of fugitives, only Preis had meetings with my father. He came covertly to the manor house and received food and milk for his whole family, free of charge, of course. Both he and my parents tried to ensure that as few people as possible knew about his visits. Nevertheless, all those living on the manor must have known – it was impossible to keep secrets in such a small circle.

To this day I can recall my parents' anxiety and dread. I felt these emotions keenly and was aware of their source. I knew that they sympathized with Preis and his family and sincerely desired to help, but all help involved very real risks. Informing to the Germans was then a common means of revenge and settling accounts. Sharp conflicts occurred between the manor house and particularly its administration, as personified by my father, and the workers on the estate. Some of the latter doubtless hated my father. There may indeed have been neither Germans nor 'blue police' in the vicinity, but they could appear at any instant; an informer could, after all, see to it that his denunciation reached as far as Kazimierz. The concealment of fugitives in our home or the outbuildings could, in the long run, hardly go unnoticed by the hired hands. No one could foresee whether one of them might use such knowledge in the manner that was all too familiar.

Nevertheless, it seems (I use this form because it is precisely this fact of which I am not certain today; my parents kept a great deal from me and there are things that I suspected or reconstructed on the basis of fragments of sentences and allusions, for they never mentioned these events to the end of their lives, but it seems to me that this is how things were) that for a certain time my father made it possible for the Preis family to sleep in the manor house barn, which they entered at night and left before dawn so as to avoid attracting anyone's attention. The watchman, who patrolled the estate all night with his dogs, must have been in on the secret. Did my parents trust him to such a degree? I cannot recall. Nor do I know why the Preises stopped spending nights in the barn, for they certainly did not use it to the end. Did someone see them? Did they themselves back out to avoid endangering us? I remembered that my parents regarded them as 'very delicate' (hardly an appropriate word in this context). As if their concern for our safety was stronger than their fear for their own lives.

I do not remember how long the nomadic existence of the Opatowice Jews lasted. Not long: a week, or two at the most. After dark one evening,

Preis came to see my father. Their conversation took place in the office, just the two of them, but my mother and I knew that they were in there and that the discussion concerned some especially dramatic situation. Was it already known that the fugitives were to be rounded up? I do not know. All I know is that Preis then requested – or perhaps asked about, rather than requesting – a hiding place. For his whole family? Or perhaps only for the children? Did my father turn him down? Or was it unnecessary to refuse, since the other understood and withdrew the request? I do not know.

All I know is that at a certain moment my mother carried a large handful of sweets into the office for Preis's children. However, Preis left in a hurry and the sweets remained on the desk. When he was gone, my parents conferred. They were extremely downcast. I heard my mother say sorrowfully, 'He forgot to take those sweets for the children'.

The next day we learned before noon that the Germans and 'blue police' had come, searched the vicinity, and rounded up all the Jews who, it seems, did not attempt to flee but rather permitted themselves to be captured. The Preis family was also caught. They were all loaded onto carts and taken away somewhere.

We sat down at the dinner table in silence and gloom. When the maid carried the soup in, she said that shots had supposedly been heard not long before from the direction of Krzczonów, a village two kilometres away. My parents said nothing. No one spoke during the whole dinner. We were leaving the table when the maid came in again. She said that one of the cart drivers whom the Germans had ordered to transport the Jews had just returned. He said that they had all been shot in Krzczonów. 'All of them?' my mother asked. 'The children, too?'

'Yes', replied the maid. 'All of them.' No one said anything more.

The sweets for Preis's children lay on the desk in my father's office for several days. No one cleared them away, although everyone glanced at them. In the end, after a long time, I began eating them. Not out of greed – I had my own sweets. I remember my intentions precisely: I wanted to remove the evidence.

For fifty years, I have refrained from speaking about this matter with anyone. Nor do I think my parents ever discussed it. I have never forgotten it. It remains vivid, shameful and burning to this day.

43. The Reward

Jerzy Kucharski

I commenced working at the Furniture Factory at 204 ulica Zielona in Lwów in 1940. My close acquaintance Jerzy Auerbach, Jewish by nationality, also worked there. He and his wife lived nearby. Between the entry of the German army in July 1941 and the barbarous liquidation of the Lwów ghetto, many Jews were employed at the factory. Numerous members of the AK, the Home Army resistance movement, also worked there from 1941–44, including Cavalry Captain Antoni Kłosowski, formerly commander of the South Lwów District, who was under our special protection. On occasions, Captain Kłosowski and I spent the night at the Auerbachs' flat. All of us, but particularly the Auerbachs, were at risk. Yet this brought us closer together and we trusted each other completely. When the Germans began their brutal liquidation of the Jews in Lwów, the problem arose of saving the Auerbachs. They had certain contacts in Warsaw, which seemed to represent the only chance of survival. It was suggested that I accompany them on the train journey from Lwów to Warsaw. I agreed without reservation and travelled first with Jerzy Auerbach and then, two weeks later, with his wife.

At the time, I treated escorting the Auerbachs from Lwów to Warsaw as something normal. Whether I was afraid or even whether I was risking my life is something I would rather not talk about. I believe that I was lucky, or perhaps we were lucky together, all the more so since Jerzy Auerbach had certain 'Semitic' facial features, as opposed to his wife, an attractive young blonde wearing a gold Catholic religious medal around her neck. In spite of many quite difficult experiences, the Auerbach family survived and emigrated to Australia after residing in Warsaw for several years. Acquaintances have informed me that they tried to find me after the war.

I escorted a young Jewish woman who was also employed with me in the furniture factory to Częstochowa in 1942. I am unable to recall her name. She left Lwów with the appropriate 'Aryan' documents. As far as I am aware, she was to be placed in a convent. I am unaware as to how many Jewish women took shelter in convents, and whether anyone has written about this subject.

Now I should like to recount my own life after 1945. Following the liberation of Lwów by the Red Army in July 1944, I continued working at the furniture factory. As a Home Army soldier, I participated in Operation 'Storm' in Lwów. I was seized by functionaries of the Soviet 'Smersh' counter-intelligence agency on 2 March 1945 and transported to their Lwów headquarters in ulica Kadecka. The investigation against me lasted until the end of 1945. My interrogator was First Lieutenant Kozłof, accompanied by an interpreter. They were both of Jewish nationality. It was established in the course of the investigation that I would be charged with activity against the USSR and was liable to a sentence of twenty-five years in prison camp. During my last interrogation, perhaps in an act of desperation, I stated that I had risked my life to save people and now people of the same race wanted to liquidate me. As I remember, the young female Jewish interpreter stated, after conferring with the investigator, First Lieutenant Kozłof, that I should not boast about things that could be checked. After this conversation, I was not summoned for interrogation over a long period. Only after three to four weeks was I summoned, and my investigator stated in the presence of the interpreter that they had checked my assertion and were going to convince me that Jews, too, are capable of saving people's lives. I expressed my gratitude. It was explained to me that I could not be released. However, several documents had been changed and I was re-classified as an internee. On 31 December 1945, I was transported among a large group of Polish Home Army members to the camp in Diaghilev near Ryazan. I subsequently stayed in various camps – always as an internee – until 28 February 1949.

My investigator, Kozłof, rode together with us from Lwów to Ryazan in the prison carriage. There was an occasion for a private conversation with him when we went separately to the toilet. He told me among other things that he had been unable to do anything more for me, and that I should take care and be cautious whom I spoke to, and about what.

Upon returning to Poland I married a woman whom I had met in the prison camp, studied and went to work. I retired in 1981 and now work only as a volunteer. In general, I have led a quiet and interesting life, and have managed, as they say, to see a bit of the world. I have no complaints. Rescuing people gave me satisfaction because it succeeded. When I think that someone would want to thank me for this, I then wonder – How could I thank my investigator, First Lieutenant Kozłof? Perhaps this is the way things are in the world: you do something good for someone, and you get a reward. My reward was my life.

44. The Earth Trembled

Bolesław Kulczycki

The Red Army hurriedly withdrew from Brody on 1 July 1941. The town stood empty for a short while. Then the German soldiers arrived in lorries and on motorcycles in the afternoon. They were all shaved and better dressed than the Russians. Many of them spoke Polish; they were called 'Silesians'. The *Arbeitsamt* [Labour Office] assigned my mother to a job in the kitchen of their canteen and my father to work in the nearby lumber mill. On 18 September mother came home from work with news that a special *'Aktion'* to liquidate the Jews was scheduled for that night. Our neighbour Sachowicz, the commandant of the Ukrainian police, confirmed the rumours. Sachowicz's wife was Jewish. My parents warned Jewish families with whom they were acquainted. Some of them came to our house to hide in the cellar under the kitchen floor that we used as a larder. The hatch in the floor leading down to that cellar was covered by a rug on which a table stood. The following people hid there: Bronia (I do not recall her surname), Herman Achtentuch, Deaf Mańka (I do not recall her surname), Lusia Skulska, Runia Seltzer *née* Meles, Mr Seltzer, the commandant of the Jewish police and his wife, and Mr Kupferman. Three other people hid where we kept the firewood in the barn. Commandant Sachowicz initially tried to hide his wife and her family from ulica Gęsia at his home, but soon had to send them to us.

Our neighbours Markus Schwadron, his daughter Liza Grunfeld, and his granddaughter Greta tried to hide in their own house next door. But their hiding place was useless once a Ukrainian family moved in, so they left at night for the village of Majdan Pieniacki, under the straw in a horse-drawn cart.

The fourteen people hiding in our house had to be supplied with food, medicine, clean linen and sanitary articles. In view of the general shortages, this was not easy to do. My brother and I would visit my mother in the German kitchen and come back with various foodstuffs. Sachowicz, too, helped us with food, medicine and clothing. He also warned us about imminent repression operations. There was the further problem of care by a physician. The atmosphere in the city was getting worse and worse. There were many informers. Everyone knew that the Germans shot all the members of families that aided Jews.

When my father and I were walking down the street one day, we saw German gendarmes using their rifle butts to force Jewish people, both men and women, towards lorries. Soon afterwards, we heard volleys of machine-gun fire. People stopped on the street and said that Jews were being shot at the 'Okopisko' Jewish cemetery. The park at the Sznell estate was another killing ground. The Ukrainian police, of whom Sachowicz was commandant, took part in the murders.

Out of curiosity, my friends and I went to the park at the Sznell estate. A woman whom we met nearby told us the terrible details. The first group of victims had to dig a large mass grave. Then they had to strip naked. A machine-gun salvo cut their legs out from under them. The next group of victims had to throw into the grave those who had not fallen in when shot. Many of those in the pit were still alive and begging to be finished off. The woman had watched as a man whom she knew killed his own wife with a shovel. I remember that blood was plainly visible on the wildflowers that grew there. The woman also told us that, on the day after the executions, the soil that had been thrown over the mass grave was still trembling ...

A physician named Bilig lived and worked in Brody. He had helped deliver me. Mother and I were standing at the gate of our house when another group of Jews was being led to the rail station. Dr Bilig, his wife and daughter were among them. He gestured to my mother for something to drink. She ran inside, came right back with a cup of water, and asked the gendarme for permission. Dr Bilig and his family drank the water. No one noticed when the physician sprinkled poison into the cup. A moment later, the three of them were dead. No one took any interest in why they had died so suddenly. Poison was a valuable commodity in this bleak period. The groups of Jews kept under strict guard by gendarmes with dogs had to walk two kilometres from the centre of Brody to the train station. Those who could not walk fast enough were beaten and attacked by the dogs. Those who could not go on were killed. The wagons full of people were sent to Bełżec or Majdanek near Lublin. The Hochbergers and their daughter Gina were in one such wagon. The parents decided on a desperate act. Through a hole in the wagon, they threw their daughter out of the moving train. 'You must live!' they shouted. When the German sentry saw the little girl falling, he opened fire. Fortunately, he only managed to wound her. When she regained consciousness, she realized that she was completely naked and lying in a puddle of blood, and that two peasants were standing over her. These men had removed her clothes because they thought she was dead. What they wanted was the clothing. They did not give it back to her. But, seeing that she was alive, they decided to turn her over to the police. At that moment, a railway worker approached from a nearby hut. 'This is railway property', he announced, 'and it is my duty to turn her over to the police'. The two Ukrainian peasants walked away. The railway man led the naked, shivering, wounded girl to his hut. He brought her food, a skirt and a blouse from his nearby home. Today, Gina Lanceter remembers proudly that 'the railway man was a Pole'. Gina made her way to the church in the nearby village, where the priest helped her and furnished her with false birth and baptismal certificates. One must assume that God forgave him this untruthfulness. 'Aryan papers' were among the most sought-after items in those days. Poles produced them in cooperation with Catholic parish priests, but one must also remember the cases in which Jewish people with 'Aryan papers' were blackmailed by members of the local populace.

45. He Left and He Returned

Henryka Kuza

Ici Beje was a poor Jew. He depended on more affluent people. He came to us in the evenings, and I would go to the bakery to purchase bread for him. Once, he came in the company of a Jewish man we did not know. The stranger was carrying a religious medal and a gold cross. My mother purchased these items and asked him for a chain. He promised to bring one. One evening he turned up, all bloody and unable to speak. He stayed with us for several days. We presumed that he had been attacked by outlaws in the meadow, beaten and certainly robbed; later, this unfortunately proved to have been the case. I do not know what became of him afterwards.

Ici Beje was our most frequent guest. Since our barn faced the meadows and mother never closed the gate, we frequently encountered him there. It must have been his second winter in hiding. He never washed or changed his clothes, and smelled bad even at a distance. 'Pani Bobowska, I have nowhere to go.' Mother would take him to the stables, where it was warmer, and give him food. This happened frequently. He would leave after several nights, and then he would return.

The gendarmes from Korczyń came to take delivery of some planks from my father one day. They loaded ten horse-drawn wagons with lumber and took my father to Korczyń with them. They took him into the gaol, where Ici Beje was sitting. My father was speechless. He later recounted that he said not a word, while Ici Beje kept repeating, 'Pan Bobowski, you must think I turned you in, but I never did. Your family was very good to me.' They let my father go. Ici Beje must certainly have been shot there in Korczyń. Those were terrible times!

My next contact was with Mrs Felderman. She was a seamstress. She was hiding with my brother's mother-in-law. She slept there and came to our house during the day to sew things for my sister-in-law. When she was at our place, she stayed in a room separated by a door from the one in which magistrate Gartkiewicz had his law office. At times, she forgot herself and sang in Yiddish. The magistrate warned my mother. She understood, and he was a human being, and that was the end. I do not know what became of her later. She certainly did not survive. I can only recall what people said about her sister, who was caught while she was pregnant. I still remember – 'after they shot her, the baby was still moving in her womb'.

I had another terrifying experience. The Szwuger family had lived in our street. Afterwards, Commandant Kaczmarek, a despicable man, moved into their house. The partisans killed him. I do not know the circumstances in which one of the Szwugers' daughters was apprehended along with a Jewish man. Kaczmarek's wife supposedly promised to save her life if she would tell where she had hidden her karakul coat. The Szwuger girl told her, but Kacmarek's wife did not save her. It was winter. The neighbours' garden lay between our house and the local prison. With the trees bare, we could see everything. The Szwuger girl and that man were led outside. I watched as a 'blue policeman' shot her. I know that Hąc and Gołda were there. Now I cannot remember which one it was, but it was one of those two. A gendarme shot the Jewish man.

Mrs Preis's son visited us after the war to ask if his mother had left anything with us. My father returned everything.

We did not help much, but we did what we could. I need not be ashamed of my parents. They acted like human beings.

All of that is in the past.

46. A Drop of Water

Maria Morawska

I was born in 1931 and lived with my parents, Antonina and Teofil Dudziński, and my sister Barbara (born in 1928) and my brother Stanisław (born in 1929) at 28 ulica Warmińska in Zielonka near Warsaw. The Germans killed my mother in May, 1941. These words about myself should suffice as background for this account.

*   *   *

The Germans established a ghetto in Zielonka just after the Russo-German war of 1941 began. They designated for this purpose the buildings of the summer camp where Jewish children had spent their holidays before the war. People were crowded in there from the surrounding localities of Zielonka, Marki, Pustelnik and others. A fence, not particularly closely guarded, surrounded the barracks. The Jews could go 'to Zielonka' to shop – in other words, to the centre of town, where the shops were. We also went there to shop. One day, perhaps in the summer of 1942, the Germans issued a ban on leaving the ghetto or perhaps ordered the enforcement of a ban that had been issued earlier. A 'round-up' of people found outside the ghetto was organized. I was in the 'shopping district' then. I saw how Jews were pursued, caught and beaten. The policemen who did this were themselves, unfortunately, Jewish. (All the inmates of the ghetto wore armbands with the Star of David.) I returned home terrified. My father was sitting on the porch with a man I did not recognize. From their conversation I deduced that he was one of the Jews being pursued, and that my father had offered him shelter. The police walked past without entering the houses. When the round-up was over, the man went 'home' – to the ghetto. Soon after this event, the Jews were transferred to the 'central' ghetto in Warsaw. I was not in Zielonka the day they liquidated the ghetto. When I returned several days later, I went to the empty barrack with other children. In the concrete rubbish tip near the former ghetto laid a man's body, barely covered. I recognized him; he had visited my parents. His bent knee stuck out of the tip.

* * *

It must have been 1942. My father bicycled to work by way of Ząbki. One evening he came home dreadfully upset. He told us what had happened: on his way home, he had to wait at the rail crossing in Zielonka where a goods train was standing. People, Jews, being carried to the ghetto in Warsaw were inside the cattle wagons. It was raining. German soldiers guarded the carriages. At a certain moment, an arm holding a tin cup emerged from the little window in one of the carriages. A man was trying to collect some drops of the water running off the roof of the carriage. A German cocked his rifle. The man did not see the German. The German fired. He hit what he was aiming at.

* * *

We survived the war in great poverty. My father had no talent for buying and selling, which was the foundation of existence then. We therefore rented out a room to 'summer holiday-makers' from Warsaw during holidays. Among those who lodged with us were the Fuerskis and the Waluśes. I think Mr Fuerski was a dentist. They were a Jewish family, of which everyone was aware. They lived in Warsaw with a Polish family and had Polish documents. Those Poles also came to Zielonka for their holiday and lived with us or with our neighbours, the Czupryniaks. They had two lovely little sons for whom I often acted as babysitter. Their father played the violin beautifully. Unfortunately, I am unable to recall their name. The Germans came one night for the Waluśes, who were staying with the Czupryniaks. They led them out of the house and shot them at the clay-pit. They were said to have been denounced by an informer from Marki (they had taken the train from Warsaw to Marki). The informer was shot in 1944 by soldiers of the Polish Underground. I do not know if they were from the Home Army or some other army, because we were deported on 4 September 1944 and did not return to Zielonka until May 1945. Fortunately, the Fuerskis survived the war.

* * *

A short way down ulica Warmińska from our house lived Pani [Mrs] Wanda, *née* Fitze, Olbrychska by marriage. Pani Wanda had a flat in Warsaw, in the Tamka district, I believe, and a small house in Zielonka that she had inherited from her parents. She once brought from Warsaw a small, fair-haired girl of 7 or 8 years old. The girl called Pani Wanda 'Auntie'. We loved playing with her because she was very intelligent. Later, the little girl went away somewhere. We knew that she was Jewish. She supposedly survived the war.

Pani Wanda's garden abutted a plot of waste-ground where an enormous clump of blackberry bushes grew. We often played among those bushes and we noticed how a heap of pure golden sand began appearing there. We all surmised that a tunnel was being dug from Pani Wanda's house to the house next door. It was known that Pani Wanda frequently harboured Jews. The Germans had carried out repeated searches of both houses, without ever finding anyone. After the war, perhaps in 1947, while spending the holidays with my aunt in Bielsko-Biała, I met a dentist of her acquaintance. It turned out that both he and his wife had hidden throughout the war in Pani Wanda's house in Zielonka, where they had dug a shelter (hence the yellow sand). The shelter had been concealed beneath the coal stove in the kitchen. When the Germans made one of their frequent searches, they never suspected that the entrance to the shelter could be there. Pan [Mr] Isenberg, as I believe the dentist was named, recalled how his wife had once come down with a coughing fit during a prolonged search. He had had to cover her mouth with his hand, nearly suffocating her. When I met them, they had a delightful little son. They emigrated from Poland a few months afterwards. They also helped Pani Wanda emigrate to the United States, where her husband had ended up after the war.

An acquaintance, a certain Pan Godlewski who passed as a Pole, used to visit my half-sister Stefania Kozerska. When the grown-ups talked among themselves, they worried that if the Germans caught him they would have no trouble confirming that he was Jewish, and I knew what they meant. One of my playmates was Oleńka (she lent me Sienkiewicz's *With Fire and Sword*), who stayed with neighbours along with her mother and grandmother or aunt. Everyone in the neighbourhood knew that they were Jews. Mr Godlewski fortunately survived the war. I do not know what became of Oleńka and her family.

Zielonka, a small locality outside Warsaw, was an asylum for many Jewish families during the war. I was a child then and remember only fragments from those years. Perhaps there are others still alive who remember more.

47. The Rescued Little Girl

Janina Okęcka

It was August, 1942. I was 19 years old. I had been sworn into the Home Army resistance movement half a year earlier. Twice a week, an older sister and I went by buggy or on horseback from Mordy, where we lived with our family, to Hruszniewo, for a clandestine first-aid course. On one of those hot August days we were returning, as always, along the road through Łosice. I saw something terrible there which, of course, I could not understand at once. Łosice was deserted, the houses empty, the doors standing open, terrible disorder and things discarded and strewn about everywhere. It was apparent that some great crowd of people had passed through in a hurry, in a panic. Someone told us along the way that the Germans had driven the Jews out of the ghetto and taken them somewhere on foot. We rode through that small town without stopping and continued on to the road from Łosice to Mordy. I will never forget what I saw on that fourteen-kilometre ride.

All along the road, in the ditches and on the grass strip, lay the bloody corpses of what were predominantly old people, who must have been unable to keep up and had been killed on the spot by the Germans. I do not know how many of them there were, even approximately. It was appalling. Then we rode through Mordy, which looked the same as Łosice. At last we reached home, where we were finally told what had happened a few hours earlier.

The Germans had driven the whole Jewish population of both small towns on foot to Siedlce. One of the teachers (a Jewish woman) from the public primary school in Mordy had given her year-and-a-half old child to my older sister with a request that she save her (my sister has written about this on p.148).

When I reached home after that awful ride, my sister and that little girl were sitting out in the garden. It was important that as few people as possible found out about the child. Our father, who had been in Siedlce that day, returned an hour later. His face was ashen and he related in terror how on his way home along the Siedlce road he had met that tragic procession. How some of them (after all, they knew who he was) had begged him to help as they made way for him to pass. The Germans screamed, drove the people away, and ordered my father to keep going. How horribly powerless he had been in the face of such force, how he had been ashamed of his (momentary) freedom. It was a terrible day. Our aunt took the Jewish girl with her to Warsaw as her own child three days later. For some time, she kept her at home with her own children, but as a result of blackmail from various people she had to give her to an orphanage. She placed her in the home for children run by Pani [Mrs] Strzałecka (so lovingly remembered in the book by Władysław Bartoszewski, *Who Saves One Life*).

48. The House at the Crossroads

Jerzy Rożniecki

Our house stood at the very beginning of a two-kilometre-long, one-street village that stretched all the way to what was then the border of Warsaw and Łódź provinces. Approximately four kilometres away ran the asphalt 'autostrada', as it was called, linking Katowice and Warsaw. The nearest town was Mszczonów and in the other direction, slightly farther away, lay Biała Rawska and Rawa Mazowiecka. Geography or History saw to it that at least three waves of refugees, homeless unfortunates, passed through our village during the war. The first house at a crossroads is always an encouragement to rest on the bench, to ask for a glass of water or something to eat, to request a night's lodging somewhere, in the house or in the barn. Despite the poverty of the ten *morgs* [about 60,000 square metres] of sandy soil they owned, my parents were hospitable and sympathetic to suffering.

The first wave of refugees came ahead of and behind the front. I remember a refugee from Poznań who feared, with justification, that the Germans would persecute him for membership in the Polish Western Union. I remember that Feliks Dzierżanowski, a favourite conductor on Polish Radio, stayed with us. There were many others. A cavalryman demobilized himself and was given civilian clothing. I remember that he came from Garwolin.

Nearby, German airplanes carried out daily massacres on the 'autostrada'.

The second wave was Jewish and usually passed through at night. It must have been 1941. The ghettos in small towns were being liquidated. I do not know what was left to liquidate in Mszczonów. Lying on the flank of the Kutno campaign and taken twice by the Germans, the town had been thoroughly demolished and burned. The leading citizens, including Dr Zacharewicz, the parish priest, and perhaps the canon, had been taken as hostages and then shot. Yet people still lived there.

In connection with the deportations and decimation, many Jews had scattered into the nearby villages. Our village left a lot to be desired as a place of asylum. There were no woods close at hand, and at the far end lived a dozen or more families of German settlers, known during the war as *Volksdeutsch*. Nevertheless, Regina – Rywka in Yiddish, or perhaps

Tojbe or Nuta – sheltered with us for several months. Her father had worked at home as a tailor, selling drill trousers for boys at a stall on market days. She impressed me with her energy and resourcefulness. She helped in the field. That was safest. The grain and the furrows between the potato bushes provided hiding places. When the searches and public executions grew more frequent, she vanished. However, she survived, since she visited my parents after the war. I was already at boarding school in Skierniewice then and did not see her.

I was, on the other hand, a remote witness of the death of her two brothers. The gendarmes were pursuing them. One was shot in the chase. His body was loaded onto a two-wheeled cart and the other brother, after being beaten by the Germans, had to pull the cart to the place called 'the Hill' in the forest near Huta Piekarska. They made him dig a grave and shot him. The filling in of the grave was left to 'Aryans', whose ancestors had not been guilty of the crucifixion of Jesus and who had not themselves been blamed for ritual murder and all the woes of this world. For at least a year afterwards, yellow sand indicated the site of that unmarked grave.

There was terror in the air – fear, pathetic helplessness and sympathy. The extracurricular indoctrination with 'civic behaviour' – 'system of values' would be too grand a definition – proved ineffective and collapsed. My generation played its part: I was not called 'boy', but rather 'young man'. It happened during the occupation, which is fully understandable. Brochures and leaflets said that Churchill was a Jew, that English capital in Jewish hands lay behind the war between England and the Third Reich and Jewish communism behind the war with Russia, and that Jews mean typhus. Looking back to pre-war times, however, I remember that 'a Jew drinks blood without leaving a hole in the skin' or that our country consisted of 'Polish streets – Jewish real estate'. I would define the propagators of those slogans as lumpenproletariat-hayseed nationalists. The badge of the notched sword surrounded by a ribbon and worn in the lapel was supposed to recall that 'King Bolesław the Brave ordered the Jews to be slain'. I remember the sign, painted on the stucco, on the house at the Warsaw Road corner of the town square in Mszczonów: 'Christian Bakery'. I can even remember the owner's name. For all my naiveté, I knew that this was not a mark of piety, but rather an injunction against buying from Jews. Nevertheless, the kaiser rolls bought from a Jewish stall on market day tasted best to me. I can remember a monthly brochure in a blue cover (the title escapes me), borrowed from better-off neighbours, where there was a lot written about the bulwark of Christianity, about – to put it in contemporary terms – values, and also about the threat to Poland from Jewish-communist freemasonry. I did not yet know what freemasonry was, but I imagined that it must be something fearful indeed. I drew similar knowledge from the *Holiday Gazette*, also borrowed because my father would subscribe only to agricultural periodicals. I remember precisely how the title formed a semi-circle. I read there about the successes of the Italian air force in Abyssinia and the victories of General Franco, aided by German aviators.

And then our turn came.

Another Jewish girl, also named Regina, stayed with us for several weeks. It was the first time I had met such a cultured, well-educated and, as I thought then, un-Jewish Jew. She attended *gimnazjum*, or perhaps even *liceum*. She told me about her 'real' school. I had just started attending a clandestine *gimnazjum*, and must certainly have blushed during those conversations. She had a lovely voice and enjoyed singing. I recall two sad songs. One had been written after the death of Marshall Piłsudski: 'It's not true that you are gone, It's not true that you're in the grave ...' The other was: 'Little town of Belz, my beloved Belz ...'

Despite her completely 'Aryan looks', as they were then termed, and her total cultural assimilation as it is now called, she stood out like a sore thumb in a village where everyone knew everyone else. If she went into deep concealment or into an urban environment where she could lose herself in the crowd, then, with the traits I have mentioned and a bit of luck, she might have survived.

Little Chaim or Henryk, along with his father, a room painter, showed up at harvest time. His father painted our rooms and those of our neighbours, while Chaim helped bale the grain and run the threshing machine. Our shared duties including arranging the sheaves in mows and treading the straw into piles. We had a rough-and-tumble good time. We were more or less the same age. After several weeks, they too vanished into the twilight.

I also remember how my father and I stripped, cleaned and test-fired two pistols in the cellar. They were Belgian FNs, seven and eight in the barrel, as people said in those days. This was a rather dubious weapon, rather for civilians; a Walter or a Parabellum packed a lot more punch but was harder to come by. They were supposedly destined for the Warsaw Ghetto. By what route, my father never said.

The third wave of refugees followed the Warsaw Uprising, either directly or through the Pruszków camp. Perhaps a little before that our neighbours, a worthy and respected family, had an elegant (as I thought then), educated, but sad and very restrained lady living with them. I do not recall her surname. She had a 6- or 7-year-old son, who came to visit us sometimes. The neighbours whispered that this was a Jewish family, but there were so many newcomers by then that this hardly made any special impression. However, when troops of Vlasov's army were quartered in our village in the late autumn, the mother and her son vanished. They surely survived.

In the summer of 1943, between the second and third waves of refugees, our village was subjected to a sort of pacification. A German army lorry or two drove in and, on the basis of a list, more than a dozen men were taken along with their whole families including small children of both sexes. They were tortured and, two days later, shot in the woods between Jaktorów and Międzybórz. They also came for my father, but he had been cautious enough to spend the night in hiding. Since the Germans were taking hostages, my mother and I left the house. Neighbours looked after our belongings. Things quieted down later and we returned.

I am unable to come up with a moral for this story ...

49. An Unknown Event

Wacława Skrzeczyńska

I have decided to make my own small addition to the history of the martyrdom of the Jewish nation. I want to describe facts which I have never read about anywhere, because I would not want them to be forgotten.

I was arrested by the Gestapo on 11 September 1942, in Warsaw. I underwent interrogation in Aleja Szucha [No.25 was the Gestapo HQ], was imprisoned in Pawiak-Serbia [Women's section of the Gestapo prison in Warsaw], and on 17 January 1943 was sent first to Majdanek concentration camp and later to Ravensbrück.

At Majdanek I made friends with Teodozja Wójtowicz from the next bunk, a beautiful red-haired Latin teacher who also knew other languages. She was a Jew on 'Aryan' papers. I cannot remember how she had landed in Majdanek. We worked together in the sewing room. I had contact with Czech Jews who brought striped uniforms, underwear and socks from the clothing storehouse for us to repair. The Jews in that command were in close contact with one of the underground organizations, probably the Home Army in Lublin. As far as I recall, a lorry took SS uniforms and underwear to the laundry in Lublin from time to time. The Jews working in that command were in contact with Wacław Szyszko (now deceased). Wacek worked in the pharmacy located near the laundry and (possibly together with others from the organization) supplied them with weapons hidden among the parcels of clean SS uniforms and underwear delivered on the lorry. The Jews then concealed these weapons in the clothing storehouse. From 7 May to October 1943 I obtained parcels of clothing, cigarettes and occasionally rolls with kielbasa from one of them, Tibor Lovenbain. I wrote a first letter to him requesting soap and a comb, since I had terrible lice. I continued this correspondence with Tibor, concealing letters in the socks or striped uniforms carried back and forth between the sewing room and the storehouse. He wrote in Czech, and Teodozja wrote replies in my name. She often read out Tibor's letters to me. He was convinced, like their whole group, that the Jews were doomed. They would never forget what they lived through on 3 November 1943 [on that night 18,000 Jews were shot at Majdanek]. Teodozja Wójtowicz survived the third of November and it was she who told me about that group. (Frycko, the leader of the group, conversed and corresponded with her.) The group included fifteen to eighteen persons, and they had arms and ammunition. She knew that they intended to defend themselves. They died with guns in their hands as heroes in an uneven battle, without a chance, defending the dignity of people who had been sentenced to death only because they were Jews.

Teodozja Wójtowicz was denounced, and on 12 November 1943 we watched from the window of the sewing room as an *oberka* [female SS overseer] chased her on a bicycle. With the bicycle wheel almost grazing her heels, Teodozja ran as far as the fifth field, where she was executed. This fact is known to my friend, Szoszana Kliger (at Majdanek: Anna Grzęda), who survived by a miracle and settled after the war in Israel. I maintain very cordial contact with her (she visited the land of her birth in 1988). Szoszana and I slept side by side on a bunk. I treated her as a younger sister, and so she has remained until today, close to my heart. I was in the fortunate situation of sometimes receiving modest parcels from my mother and from Tibor. Several other Jewish women survived thanks to sisterly help from their Polish fellow-prisoners.

Tibor, Frycko and Laci will always remain in my heart and my memory, as will many others who are gone. I have wanted to write about this for a long time, but only those who lived through that nightmare can understand how difficult it is, even years later, to remember. I simply lacked the strength to re-live those days in memory, and the pen dropped from my hand.

Today I am 70 years old and am scheduled for an operation tomorrow. I do not know if I will survive. That is why I ask for forgiveness for the chaotic nature of my account, but I have too little time for a calm and detailed one. I would only like those who survived the Holocaust to know about this small group of Jews who died as heroes. Thank you.

50. Ingratitude? Amnesia?

Krystyna Usarek

I met Mrs Zofia Bartel when I was still a child and she served me as an example of what a Jewish woman looked like. She was a very good-looking woman, and I would even say pretty, if it were not for that nose. It was large and had a characteristic hump (a favourite target for the malice of all anti-Semitic publications, not only in Nazi Germany but also here in Poland). That nose betrayed her origins.

So it was: it betrayed her, for it had always seemed to me that she would have preferred to forget that she had been born Jewish. She was married to one of my father's university friends. Our whole family visited them, and they visited us. She never mentioned her origins, nor did that subject ever come up in conversation. Everyone sidestepped it delicately, and only after they had gone home would my parents exchange remarks that allowed me to see how things actually stood.

She only ever mentioned that she and her sister had attended the Popielewska-Roszkowska *gimnazjum* [high school], a hint about the affluence of parents who could afford to send two daughters to a private school. However, neither that sister nor anyone else from her family ever attended her name-day parties or those of her husband, Oskar. At the Bartels', as a rule, one met only Mr Bartel's friends and colleagues (and, in later years, his former students – he taught history at the Rej *gimnazjum* before the war).

The Rej school was Protestant, Mr Bartel was a Protestant, and Mrs Zofia Bartel had been baptized before their marriage in the Augsburg Evangelical rite. They attended Sunday services together at the church on Małachowski Square, and she once confided to me that she would like to take vows as a deaconess. A person of quick intelligence and wide intellectual interests, she spoke fluent German and Italian in addition to her beautiful Polish.

It would be difficult to specify the degree to which she had managed to forget about the fact that she had once been Jewish, before the time came when the dangerous truth was brought home to her that she was still Jewish and that she had that nose of hers.

Each inhabitant of the General Government was required to submit documentation of 'Aryan' origins to the Nazi Occupation authorities.

Those who could not submit such documentation went to the ghetto, which they were forbidden to leave under pain of death. The death penalty also extended to all those who remained on 'the Aryan side' as well as to Poles who rendered them any sort of aid. Mr Oskar Bartel acquired for his wife the documents of one Jadwiga Idzikowska, deceased, as supplied to him by a Catholic priest from St James's Church. For a time, she even took shelter at the rectory there.

One late afternoon in 1943, however (when it was already dark, since it was October), she came to our home at 29 ulica Siedlecka. This was in teachers' quarters on the school grounds; the school building had been taken over by the *Wehrmacht*. Anyone wanting to visit us had to show a pass to the German sentry, as well as registering at the school office. Mr Oskar Bartel went to register while his wife, showing my mother's pass to the sentry, entered the gate. She had wrapped a scarf around her head in the hope of softening the impression made by that nose of hers, and fortunately the German sentry did not pay very close attention. Once again the old sayings proved correct: it is darkest under the lamppost, it is safest in the lion's den. This was, however, a risky security.

My father had been appointed by the Polish government-in-exile in London as head of clandestine education in the Praga district of Warsaw, and clandestine education, for teachers and students alike, was punishable by death. I was a courier for the underground 'grey' scouts' resistance movement. Mother, on the other hand, having lost her post as headmistress of Primary School No. 126, was running a shop in the demolished Haberbusch and Schiele factory at 59 ulica Żelazna. There, she sold rope sandals with linings made from red Nazi flags bought at the Różycki street market – with the swastikas removed, of course. The very act of unstitching the swastika from the flag was punishable by death. Her shop was also a distribution point for the underground *Information Bulletin* newspaper and, to make the set of capital offences complete, my mother was hiding a Jewish woman in the wardrobe.

She had been hiding her there for eighteen months. The fugitive was a total stranger who, being marched along ulica Żelazna to a work assignment, had read the shop sign and dived inside. 'Mrs Usarek', she said, 'you do not know me, but I was a teacher at the Praga Jewish School and I heard people say that you are a virtuous woman. Please save me. Please give me a place to hide!'

This person, whose name I never even learned, had neither money nor ration cards. She shared our potatoes and beets, our bread and margarine for almost two years until we were arrested in April 1944. (Afterwards, until the outbreak of the Warsaw Uprising, she was taken care of by my mother's former colleague Władysława.)

So it was that Mrs Bartel, alias Jadwiga Idzikowska, became our 'second Jew'. She lived with us for six months. She could not, of course, ever set foot outside the flat or even show herself at the window. However, she observed from a safe distance back from the kitchen window how the German soldiers formed ranks, marched, sang, climbed into lorries with tarpaulins over the back to drive off on a 'mission', and how they returned exhausted by the 'work' they had done.

At the beginning of April she announced that she was leaving. Mr Oskar Bartel had found a hiding place for her at a manor house near Dęblin. We spent a long time urging her to reconsider her decision. There was a curfew from eight in the evening until six in the morning, and it was forbidden to be on the streets during this time without a pass. She would have to walk in front of the sentry while it was still light, make her way to the tram terminus near the Basilica (often used by German soldiers going on leave), walk from the tram stop at ulica Targowa to the Eastern Station, and finally ride a hundred kilometres in a crowded train. I was brutal. I handed her a mirror and told her to look at her profile. 'Yes, I know what sort of nose I've got', she said. 'I'll have plastic surgery as soon as the war is over. But for now, I'm leaving!'

She left on Holy Thursday and arrived safely. She encountered no evil people, no stupid people, and no Germans along the way. She met no one infected with 'racial hatred,' none of those asinine Poles who are convinced that 'the Jews must bear their punishment, because they crucified Jesus'. She must, on the other hand, have met at least two or three hundred people who knew what she was as soon as they looked at her, but pretended to see nothing. Just four months later, she was free. She survived.

But the Gestapo came for us at night, the following Thursday, exactly a week after her departure. Our arrest had nothing to do with Mrs Zofia Bartel. The Gestapo officer at their headquarters on aleja Szucha [in Warsaw] screamed 'You should all be shot and hanged! You are ALL in the Resistance!' (There were a hundred of us, and I supposed that he must have been right.)

Forty of the hundred were shot forthwith, and the other sixty sent to concentration camps.

It was pure chance that we were among the sixty, and not the forty. We had known from the moment of our arrest that this was a pure revenge operation. And nevertheless I recall the wordless triumph with which we looked into each other's eyes. We were thinking that, whatever became of us, Mrs Zofia Bartel had survived. That was our victory over the Gestapo who swarmed over our flat, over Hitler and the whole Third Reich! Such a splendid feeling at such a dramatic moment.

We often met Mrs Zofia Bartel after the war. She and her husband were both especially kind to us, and also extended that kindness to my daughter. Yet although Mrs Bartel's Occupation experiences became generally known (to the degree that a friend of mine heard two people talking on a bus about how my parents had sheltered a Jewish woman), she never managed to submit the required affidavit to the appropriate authorities. Nor did she do so for any of the other people who sheltered her. I sometimes found myself on the point of saying something to her about this, but my courage always failed me: she so wanted to forget about the fact that she was Jewish ...

And the other woman? My God, we have not the slightest idea what became of her. My mother's colleague Władysława had left her shut up on ulica Żelazna, as usual, when the Uprising broke out. The Germans must certainly have broken into the shop and killed her. The *Kampfgruppe Reinefarth* murdered approximately 50,000 residents of the Wola district on 5 and 6 August. She may have died as a Jew, she may have died as a Pole, but the fact is that she must have died after years of hell.

My parents have not got a Tree of the Just in Israel – nor have thousands more Poles who risked their lives to save others from annihilation.

51. Alibi for a Girlfriend

Regina Wojcieszuk

My parents and four younger siblings and I moved to Wołomin in 1937. I was twelve then. We lived on ulica Warszawska. Our next-door neighbours were the Muszkatblats, a Jewish family of seven people. The friendship that I formed with one of their daughters, Pola, has lasted until today. We were the same age. During the Occupation, my family did what we could to help the Muszkatblats. I remember entering the ghetto under the barbed wire, at a place where there were sand piles. I looked for the least visible and safest place. Sometimes I took a modest food parcel, and sometimes only words of encouragement since we ourselves often had nothing to eat. The ghetto was liquidated, as I recall, in 1942. As soon as I heard the news I ran to my familiar crossing point, but there were sentries everywhere. All I could see beyond the barbed wire was how the Germans were brutally evicting women, children, elderly people and those in the prime of life from their dwellings. They drove them with screams, gunfire and blows of their rifle butts to the assembly point. It was a horrible sight. Our friends were there on the other side of the barbed wire and I was helpless. There was nothing I could do to help them. However, that was not the end of that terrible day. The door of our flat opened in the evening and there, like a ghost, stood Mrs Muszkatblat. She was in a dreadful state. When she had recovered a bit, she began telling us what had happened in the ghetto.

The liquidation had begun early in the morning. She had been alone at home with her husband, who was ill, and her daughter Pola. When her son Kuba had learned the previous day about the planned liquidation of the ghetto, he had taken their youngest daughter Lila with him and gone to hide in the nearby woods. They had agreed with Pola that if any of them survived and managed to escape, they should meet in the village of Rostka [a small village, near Wołomin]. The Muszkatblat's neighbour had run to their flat and shouted that the Germans were throwing people out. So Mrs Muszkatblat had ordered Pola to flee and had remained with her husband. Some time later, two German soldiers entered the flat. They dragged her away from her husband's sick-bed and threw her out of the flat. When she reached the courtyard, her only thought was to hide somewhere until she could go back to her ailing husband. She sat in a cranny for several hours. Then she began sneaking back towards home. An awful sight awaited her there. Her husband lay in bed, dead. He was shot full of bullet holes. She remembered nothing more. She had no idea how she had found her way to us. That was the end of Mrs Muszkatblat's story.

The second scene took place several days later. Despite all our urging and persuasion, Mrs Muszkatblat decided to travel to Małkinia to look for the village of Rostka and her children who were supposed to be there. I should explain that Pola had an acquaintance in Rostka with whom she did some business. Those acquaintances had not known that she was Jewish. At the beginning of the war, I gave Pola a birth certificate with an 'Aryan' name, and she had been using that document. Furthermore, no one in the Muszkatblat family had Semitic features, a fact which made it easier for them to move from place to place. We therefore decided that I would accompany Mrs Muszkatblat to the station, buy her a ticket, and act as if I were seeing off a relative. Before leaving, we agreed that she would send word if she found the children, and would return to us if she did not. We thus set out full of anxiety and worry. Germans and 'blue police' swarmed in front of the station. Our hearts beat faster. There were even more of them at the ticket windows and in the waiting room. They were all watching everything carefully. I bought the ticket and we sat down on a bench, chatting as if everything were normal. In my thoughts, meanwhile, I was beseeching all the gods that no anti-Semite or other unthinking, stupid, little person would appear who, without even considering the consequences, would point a finger and say '*Jude*' [Jew]. Wołomin was then a small town with a population of eighteen thousand. Ulica Warszawska ran right past the station. It would thus be very easy to encounter the wrong person. The train was finally called. People began shifting about. A German gendarme with a dog on a leash looked closely at everyone going onto the platform. To make it all seem as natural as possible, I kissed Mrs Muszkatblat farewell, helped her onto the train, and waved goodbye. As the train moved out, I felt lightheaded, and my legs could have been made of cotton wool. I had to sit down in order to get a grip on myself. I dreamed that scene with variations for a long time.

Mrs Muszkatblat's younger daughter visited us some time later with news that their mother was with them. She also asked me to go to Rostka for a few days to help them. I went, passing myself off as their cousin. During the several days that I was there, Mrs Muszkatblat told me an incredible story. Was it a miracle, fate, or coincidence? Here is her account of her journey to Małkinia. After getting off the train, she wandered the streets for a time. Then she went to the rectory where the priest gave her something to eat. After that, she went into the church and prayed fervently. On her way out, she saw two teenage girls playing hopscotch in the courtyard. She went up and asked if they had heard of a village called Rostka, where her daughter Pola lived. One of the girls said that she was from Rostka and knew Pola. She had come to Małkinia for market day. She promised to lead Mrs Muszkatblat to her daughter, and did so. Mrs Muszkatblat returned to Wołomin with Pola and Lila in 1945. In May of that year they migrated along with us to Piła in the Recovered Territories.

Her wartime experiences destroyed Mrs Muszkatblat's nerves. She died in a psychiatric hospital several years after the war. Her son Kuba had died under an assumed name at Pawiak prison as a Polish underground activist. Her daughter Rachel died at Treblinka.

Pola has lived in Israel since 1957. On her recommendation and thanks to her efforts, my family and I received the medal of the Righteous Among the Nations. Pola also invited me to Israel. I was refused permission several times and did not manage to go there until 1987. My husband went with me then and we spent several months as guests of Pola and her husband. We travelled the length and breadth of Israel, with my friend accompanying us everywhere. She wanted us to see as much as possible. She and her husband showed us a great deal of care, cordiality and love. And, despite our objections and despite the fact that they are not wealthy people, they insisted on covering our expenses down to the last detail.

Finally, a small digression. I was brought up to believe that what counts is not nationality, skin colour or religious denomination, but rather humanity. I hope that what I say has some authentic Christian value.

52. Morphine

Alina Margolis-Edelman

My mother was a pediatrician and specialized in tuberculosis among children. In the ghetto, she worked first at the Berson and Bauman Hospital on ulica Śliska and, after the liquidation of the 'Small Ghetto', at the hospital on ulica Leszna. Later, later, no one knows why, the Germans set aside a bit of space at the *Umschlagplatz* for a children's hospital. It was not, of course, a real hospital, but rather merely a place to die in. At least the children could die in bed, even if there were two, three or four of them to a bed, even if they sometimes lay on the floor. Almost all of them had diarrhoea. They died quickly and looked like dirty, dried-out wax dolls.

One of the patients was a girl of 4 or 5 years old, the daughter of one of the nurses who had worked with my mother at the Drop of Milk, when the Drop of Milk [a charitable organization for children] was still operating in the Ghetto. The nurse in question, no longer young, was completely alone. That little girl, Renia or Reginka, was the only good thing that had ever happened in her life.

Now Renia or Reginka lay in one of the filthy beds on the upper floor of the building on the *Umschlagplatz*, waiting with the other children for the day or hour when she would be taken to the cattle wagons. Her mother was not there, of course. In that hell, there was no question of being with one's child.

If the hospital had been a normal hospital and Reginka had been receiving normal care, there would have been no reason for her to die. But at *Umschlagplatz*, there was a different issue: it was not clear whether or not she would die quickly enough. If she did not make it, she would be thrown into the cattle wagons.

She made it.

I learned about this afterwards. On my way back to our room in the fourth-floor flat, I saw Reginka's mother kneeling in front of my mother and kissing her hands.

My mother had injected Reginka with her morphine. Today everyone knows the story, so there is no point in repeating that morphine and cyanide were then worth their weight in gold, that only the chosen few had access to them and that a small capsule in one's pocket provided a miraculous sense of safety, protection and the option of escaping at any given moment.

To give someone your morphine or cyanide meant renouncing a peaceful death of your own, at a time of your own choosing. It meant renouncing escape from the cattle wagons, from the Golgotha that others could not avoid.

53. A Slice of Bread

Krystyna Tarasiewicz

It was January 1943. We had been transported from Pawiak [prison in Warsaw] to Majdanek the previous day, and had spent a dreadful night in a barrack with broken windows, no straw mattresses or even any straw, and no lights. They drove us out for roll-call before dawn, lined us up and counted us. When we were finally allowed to stop standing in rows, we decided to try to establish where we were.

My first impression, the first image that I remember clearly, was this: an emaciated prisoner in camp stripes, with a Star of David sewn on his blouse, was sitting on a heap of smouldering rubbish. His dark eyes burned with hunger. It was plain to see that he had lost any sense of what was going on. I gave him a slice of bread that I had brought from prison. Pressing it into his hand, I could tell from the way he looked at it that he no longer had the strength to raise it to his lips. In his agony, he consumed the bread with his eyes.

I was 16 years old. I had been arrested for belonging to an illegal scouts' organization in Warsaw. Later, during my three years in the concentration camps, I was often as hungry as a person can be without starving to death. But that first scene of the human tragedy has stuck in my mind so precisely that if I knew how to paint, I could reproduce it like a photograph.

I spoke about it in Düsseldorf, as a witness in the trial of the Majdanek war criminals.

54. Typhoid Fever

Feliks Emil Rathauser

The Nazi rulers of Lwów commenced one of their largest anti-Jewish extermination operations on 10 August 1942. The fact that my Soviet passport identified me as a Catholic Pole had no significance in the light of the Nuremberg Laws. The death sentence on all non-Aryans covered me. Yet it seemed that my horrid and dangerous job combating the lice infestation and typhoid fever that the Germans dreaded could offer me a stay of execution (the inscription '*Fleckfieberbekämpfung*' – Typhoid Fever Prevention – surrounded the Star of David on my armband).

Every day, the Jewish District Sanitation Office gave me a long list of flats infested with lice and infected with typhoid fever – dwellings of abject poverty. The lice literally devoured the skeleton-people who had been wasted by months of starvation. Patrols feared to hazard infection by moving the corpses, leaving the job to us – to me and my co-workers in the anti-typhus service.

I was surprised when it turned out that – surely because of the need to reach some previously established target figure – the privileges of the anti-typhus service had been invalidated on what was said to be the last Saturday of the operation. I had just left my flat and was walking down ulica Bernsteina when a Ukrainian police patrol called to me from across the street and ordered me to join a group of several Jews they had apprehended. I explained my role in the campaign that the German authorities had mandated against typhoid fever and showed them my armband, but to no avail. These police might not have understood German.

They led us on a roundabout route to Teodor Square behind the Grand Theatre, where they made us stand with our faces against the wall. We could hear them cocking their rifles behind us. I crossed myself and began reciting the rosary in a half-whisper. An old Jewish man in traditional dress, with a long white beard and side curls, stood to my right. He prayed in his own language, rocking back and forth in the Jewish manner. Several minutes later, a Jewish policeman appeared from somewhere. I was deep in prayer and his presence startled me. I surmised from his conversation in Yiddish with my neighbour that the older man was his uncle. The nephew was promising to intervene with the Ukrainian police. However, the old man replied unexpectedly that he had had enough of life, and preferred that his nephew intervene on my behalf. Although it seemed to him that I had been baptized, he had once been my patient in the clinic and was convinced that I was an unusually honest and skilled physician. My life was therefore far more worth saving than his own – he was old, alone and useless, and his whole family had already been murdered. His nephew, the policeman, carried on a long discussion with our guards, but their gestures indicated that his intervention was fruitless.

The police therefore moved us along to the courtyard of the police station at 23 ulica Kurkowa. By now, there were about twenty of us. I had lost all hope.

The courtyard was full of leaves from nearby trees. There were also several tree trunks with axes stuck in them. We were ordered to go to work. We could choose to gather the fallen leaves or chop the tree trunks. I decided to go after an SS man with an axe before I died. Nothing in my biography foreshadowed or offered motivation for such a thought, and later I would often wonder about it. Yet without the slightest hesitation and before anyone else in the group moved, I took hold of an axe and began hacking away at the wood.

An SS man approached me a moment later. I could feel the blood rushing to my head and I must have blushed. The SS man asked what I was doing. Although the answer seemed senseless to me, I replied, 'I am chopping wood'. I was concerned with not seeming to be an idiot, while he was trying to understand how an anti-typhoid service worker could have ended up being arrested. I ventured the supposition that the Ukrainian police could not read German. He mumbled, 'You may go'. I must have hesitated too long, because the SS man suddenly screamed '*Los!*' [Get out!]. He led me to the entranceway and ordered the Ukrainian sentry to let me out. The sentry did so, adding a powerful kick on his own initiative.

55. The March of the Women Prisoners

Jan Tylicki

Despite the decades that have passed since those events, the quiet plea that I heard then from two women, *'nicht schiessen, nicht schiessen'* [don't shoot] will remain in my memory to the end of my life. The event that I wish to write about occurred in my family home in Śliwice during the cruel winter of 1944–45.

The Germans had been withdrawing westward day and night along the road through Świecie on the Vistula, Czersk and Chojnice. The front-line was approaching from the Vistula, bringing liberation from the Nazi Occupation. Since I had turned 15 in 1940 and throughout the Occupation I had been working as an agricultural labourer for a German on the land that had belonged to the local parish. I worked as a Pole, for my family had refused to apply for a place on the German nationality list. Since November 1944 I had been forced to spend my nights in the parish barn and watch over the pigs that had not yet been [removed and] taken west by the Germans. The German woman who administered the estate permitted me to visit my home during my free time, usually in the late afternoon. On a day when I was on my way home as usual, I passed a long column of women led by an armed SS detachment. Near our home, the column turned onto the road to Czersk. It was an appalling sight. I hurried home. I remember that the garden gate was open. This caught my attention, but I merely shut it behind me and went indoors. Only my mother was there, and we began talking about the column of women being led towards Czersk by the SS. Later, my mother asked me to go to the barn and pitch some hay down from the loft for the goats. When I climbed up the ladder, two young women covered in tattered blankets emerged from the hay pleading: *'nicht schiessen!'* The sight of them horrified me. I ran quickly inside and informed my mother. We went back together to find them. They were hidden in the straw, very frightened, as were my mother and I. They wore ragged denim garments under the blankets, and had their hands and feet wrapped in rags. They were frozen and emaciated. Since they did not speak Polish, we began communicating in German. They told us that they were Jewish and that they were both around 20 years old. One was from Austria and the second from Czechoslovakia. They had taken advantage of a moment's inattention by a sentry and of the fact that our gate was open, and had managed to reach the barn. They begged us for help. Mother and I agreed that we had to protect them from death. This was not such an easy matter, however, since there were Germans everywhere and aiding Jews was a capital offence. We decided to do whatever we could. They were taken into the house in the evening. Mother washed them, dressed their wounds, and gave them clean clothes. She burned their lice-infested rags in the stove. Then she fed them and hid them in the cellar beneath the house, from which for reasons of security they could come out to use the toilet only at night.

The next day, the Germans ordered the local Poles to gather the corpses of the Jewish women who had died from SS bullets during the march. The bodies of sixty-five Jewish women were collected from a six-kilometre stretch of road and buried in a mass grave in the Śliwice parish cemetery. The German police also searched the houses along the march route that day. Thank God, they did not find our Jews. The only people who knew that they sheltered with us until liberation were, aside from my brother and sister (my father had died in 1932), the cook from the rectory who gave me food for them and an Austrian *Wehrmacht* chaplain who supplied us with medicines to treat their frostbitten hands, feet and faces and also helped us avoid unexpected visits from the Germans. We learned from the women that they had been evacuated from a camp at Grodno near Toruń in late autumn 1944. They came out of hiding after Red Army soldiers entered Śliwice on 20 February 1945. The fear for their lives and the lives of our family was at an end. At the beginning of March, the Jewish woman from Austria was taken to the Red Army hospital at Świecie on the Vistula. There were fears that one of her feet would have to be amputated as a result of frostbite from the march westward. The second, a Czech named Ela, was supplied with money and food and set out by train for Czechoslovakia in the spring of 1945. I do not know what their subsequent fates were. They never contacted us. But neither did we try to trace them or get in touch. We regarded rescuing the women as a normal, Christian act.

56. A Physician

Boguslawa Golachowska-Szczygłowska

I am a physician. During the German Occupation, I worked at the hospital and the glass factory in Krosno on the Wisłok river.

* * *

A forester came to the hospital one day in December 1943 and told about a Jewish family living in the woods in a dugout they had built. He had been leaving potatoes and food for them, but now they were ill. They had fevers and diarrhea and he did not know how to help them. I conferred with the nuns who worked in the contagious diseases section and they all agreed without hesitation to accept them as patients in the typhus ward (the Germans never went there; a sign warned: *Seuchengefahr* – dangerous contagion). I filled out hospital admission forms for Stanislaw Guzik, Janina Guzik, etc. (this was the most common surname in Krosno). That same day, the forester delivered them in a cart of hay. The nuns bathed them, shaved their heads and hung medallions around the necks of the children. They spent the whole winter recovering, with no one to bother them. Things only turned dangerous when the children, now healthy and with their red hair growing back, began sneaking out into the garden. That was when the director of the hospital, Dr Zygmunt Lewicki (head of the medical service of the Home Army resistance movement in the Krosno region), summoned me and said that we could not go on sheltering them because the whole hospital could suffer. We could already hear the artillery from the east. The Red Army was drawing near. Home Army soldiers led the 'Guzik' family into the forest at night and ordered them to make their way eastward. I do not know what became of them. Nor do I know their surname. I hope that they survived until liberation.

* * *

During the battle for Krosno in September 1944 a Jewish couple was admitted to the hospital. He was a physician (a morphine addict), already on his old age pension. When the Soviet bombs fell on the town, he thought it was a thunderstorm and decided to close the windows in the hospital barracks. A bomb blast tore off his arm. He died soon after. What happened to his wife? What were their names? I do not know. This was another case where the nuns admitted them without hesitation and cared for them tenderly.

* * *

A group of doctors learned English during the Occupation. The teacher was a pleasant, middle-aged lady. She did not live in the ghetto or wear the armband, so we had no idea she was Jewish. On the day when they deported the Jews from town, they ordered them all to lie down on the street and then threw them into the wagons. When they threw in an old woman, our teacher suddenly rushed to the wagon and jumped in after her. It turned out that the old lady was her mother. I do not know what her name was. She could have saved herself. She was not at all the Jewish type, but she voluntarily went to her death with her mother.

* * *

A group of Jews worked in the glass factory. A young Jewish woman came to me one day to complain that she was in the fourth month of pregnancy and was bleeding. I gave her sick leave and medicine and ordered her to stay in bed. I was summoned to the Gestapo. Never knowing whether I would return home, I dreaded going there. The Germans talked to me and warned me that if I treated Jews or gave them sick leave from work, they would send me to Auschwitz. This time, I returned home and went on treating Jews (although I no longer gave them sick leave from work).

PART FIVE

REMEMBRANCE – PART OF HUMAN CULTURE

Introduction

Remembrance is a central element in human culture and particularly so with Jews and their long history of suffering. Before he was murdered by the Nazis in Riga in 1941, the distinguished Jewish historian, Shimen Dubnow, proclaimed '*Farshraybt!*' – 'write it down'. The Warsaw historian Emmanuel Ringelblum also knew that the unprecedented situation of the Jews in Poland during the war had to be remembered accurately, and therefore set about creating his *oyneg shabes* archive. The testimony of survivors and witnesses after the event is of equal importance. It is often the personal insights and the details which convey to us the true horror of what happened. The oft repeated refrain 'I saw it with my own eyes' is testament to the need to be believed.

Jerzy Ertelt (59) recalls 'the sweetish odour ... of burning bodies ... afterwards we were unable to eat the meat dinner we had been looking forward to. We felt like throwing up for a long time.' Zbigniew Lisowski (62) depicts the 'killing fields' near Jaszuny, Lithuania: 'Hands stuck up like the stalks of plants from that ground lacerated by spades and bullets ... The whole area was whitened, like the last snow melting in springtime, with prayer books or pages torn from them.' His is adjured by his father to "Remember all of this well'. Kazimierz Wolff-Zdzienicki (67) describes a procession of emptied prams coming from the gas chambers of Birkenau, as the conductor of the camp orchestra stops momentarily and leads them into Chopin's Funeral March, much to the annoyance of the SS commander. Przemysław Sadowski (69) goes into a restaurant in Radom and encounters 'an elegant SS officer', upset that his dog had been run over that day. The same officer had earlier that day organized the murder and deportation of Radom's Jews. In Będzin, the 7-year-old Teresa Słocińska is mesmerized by the distant view a young man with a red handkerchief round his neck (71) until her fascination turns to horror, when she realizes it is blood spurting from a wound in his neck.

For some the re-telling of the stories is a relief, the terrible memories at last finding an outlet. For others it is the right thing to do: Alina Adamowicz (72) writes her account 'to be able to give vent on paper to my feelings, but above all so that something of these people remains behind'. Where they were mere witnesses of horrifying crimes, recording their memories is the only way they can help those victims.

57. Ponary

Andrzej Czajkowski

When I got out of Kowno prison in August 1941, my only document was my release order from *Kauno Sunku Darbo Kaleimas* (Kowno Hard Labour Prison) and a one-time travel pass from Kowno to Wilno.

However, I used that pass over and over because no one ever punched it. Because I bought and sold things, I travelled regularly between Wilno and Kowno.

There was no chance of getting on the train in Wilno itself. They checked everything very carefully at the station. For that reason I always walked to Ponary, the next station in the direction of Kowno.

Thousands of Jews from Wilno and the surrounding areas were systematically murdered in the woods not far from Ponary station, beginning in August 1941. I walked that road many times and observed the different phases of the extermination operation in all its primitive brutality.

Small groups of Jews dug the mass graves, and they themselves ended up in the graves they dug. Afterwards, lorries with canvas covers on their platforms drove up under heavy escort. There was always a bus full of drunken Lithuanian *szaulis* collaborators at the end of the column. Their shouts and roars rang out through the open windows of the bus. Sometimes they sang in Lithuanian. I never saw a German uniform, either in the convoys or at the execution site.

Szaulis means 'rifleman' in Lithuanian. These riflemen made up units of the fascist Lithuanian police and were also used to fight the Home Army partisan units. It is no surprise that the Home Army fought back, and that the well-organized and courageous Home Army units made short work of the cowardly *szaulis* bands who only acted like heroes when they were up against unarmed civilians. Many of them died.

The site of the murders was neither fenced off nor concealed in any way. The sparse pine forest offered no cover. The unloading of people from the lorries and the ceaseless beating with rifle butts and shovels could be seen clearly. Terrible screams and groans could be heard, and it all went on to the accompaniment of salvos of gunfire and the explosions of grenades. In the bushes nearby, the heroes raped girls.

A dozen or so healthy men were left to strew lye over the corpses and cover them with a thin layer of earth, not even a metre thick.

These workers were themselves killed at the edge of an empty grave. Carrying personnel who were in even better humour than when they had arrived, the vehicles drove back towards Wilno. No one guarded the site of the killings. It was possible to take a shortcut to the station right past the graves. Vodka bottles lay everywhere in the grass nearby.

The summer of that year was very hot, and the older graves gave off a fetid odor of decaying corpses. The earth settled over them and after even the lightest rain it congealed, sealing in the escaping gasses, so that the surface rose and fell. Bubbles, white from the lye, formed on the surface.

Can anyone forget such a sight?

58. From the Prison's Window

Stefan Czerniawski

It was the summer of 1942. The morning fog, stretching in a wide band along the River Nida on which the town lay, crept through the wide-open window of our cell in Pińczów prison. A new day was beginning. What would it bring for us prisoners? We heard the pearly twittering of the lark climbing vertically upwards or diving towards the rye-field. The day before, we had finished harvesting the fields administered by the prison authorities.

I was alone in the cell because the rest of the prisoners had gone out to weed the carrot patch and destroy the caterpillars that were devouring the leaves of kale and cabbage. It was 'application day', on which the prisoners' families could supply them with a bit of food – there was no way to survive for long on the prison rations – and also, if they had managed to obtain permission from the prosecutor, have a visit with the prisoners. The window of our cell looked out on the prison gate. I could thus see the guards and prisoners milling about. The latter were watering the flowers and vegetables that grew in the beds along the long prison building, which stood more or less in the middle of a spacious yard surrounded by a high wall with watchtowers.

I could observe everything without difficulty because the Pińczów prison had 'normal' windows, except that they were barred. The buildings had supposedly been an army barracks that had been adapted as a prison before the war.

The twittering of the skylarks was suddenly and brutally drowned out by two gunshots, one after the other.

I wondered what had happened.

Gunshots were nothing new in Pińczów. Previously, however, the condemned men had usually been led out of the prison. They were taken to the old firing range at the foot of the hill near the prison, which was used as an execution site. Today, no one had been taken there. Then, two people handcuffed together were led into the prison courtyard by a 'blue' policeman. They were stood against the wall of an outbuilding next to the prison gate. One of them might have been around 20 years old, and the other perhaps 10. The older one was pale and weak, and leaned against the wall built of the local sandstone. He slumped lower and lower. Only now did I realize what had happened. A red bloodstain was visible on the wall as the prisoner sank down. A puddle of blood formed at his feet. He had lost all will, he had given up. The other boy, handcuffed to his brother (as it later turned out), who had been shot and was certainly dying, looked on in extraordinary despair as life slipped away.

However, no one paid any attention to these two. Only when the man who had been shot rolled over and pitched onto his face without any sign of life twenty or so minutes later were the handcuffs taken off. The wounded man was carried to the prison hospital where he died shortly afterwards. His little brother was murdered in the prison the next day. We later learned the whole story of what had happened.

The 'blue police' had found those Jewish brothers somewhere in the cellar of a ruined house in Pińczów. They were handcuffed and escorted to prison. They must have hoped to escape and made a run for it in the crowd of people at the prison gate. The fact that they were handcuffed together hampered their flight, which had been hopeless in any case because the prison stood in isolation at the very edge of town. There were open fields all around; the brothers were excellent targets and had nowhere to hide from the pursuing 'blue policeman.'

The two shots, one of which found its target, ended that escape.

59. Fire and Smoke

Jerzy Ertelt

The street where we lived with our grandfather was called ulica Pros-
zowska. It ran north in the direction of a small town, called Proszowice,
in Cracow province. Past Bochnia, that road skirts the Niepołomice Forest. Just there, in the village of Baczków, the Germans had laid out a mass
grave for Jews. We only learned about it near the end of the war. What
happened before that?

Military motorcycles with machine guns mounted on them and dogs
appeared in our street one day. The Germans stopped at each house to
warn the residents not to go outside. They ordered them to draw their
curtains. This naturally caused overwhelming fear, since no one could
conceive of what the Germans intended to do. As I recall, the ban was to
last for several hours. German lorries with their tarpaulins closed tight
soon began passing by from the direction of town. Loud lamentations,
sobbing and screams came from inside the lorries. Despite the German
ban, my grandfather, my two uncles and I crept to the attic to observe the
street and the passing vehicles from under loose shingles. I remember
that my mother did not want to allow me to go up, but my grandfather
said, 'Let him go so that he can see it and remember'. I did not understand those words then, but they stuck firmly in my memory. While we
observed, my grandfather told my uncles, 'They're taking them to their
destruction'. After about an hour, the lorries drove back empty. The
hoods were open, and various garments blew out and fluttered into the
ditches or the fields: trousers, blouses, jackets and so on. The lorries
drove back and forth several times. Such operations went on for several
days, perhaps a dozen. It soon became known that the lorries drove deep
into the forest. From there, volleys of rifle fire could be heard at intervals. They were audible to the inhabitants of the village of Baczków. No
one, however, knew what the Germans were doing to the Jews – the
whole forest was surrounded by soldiers and entry was forbidden. The
screams, lamentations and sobbing from the lorries that drove past were
horrible, and I can still remember how the tears rolled down the cheeks
of my grandfather, a Bochnia miner. I know that my grandfather was
what is today called a tough man and that few misfortunes could upset
him. As soon as it sunk in that masses of innocent people were being

murdered only because they were called 'Jews', I was seized by the terrible fear that the same thing could happen to us, the Poles. I remember
frequently waking up sweaty and frightened, full of dread because of
my nightmares on that theme. I can also remember how my mother took
me to a doctor and described my torments to him.

MAKE-BELIEVE SIBLINGS

We were dependent on my grandparents. It was fortunate that my grandfather worked in the local salt mine and could support us. My mother made
a little money sewing, but we were so far from town that it was hard for her
to find jobs. Things were crowded at my grandfather's, but comfortable.
However, one of my mother's sewing customers told her that she should
submit a petition to the city authorities because there were many vacant
flats, and if she got one it would be easier for her to find clients nearby. The
woman also said that her husband worked at city hall and could help push
the petition along. Thus it was that we moved to ulica Trudna in the centre of town. The former tenants of the house, all Jews, had been evicted
and moved to the ghetto. A stream called the Babica ran along next to our
street, and on the other side of the stream was the barbed wire fence of the
ghetto boundary.

As it turned out, mother did not get a lot of new clients because people
were poor and having new clothes made was the last thing on their
minds. Mother spent most of her time doing alterations and mending.
There was a lot of such work and it paid poorly. At times, we ate only
once a day, and we might not have made it without help from my grandfather. An acquaintance of my mother's called one day and offered
her a job escorting two children from a Jewish family on the train from
Cracow to Bochnia. Someone was supposed to pick the children up in
Bochnia and take them to a village. My mother was offered some money
for this assignment, but what I remember as a child was how long it took
her to decide whether to accept the job, because it frightened her badly.
There were many German patrols in Cracow in those days, especially
around the train station. Furthermore, 'Semitic features' could make it
easy to identify Jewish children and adults. Some of her friends advised
my mother to turn the offer down, but our chronic need for money
finally tipped the scales. So we went to Cracow on the appointed day.
There, the children to be escorted were drilled for several hours in
pretending that I was their brother, while I had to learn their names.
There was a boy about my age and a girl a little older. I remember that
my mother wanted to turn back when she saw them, because they had

dark hair and swarthy complexions and did not at all resemble me. Only later did I learn what we were risking. We somehow got to Bochnia safely, thank God, although I can recall my mother's anxiety when German patrols were strolling around in Cracow and at the stations along the way. But the children reached Bochnia, and someone took them from us.

THE ODOUR OF BURNING

Our house stood right at the boundary of the ghetto. We could observe the life there from the window on the stairwell. The more courageous Jews tried to escape from the ghetto, usually through the barbed wire and always at night, when the vigilance of the German patrols walking ceaselessly back and forth along the barbed wire was slightly relaxed. Still, incidents where young Jewish men and women were shot trying to escape were not infrequent. Since there was a forbidden zone near the wire that Jews were not allowed to enter, the bodies sometimes lay there for many hours in the position in which they had fallen. That was an extremely shocking sight. But not the most shocking.

One spring Sunday, my mother and I were on our way to mass, as usual. It was a special Sunday, because my grandfather had 'organized' a goat somewhere and sent us some meat. Meat for dinner was rare in those days. On our way back from church, we noticed that smoke with a sweetish odor seemed to be coming from somewhere in the ghetto. We saw that a big fire was burning not far away, on the high ground in the ghetto that is still called Salt Hill. That was where the smell of burning was coming from. When we reached our staircase, we could see through the window that an old building was engulfed in flames. Nearby stood a tightly-packed crowd of Jews and many people in uniforms. Then we saw that the men in uniforms were taking people from the crowd, adults and children alike, and throwing them into the fire. We could hear the terrifying screams and cries of the Jews standing there waiting to be burned. The crematoria of Auschwitz and Birkenau must have been unable to keep up. My mother, our neighbours and I stood petrified for a long time watching this act of criminality. The sweetish odour was the odour of burning bodies. Then a German patrolling the ghetto boundary noticed us at the window and aimed his rifle at us, and another soldier fired over the roof of our house. We ran in panic to our flats. I remember that afterwards we were unable to eat the meat dinner we had been looking forward to. We felt like throwing up for a long time. I kept reliving what I had seen that unfortunate Sunday, and despite my young age I began to understand what had happened.

60. The Junkyard

Sławomir Bołdok

I was still a child during the Holocaust. I was living in Radom with my parents on the first floor of a building at 8 ulica Andrzeja Struga, at the corner of ulica Wąska. From the window, I had a view of a typical court-yard with its rubbish bins and outbuildings, and the high wooden fence of the adjacent property. What was behind that wall intrigued me: scrap iron was kept there. Confined between two buildings, the junkyard was also closed off from ulica Struga by a fence, with a gate leading inside. My parents forbade me to go there, but from the window I gazed at the 'treasures' – iron bedsteads, sheets of metal, parts of some sort of machine and various other rusty bits of junk. At the back of the junk-yard stood the little shed that served as the office of the – of whom? The owner? The junk merchant? I did not know.

The first of my wartime memories connected with that junkyard has to do with my father. He was a reserve cavalry officer and as such had two swords at home, an officer's parade sabre and a second field sabre that recalled his service in 1920. Another souvenir of his from that first war was a revolver that, if I pleaded enough, he would take out of his desk once in a while and let me hold. In September 1939 he had been evacuated eastward with the State Forestry Board and been captured near Równe by the Red Army. He escaped by some miracle and one of the first things he did when he returned home was to wrap the sabres and the revolver in an oiled cloth and carry them at night to the fence, where he prised up a board and slid the weapons out of sight in the junkyard. He must certainly have counted on retrieving them in a few months, once France and England defeated the Germans.

My next memory connected directly with the junkyard was the moment when they set up the ghetto. I saw – and it made a great impression on me – the construction of the wall and gate at the corner of ulica Wałowa and ulica Żeromskiego, which was followed directly by the resettlement of the Jewish population. That must have been in 1940 or 1941, when my father was still alive and I was 9 years old. The estab-lishment of the ghetto stuck in my mind because it left some flats empty in the 'Aryan' part of Radom, and a family from Poznań that had been quartered with us moved out to one of those flats. The most dramatic event connected with the junkyard was the round-up carried out by the German police and gendarmes. Very early one morning, shortly after the establishment of the ghetto, loud noises from the junkyard awakened my family. From the window we could see how the police and gendarmes were leading a woman and some children from under a piece of sheet metal and back to the shed where a man was standing. When they had finished searching the whole junkyard, they led the people out. It was only then that I realized they were Jews, because I had not previously cared about who the junk-dealer and his family were. I do not know what happened to the junkyard, because my mother and I had to flee after my father's arrest. We went to live somewhere else. So the sabres and the revolver were lost, and my father died in 1942, and I am sure that no one survived from the junk dealer's family. A half a century has passed since these events, and although I am hardly an important witness to history, perhaps my recollections will add something to the image of those times.

61. The Extermination of the Roma

Krzysztof Galon

Did anyone from Wolbrom survive? I remember that, as I grazed the cows beyond the woods far from town, I kept seeing groups of Jews or individual persons wandering between the fields with madness in their eyes. They feared meeting anyone, and avoided even me, a 10-year-old boy. This hurt me because I wanted to talk with them, just as I had done at my parents' house before the war, on the many occasions when they stopped. Something terrible had happened in their minds. A fear of everyone paralyzed them and impelled them to keep going eastward, where they thought they would find aid. But did they find it? The front line was still far away, somewhere in the depths of Russia and on the steppes of the Ukraine. And so they died alone of exhaustion and cold in the fields and forests. Living on blueberries and the potatoes buried in the fields, they did not come out of the forests until winter.

On my way to school in the next village, I once observed a rag, a scrap of cloth covering a figure in a snow-drift. I drew closer and saw that it was an old Jewish woman. She seemed tiny and fragile; her unreal-looking glassy eyes like ice crystals, like pangs of conscience, looked at me. I thought she was alive. I took out a sandwich. I thought she had only fainted. Unfortunately, she gave no sign of life. I picked up her hand and it was as stiff as bone. To this day I can see the gaze of those uncanny, glassy eyes looking accusingly at me, or perhaps that is how it seemed then. When the ground thawed in the spring, the peasants buried her at the edge of the nearby forest.

I grazed cows the following summer. On hot days, I walked to a spring to cool off and have a drink. A man from the forest came there. He looked Jewish. I remember that he had curly black hair and a high forehead. He must have been between 30 and 40 years old. He did not have much to say aside from remarking that it was hot, or that the water was cold. Rather avoiding conversation, he would fill a jar with water and go back into the forest. Sometimes, as I strolled among the pines, I would see him gathering blueberries. At other times I would see a woman carrying a basket and walking towards the forest from the direction of the village. Later, I would see her going back the same way. I wondered if she was taking him food. She must have been doing so, for the man in the forest could not have survived merely on blueberries and water from the spring. The [Polish] 'Blue Police' came one day and went straight to his hiding place. He was shot as he slept, and buried on the spot. Peasants dug the grave under orders from the police. A local forester was suspected of having informed. He was punished severely for that and other misdeeds. Just before the end of the war, a grenade was thrown into his house, leaving him with severe injuries. Before the grenade attack, I had felt guilty for the death of the Jew. I had known something about his hiding place, although I had not told anyone. The forester knew the woods like the palm of his own hand. He had also been terribly opportunistic, and must have reported the Jew to the police.

The partisans did not tolerate informers, so they levelled their punishment.

After the destruction of the Jews, it was the turn of the Gypsies. For a certain period of time, Gypsies had occupied flats in several houses in Dziadówki, close to the nearby village of Ibramowice. They lived comfortably and happily. The wives smuggled contraband across the border between the General Government and the Reich. As 'wealthy' families, they scorned fortune-telling and theft. They must have regarded themselves as an elite among their people, for their pride was obvious. When the women returned from the border, there was dancing and drinking all night to the accompaniment of their own orchestra. They lived in friendship with the peasants. They were treated kindly throughout the neighbourhood.

I remember the night of a sudden thaw after a hard frost, when the snow became heavy and the sky and the trees blackened. My father awoke us in the middle of the night, shouting, 'Get dressed fast, children! The Germans are shooting people.' We ran outside half-asleep. We could hear individual shots and volleys from Dziadówki. We waited fearfully for dawn and news from neighbours. All the Gypsies, more than forty of them, had been shot. By a miracle, two small gypsy girls had survived. The next day, their landlord turned them in at the sentry-post in Wolbrom. Whether he was following orders or acting on his own, I cannot say. I saw the two little girls, half-covered in the straw, riding on his sleigh. No mercy was shown them. The sentry on duty took them behind the station and ended their short lives with his rifle.

62. Still Life

Zbigniew Lisowski

The concert of death usually began at dawn. The machine guns were the main 'solo' instruments in this satanic orchestra. But there were also frequent individual shots that somewhat upset the rhythms of the unending series that could go on without a break from early morning to late in the evening. They obviously 'worked' shifts. As far as I can remember, the main operation by the Lithuanian death squads lasted for two weeks. Those malevolent 'echoes of the forest' reached us from a wooded hill near Jaszuny, ten kilometres away, where there were mass shootings of Jews. The sound of the gunfire bored into our ears like drills, seeming to penetrate with their sharp points right into our brains, throbbing deeper and deeper, ripping all the fabric of our nerves. We ate our meals at night, because we could not keep any food down during the day. We barely spoke during the day. Each of us experienced silently and alone the tragedy being played out so near at hand.

Immediately after the main operation by the death squads, my father decided to take me with him to that horrible place near Jaszuny, so that I could someday 'bear witness to the truth'. To this day the terrible sight has remained with me. If I were a painter I would resort to tragic irony and title it 'Still Life with Hands and Prayer Books'. Hands stuck up like the stalks of plants from that ground lacerated by spades and bullets. They jutted towards heaven as if calling out to God for vengeance on the malefactors. The whole area was whitened, like the last snow melting in springtime, with prayer books or pages torn from them.

'Remember all of this well', my father whispered hissingly. We went home in silence. I came down with a fever that night.

63. The Prophecy

Józef Łasiński

I was born and brought up in a village near Kielce. My childhood and youth passed in that characteristic atmosphere where the most vital and colourful elements of local tradition and culture were handed down by word of mouth. Our Jewish neighbours played an important role in this oral culture. I did not know them before the war, because I was only an infant then. Now, like a speeded-up film, I remember how, in late 1942, two young Jews fleeing from the Nazis appeared in my parents' impoverished home, hastily rolled cigarettes for themselves, and ate some bread. They were in such a hurry that one of them took a hot coal from the stove to light his cigarette and dropped it down his own sleeve, burning himself. He jumped up and began waving his arm about, trying to shake the hot coal out of his sleeve. We children burst out laughing as we watched. My childish imagination was still innocent of how these people would be tormented bestially.

All the Jews from the surrounding villages ended up in the ghetto that the Germans established in Radoszyce. For some time afterwards their abandoned homes remained, along with endless stories, more-or-less exaggerated biographies, and legends. The Jewish tailors were gone, along with the itinerant traders who, like wandering nomads, seemed ubiquitous in the tiny villages. Once in a while, my mother would fall into a reverie, forget about the fact that they had been deported, and speak as if they were still among us. Then I would ask her in my childish way where they lived now. My mother would break off her tale. A sad, nostalgic look would come over her face, and she would snap, 'What do you mean? Don't you know the Germans murdered them all somewhere?' Even that 'somewhere' deepened the tragedy of the nation that had been killed in locations that the murderers had tried to keep secret.

To ease the work of the barbarian machinery and create or maintain an attitude of passivity among the local Polish population, an idiotic 'prophecy' was spread – I do not know by whom – that the disappearance of the partridges from the fields would signify that the Jews were no more. Since hardly anyone ever saw a partridge in those uncommonly frigid wartime winters, people heeded that 'prophecy' and read it as a sign of 'Providence'. The common thinking ran: 'It obviously had to be so, because it was prophesied'. How many similar 'prophecies' are still accepted in that countryside under the absolute subjugation of the Church!

Every one of my returns to my native countryside summons up again the shadows of those people who were so close to us, and yet so different. They were in essence perhaps trusting and gentle in a way, since they so humbly – at least in the beginning – bore the fate of their persecution. Yet their defencelessness only incited their persecutors to greater bestiality, rather than evoking any positive reaction.

One of the few scenes that left me with a sense of fear that I cannot overcome to this day was the expulsion and forced march to the station in Końskie of a transport of Jews during the 1943 liquidation of the Radoszyce ghetto. My memory is marked forever by the silhouettes of children with huge terrified eyes, dressed in loose, muddy rags (and half a century later, tears still spring to my eyes when I see people dressed in rags). With my mother and uncle, I watched the incredible beatings inflicted on the marching people. Some fell to the paving stones. There were horrible screams from the women. Old people were beaten to death. Five years old, I was so terrified that my mother had to hug me for a long time before I calmed down. I learned then, and would never forget, how cruel people can be when they hate.

64. March of the Condemned

Juliusz Olszewski

This scene has oppressed me since childhood. During the war, I lived with my parents in the village of Bidziny (in the former Opatów district, Kielce province). In 1943 or 1944 I witnessed how 'Kalmyks' drove a long column of Jews through the village along that same road. [Kalmyks were a Buddhist people originating from Western Mongolia, living on the North-Western shore of the Caspian Sea. Because of their persecution under Stalin, some Kalmyks collaborated with the Germans when they occupied their area.] They were probably Jews from the Sandomierz ghetto. I joined a small group of children that followed the column for some time. At a certain moment a tall, very thin man who was obviously having trouble walking began falling behind. He was supported by a woman and two small boys who kept crying fearfully, '*Oy, tatyni, Oy, tatyni*'. Today (although so many years have passed!) I can still see how a sentry unshouldered his rifle, pushed the woman aside with the rifle butt, kicked the boys, shot the man at point-blank range, and then ordered the others to push the body into the ditch. I can see how the boys clung to the body of the dead man. At mass the next Sunday, the priest reprimanded the congregation for the fact that an hour later the corpse lay there without shoes or clothing ... That, too, I saw and remember.

65. A Selection

Leszek Popiel

It was a cold, overcast, November day. Rain mixed with snow was falling – the start of an ordinary, hopeless day in the camp. We had been standing at roll call for hours. The roster had already been checked, but the work units had not yet been assembled. As we waited, we noticed more and more SS men on the camp grounds. Something new, unusual and terrifying lay ahead. Our ragged prison uniforms were soaking up more and more moisture, until they formed cold, wet compresses all over our bodies. They finally told us to go back to the barracks, and then locked us in. Something bad was coming. Shivering from the cold and anxiety, I leaned against the wall at a point where I could look out through a crack and see the roll-call square. Columns of Jews stood there motionless. There were a lot of them – two or three thousand. Armed camp guards surrounded them on all sides. Machine guns had been set up at the corners of the square. A group of high-ranking SS functionaries strode onto the square at around seven a.m.

'*Jüdische Häftlinge!* [Jewish prisoners!] I have been inspecting this camp since yesterday', Sturmbannführer Haase began his speech, 'and I cannot understand how it was possible to crowd so many people into such primitive conditions. This is simply inhuman. We must do something immediately. Some of you are to be transferred to the Heidelager camp (Pustków), where there are completely different, far more decent conditions and splendidly equipped workshops. For the moment, of course, we are able to transfer only the most highly-skilled craftsmen there.' In conclusion, he began calling out the skills that were needed and asking volunteers to step forward. After a moment of mistrustful hesitation, the Jews began stepping out of their ranks and walking to the new formations. In the meantime, Hauptscharführer Josef Grzimek, the *Lagerführer* – the commandant of the camp there at Szebnie – joined in and started protesting that all his best workers were being taken away. An apparently paradoxical situation arose: two SS men arguing over each skilled Jewish worker. The rain had turned to large snowflakes. The ground turned white and it was getting colder.

'The prisoners are freezing', Haase screamed. 'They will become ill. Bring them hot coffee at once!'

'What's going on here?' I wondered out loud.

'Liquidation', whispered *rotmistrz* [cavalry captain] Andrzej Skarżyński, a former officer and my fellow prisoner.

Yet why were they going about it in such a perfidious way? I could not understand.

In the meantime, a steaming coffee urn was brought out. 'Ladies first', said Grzimek solicitously. 'Why not call out the orchestra?' mused this slaughterer of the Jews. The Jewish camp orchestra was quickly assembled and began playing a concert of the Viennese waltzes so dear to the camp commandant, SS-Hauptsturmführer Hans Kellermann.

'Move around! Move around to stay warm', Grzimek urged. The hours went by. Those who had not been offered the chance to travel to the supposedly new and luxuriously outfitted camp drifted away. Kettles of soup were brought out, but there were no bowls or spoons. The Jews scooped the soup up in their hands, which upset the SS men and Jewish police. It was getting dark. The column of more than two thousand 'selected' Jewish prisoners was surrounded by armed SS men with dogs on leashes. Bright spotlights illuminated the main streets of the camp. The columns set off towards the gate. The comedy that had been acted out since morning was drawing to a close. The first shots rang out during the march through the camp, and motionless, bloody human remains fell onto the snow.

4 November 1943 was drawing to a close at the Szebnie concentration camp near Jasło.

66. In the Closed District

Lech Poraj

She remains extraordinary and enthralling in my memory, and neither time nor forgetting will ever eclipse those childhood emotions from more than half a century ago – emotions that I encountered in a Łódź courtyard around which loomed the peaks of filthy tenement houses. All the children called her Rutka. They never kept her out of our games, although she was different, more delicate somehow, with legs as slender as sticks, pale skin, thick curly hair the colour of ripe chestnuts, and large brown eyes. She had certainly never been baptized, for she was Jewish, as we all knew. Rutka stuck to us and, as I thought, particularly to me, with the trustfulness and sincerity that is given to small children.

She was the only Jewish child in our building, and perhaps in the whole street. I cannot say what it was that led her mother to take up residence in this district where the residents were mostly industrial workers and German shopkeepers whose families had lived for several generations in the melting pot of the 'Promised Land' of Łódź . My family had moved into that old building, where there were no toilets or running water, after our suburban villa and garden were confiscated by the victorious master race at the beginning of the war. We lived next door to Rutka in the dark corner of the back courtyard. The sun never reached our flats. This made the spacious courtyard all the more of a paradise for us children.

Rutka's mother was usually sewing something on an old Singer machine. We could hear her coughing late at night as she worked. The coughing was hard to take; it kept us awake. But we children had our own world of things we were interested in and things we imagined, and adults' problems seemed as distant as the moon. We loved to play in the rubbish tip in the courtyard. It was partly set into the ground, and we competed to see who could jump farthest into it. Being a little bit older, I did better than Rutka. Then she would get angry, and I would let her win just to see her tears of joy. I made up for this with my skill at hanging upside down from the iron frame where rugs were beaten. Then she would look admiringly at me. The only thing that could get me down was when good-natured Frau Bibolt, who seemed to be spending her retirement staring out of her second-floor window, shouted that I should stop before I broke my neck.

I often led Rutka by the hand through the nearby streets. We sailed sticks or paper boats in the blue-gray liquid that ran through the gutter, to watch them disappear down the grates. I taught Rutka to gather the cigarette ends that uniformed men nonchalantly threw to the pavement. We followed them assiduously, and when we got back to our courtyard we would unwrap the butts and make new cigarettes in German Juno papers. Rutka did not join in the clandestine smoking. We all thought she was too young, and her delicacy and frailness made us feel protective. We let her play only tag, hopscotch and hide-and-seek. It seemed to me that she was such a subtle creature that we had to guard against injuring her.

Therefore, I could not understand the vehemence with which Jadzia, the porter's daughter, once called her a 'little Jewess'. I felt that the other children were as outraged as I was. I liked Rutka best when she walked around the courtyard after her mother had braided her red hair into two pony-tails and tied them with a big bow. I wanted to be her page, her knight and, in the secrecy of my soul, her husband. We often played house in the corner of the courtyard. I pretended to be drunk, to want to sleep, and to pay no attention to my wife. She took it very seriously; her voice wavered and broke, and she shed big tears. Then I would laugh to bring our parody of adult life to an end.

We sometimes saw old Szleser, with his Kaiserian moustaches and the gold buckle across his round belly, helping a woman drag her husband out of his basement beer-hall. We followed such street scenes with rapt attention. Only later did I realize that Rutka seemed to be growing more reluctant to poke her head out into the street. Later still, it dawned on me that this was because of the fact that she did not wear the armband with the yellow star when she was in the courtyard. I also came to realize that our little paradise was surrounded by great evil; Rutka knew this before I did. The warm spring winds that followed the harsh winter of 1940 reached even into our gloomy courtyard and seemed to blow that evil away.

Staś opened his high window and played sentimental melodies on his gramophone. We would stop playing and sit on the old well listening to the lyrics of Polish love songs. The German language had been growing more and more oppressive, and by then Polish was used only in talking to family or close friends. So we sat listening as Staś, so young and pale, reclined his head on the pillow near the window and coughed out what was left of his lungs. When he died, his gramophone and broken records lay for a long time on the rubbish tip. Those were the days when the enthusiasts who wore the swastika, some of them our old neighbours, were going around plundering Polish flats and ripping the fur collars off our mothers' coats. That was supposed to be the Polish contribution to the *Ostfront*. They smashed Staś's musical world to bits.

But by then, Rutka was no longer around. I do not remember exactly when people began whispering about the resettlement of the Jewish population in Bałuty, the oldest district in the city, with its stink of sewerage and dilapidated tenement houses. That was when some of the Slavic Aryans showed their true selves – despite all the dangers of the occupation, they greedily bought up vacated Jewish properties for a song. Their greed blinded them to the fact that they were next in the queue for extermination.

In our home, the feeling was one of sympathy. We had become good neighbours with the Lebenbaums, and my mother often shared her rationed margarine or bread with them. We admired the Lebenbaums' will to live and their determined fight, totally alone, to protect their child. We could do nothing to help them; we were frightened ourselves. Only old Bednarek, a weaver from the I.K. Poznański Mill, dared to demonstrate his sympathy. While the whole building watched, he constructed a two-wheeled cart so that the two women would have some way of transporting their possessions to the ghetto. We children stood watching, knowing that the cart was for our Rutka. She no longer played with us. She had taken to sitting at home, as if she were already trying to forget us. I sometimes glanced at her window in the hope that she would come out, or at least wave. But the curtain never stirred. Rutka was preparing herself for a different life, although it is hard to say how much of her will was in that preparation.

There was never any real leave-taking. Perhaps we had all been too dulled by the occupation – by the fear, the shortages, the round-ups, the arrests. Perhaps we had become numb, indifferent and complacent because of the sound of thousands of feet on the cobblestones or the muffled conversations outside our window after the night-time curfew that made it impossible to sleep. We were still secure! In any case, like our mothers, we children watched in silent fascination on the early afternoon when Mrs Lebenbaum harnessed herself to that two-wheeled cart containing her miserable possessions and set out along with her daughter for an unknown fate. I do not know how long we went on staring. I remember that I ran out into the street, and saw how they turned at the first intersection. The little girl was walking beside her mother. What I could see best from that distance was the big white ribbon in Rutka's hair. She only looked back once, as if she knew that I would be the one who would watch them the longest. Then she disappeared around the corner.

Memories of Rutka returned in waves through the months of occupation. Our courtyard games continued as we grew up by degrees. The adult
world weighed down on us more while the desire to escape from the op-
pressiveness of the war kept us tied to the childishness of our imagina-
tions. Yet Rutka was still there in that make-believe world. More than once,
I climbed on a number 8 tram and rode towards the ghetto. From adults,
I had adopted the concept of the ghetto as a district of Jewish poverty, terrible overcrowding and even more terrible hunger. In the tram, I tried to
get a window seat. I would scratch at the layer of blue paint that had been
applied to the windows of all the Łódź tram cars because of the blackout.
The conductors would either shake their fingers at me or pretend not to
see, while I anxiously watched the street. Ulica Zgierska ran through the
ghetto from one 'Aryan' part of town to another. The tram did not stop
there – the old tram stops had been taken out of service.

Surrounded by the many barriers of barbed wire, the Jewish district
was like an outdoor exhibit when seen from the tram car, a sealed box
with glass walls. People wearing the yellow Star of David swarmed
beyond the wire. The people on the two wooden bridges running above
the tram line looked like dots. To me, a 10-year-old boy with Slavic looks,
the crush of people in a small space seemed terrifying. Then there was the
noiselessness and the way thousands of pairs of eyes looked from beyond
the wires at the passing tram. I remember how everyone in the tram
would fall silent then, while I feverishly scanned the thousands of pairs
of eyes beyond the wire for a small girl. I knew how powerless I was, and
fear of the people with rifles paralyzed any hope of rendering aid. I would
ride to the terminus and then ride back, usually on the same ticket – with
the conductor's assent. I would stare again into the alleys of the passing
ghetto. Perhaps I would see Rutka this time. I always took those journeys
to Bałuty by tram alone, and I took them countless times.

There were fewer and fewer people behind the wire, and the wooden
bridges over ulica Zgierska were empty. Seldom did I see anyone at all. I
did not yet know what had happened to the Łódź ghetto, and I do not
think that any of the adults around me knew the truth, either. Sometimes
I would sit in the first, 'Nur für Deutsche' [Only for Germans] tram car in
order to be able better to look for little Rutka in those gloomy streets, without being crowded by other passengers. Vacancy and silence yawned beyond the wires. There was never a girl there with a white ribbon in her
chestnut-coloured hair. I could feel the strength of my longing to return
to what was gone. It seemed that I could hear the beating of my young
heart in that silent ghetto. And so it has remained ever since, whenever I
walk alone through the old streets of the Bałuty district in Łódź.

67. The Prams

Kazimierz Wolff-Zdzienicki

It was a Sunday in June. The hot sun had dried a crust over the mud of Birkenau. The roads sounded hollow when work units walked along them. Yet it was Sunday, a fortuitous Sunday.

The units did not go out to work, although round-ups were sometimes held on Sundays, especially for the 'airplane' unit. The orchestra sat outside the block supervisor's room near the Main Gate. It was a good orchestra – after all, you can find some superb musicians if you have millions of people to choose from. They had once given symphony concerts around the world or played in the grandest opera orchestras and the most elegant nightclubs. Now they wore scratchy striped uniforms instead of tails. The repertoire was varied: symphonies and concertos, but also folk dances, operetta melodies, marches and dance hits.

When the orchestra took up its position on Sundays, crowds of prisoners pressed towards the gate, sitting in the ditches beside the road, standing outside the kitchen buildings – and listening. They forgot that they were in a camp surrounded by electrified barbed wire or that the SS men in the towers wielded not only their cold stares, but also machine guns. The music came from another world; it was a strong gust of freedom.

So it was that day in late June, 1944. The Hungarian transports had stopped a few days earlier. Of the hundreds of thousands of people brought from the land of the czardas and Tokay, only 60,000 had been registered as prisoners. The rest – smoke. The orchestra began to play. We listened. They played beautifully. One melody followed another, when something running along the road outside the camp diverted my attention. Something was glimmering there. I strained to see – was it cyclists, or prisoners with new shovels? At first, I could not understand what it was. After a minute or two ...

A column, the likes of which I had never seen, was approaching from the direction of the crematoria and the main warehouses where the possessions of the victims were collected. Several hundred female prisoners were walking in orderly ranks of five, each pushing an empty pram. The head of the column was gradually approaching the gate of our camp. In the vanguard marched a tall SS woman with a beautiful Alsatian. Other SS women surrounded the column.

The orchestra was playing a waltz. The tall concert-master, a grey-haired Frenchman, swayed to the melody. The women had scarves around their heads, and their heads hung low. Many could not hold back the tears, and their sobs carried over the sound of the music.

The prams were varied. Some glistened with chrome and enamel, while others were old and scratched. There were new limousine models and old-fashioned ones on high wheels, there were prams for newborns and toddlers' strollers. The prams rolled along in rows of five, empty prams.

The sobs of the women and squeaking of the prams distracted the concert-master. He looked around and froze in mid-beat. The orchestra lost the tune and fell silent for a moment. Everyone had turned towards the road. Prisoners who had been sitting on the ground stood up. One by one, they began removing their caps. The concert-master glanced at the orchestra, then at the SS men standing at the gate, and raised his baton. He brought it down twice in a slow, measured movement. When he brought it down the third time, Chopin's funeral march began.

The parade of empty prams passed through the gate of the Birkenau Men's Camp to the strains of the march. The head of the column turned towards the ramp. The prams were being sent to Germany ...

When the backs of the last of the women pushing the trams were out of sight, an SS man began screaming at the concert-master. He cursed him and ordered the orchestra back to their barracks.

The Sunday concert had been uncharacteristically brief.

68. A Street Not at all Cheerful

Stanisław Zalewski

We were living then on ulica Wesoła in Hrubieszów. 'Wesoła' means cheerful, but no name could have been less appropriate. The next street, which I could reach through a hole in the fence, was called 'Cicha', which means quiet, but it was rarely quiet there. It was, on the other hand, merry – there was a little bordello for *Wehrmacht* soldiers in one of the houses. The soldiers waiting their turn drank beer, laughed and some-times sang. One of the girls couldn't take it any more and tried to poison herself with concentrated essence of vinegar. The whole street stank of the stuff, and she screamed through her burned throat, or rather bellowed like some exotic, unknown animal.

Three Jewish families also lived in ulica Cicha and what was important to me was that one of them produced makgigi, also known as makagigi. (For those under 60, I should explain that this was flour – in this case, bran husks – mixed with something sweet, formed into sticks and baked on a stone.) It wasn't a *metsiya*, but on the other hand it only cost a penny. I was a frequent buyer of makgigi regardless of the 'wall newspaper' on the bulletin board in the school corridor which featured rhymes advis-ing strongly against buying anything from Jews. That bulletin board was personally arranged by the headmistress under the keen eye of a *Schul-rat* [school council] official. I have forgotten those rhymes, alas, but I have been unable to forget one of the sketches accompanying that literature. An obese, curly-haired Jew (side-locks, yarmulke, hooked nose – all the requisites) was feeding an enormous rat into a meat-grinder to make sausage for naive Christians.

It was mainly in consideration of the makgigi that I noticed regret-fully that the gendarmes were driving the Jews from ulica Cicha to the ghetto at the other end of town. That whole ghetto consisted of about twenty small buildings. I have no idea how the several thousand Jews of Hrubieszów lived there. The majority must already have been deported to Bełżec or killed in town, because there were frequent mass executions in the Jewish cemetery.

One sunny afternoon I looked through my hole in the fence and noticed a commotion in ulica Cicha. I hardly need say that I ran there as fast as I could.

A boy sat on the edge of the pavement. He was younger than I, around 10 years old, or perhaps he only looked that way because there wasn't much left of him. Despite the sweltering weather he was wearing a cap and had a greenish face with very large eyes. I did not recognize him and had probably never seen him before. I wondered if he always stayed at home because of an illness, or perhaps because he was afraid.

The boy looked silently at the people around him. I remember neither fear nor despair in his eyes. He must have known that it was all over. Then he began to speak. He explained quietly that he had not come from the ghetto, that he had been hiding in a cellar with his uncle. They had run out of food and his uncle had died. 'What was I supposed to do?' he asked.

A gendarme, one of those with the metal shields on their chests, pulled up in a horse cart. I do not know if he had appeared there by chance or if someone had summoned him. He helped the boy to get up, but when the boy could not climb into the cart the gendarme grabbed him, threw him in as if he were a dead cat, and drove off.

I do not know why this has all stuck in my memory. I saw things that were far worse because that region, as everyone knows, was hardly peaceful either during the Occupation or after. I do not recall that it made much of an impression on me at the time, but today my throat tightens whenever I think of it. That's simply the way it was.

69. Pity for the Dog

Przemysław Sadowski

I was woken up by some sort of noise early on an August morning. I lay there, still half asleep, unable to understand what was going on or where the noise was coming from. There was some sort of commotion outside.

I saw my mother standing at the window in her nightshirt with a robe over her shoulders, looking down into the street from the second floor. I got up to join her. She made room for me without saying anything.

Jews were walking down the street in rows of four. They were carrying their possessions. They had obviously taken whatever they could: suitcases, parcels and kit-bags. Most frequently, they carried bedding wrapped in sheets. They were older people, men and women. I did not notice any children. The unbearable din made by these unfortunate people pierced my eardrums.

Although it had been a hot summer and the day just beginning gave every sign of fine weather, they were all walking in overcoats and worn furs. The older Jews wore long coats and had hats or yarmulkes on their heads.

They were escorted by soldiers in black uniforms. I later learned that these were Latvian SS under the command of German officers. They did not hesitate to batter their prisoners. They beat them with rifle butts, screaming at them in a monotonous cacophony. Their screams in an unfamiliar language, and from time to time in German, seemed like the barking of mad dogs.

The terrified Jews added to the insufferable babel.

Some of them, overloaded with their belongings, fell by the way. Mindless of the blows raining down from the guards, their companions in misfortune tried to help them stand. A modern, local version of the stations of the cross was taking place here in Radom. It led from the ghetto at the riverside through ulica Peretz (now Podwalna), Narutowicza, Kościuszki, Planty and Bronia to the waiting goods carriages that were to take them to the place where they would be resettled – or so the Germans had assured them.

Our window overlooked the bath house of the Arms Works near the intersection of ulica Bronia and the Planty. At the place where trees grow today and footpaths cut through the park-like lawns, there was in those days an empty plot of ground used for football practice. During the war, the SS men quartered in the nearby blocks of flats played football there. The *Kriminalpolizei* [Criminal Police] had its offices in the 'foremen's block' and the notorious Radom Gestapo was in the engineers' building on ulica Kościuszki.

We watched as, at a certain moment, one of the escorting soldiers led a man in a long coat onto the football pitch, put his rifle to his head and fired. The Jew dropped. His body jerked several times and froze motionless. One man's road had come to an end. The soldier returned to the column and resumed his duties for the glory of the German Reich, as the cavalcade continued.

I do not remember how long that procession trudged before our eyes. Mommy felt ill, leaned against me, and without a word we stood there until the end of that march of human beings abased by the 'superior' German race. There must have been more than a thousand unfortunate people. As it turned out, those chosen at the first selection in the ghetto at the riverside had been older people who could no longer be of any use to the Reich war effort. They went off to 'resettlement', which explains why they were carrying their belongings. They were led to the station by way of the crossing that no longer exists at ulica Kolejowa. I do not know where they set down their baggage, but they certainly did not take it with them. They changed trains for heaven at Treblinka. This was not, however, a ritual funeral with weeping, the tearing of hair and burial in a seated position in a sheet, so as to be ready to rise more quickly at the Last Judgement. The Germans assisted them and hurried them along, simplifying the ceremonies. The unfortunates must surely have gone as they had walked along our street, in rows of four, except that now they went through the chimneys, straight to heaven without waiting for Judgement Day.

It was almost 5.00 and I was to leave for work at 7.00. Mother and I said little that morning, and I did not touch the breakfast she set out for me. Leaving home earlier than usual, I took a longer route to Golgotha, through the Planty, ulica Kościuszki and Narutowicza, instead of my customary route.

There were signs of the procession everywhere. I counted nine bodies left on the street or at its side. Kit bags and abandoned possessions also marked the trail.

At the Planty, I saw something that made a haunting impression on me. A little girl, a Pole, knelt by the body of an old Jew. She was going through his pockets. I knew her by sight: her father, an Armaments Works employee, was in a concentration camp and she lived nearby with her mother and sister. I still see her today in Radom – she is, naturally, a mature woman. I sometimes wonder if she remembers that day, if her conscience ever bothers her.

One more sight horrified me. At the intersection of ulica Narutowicza and Kościuski, an old lady in a faded lily-coloured dress that must once have been a ball gown sat in the gutter with her arm resting on the kerb. She stared straight ahead with glassy eyes. She had beautiful features, a profile like a Greek statue, and carefully combed grey hair. She sat without moving.

Germans were on their way to work in the nearby Gestapo offices: tall, handsome SS men who looked good in their uniforms. The woman sitting in the gutter made no impression on them. They walked past, indifferent.

Despite fear at the reaction of the Germans, I asked the woman if I could help her. She did not answer and did not move, but only looked at me with eyes that saw nothing and were perhaps the eyes of madness. How could I help with all those Germans around? Perhaps she realized how hopeless it all was.

I went to work. The construction offices were nearby, on Kastanienalee (now ulica Piłsudskiego). The early-morning deportation of the Jews had made a strong impression on both the Germans and the Poles who worked there. After an hour, I went out to see what had become of the 'lily lady'.

She was gone. Nor were there any kit bags on the street. The corpses had been removed. Jewish Police had loaded everything on carts which they drove to the ghetto – the 'lily lady', too, I assumed. She certainly hadn't had long to live, if she had been alive when they took her.

Before the bodies were thrown into graves, other hands than those of that little girl had searched their pockets thoroughly, and any 'treasure' they found there might yet have been of use to those left alive.

The day was as sweltering as the ones before. My friend Adam, a Silesian who spoke excellent German and had a wide range of acquaintances among the Occupation personnel, invited me for a beer after work. There was a small restaurant near our office that served cold beer in the buffet, and although Poles and Gypsies were given a hostile glance as they entered, their papers were not checked.

We were preparing to leave when an elegant SS officer, who knew Adam from somewhere, came up to him and ordered another round of beer. As he drank, the SS man told us in agitation how his beautiful dog had been run over by a car that day. He couldn't get over it; he was so upset by that accident. When we left the restaurant, Adam asked me if I knew who the German was. I shrugged my shoulders – how should I know? He informed me that the German had been the commander of the deportation operation. His dog had meant a lot to him; a human being counted for nothing.

The next ghetto liquidation took place more quietly, at night, without any marching through the streets. The Reichsdeutsch families who lived downtown, unaccustomed to the barbarity of their countrymen, had supposedly lodged a complaint about the way their peace had been disturbed.

When I walk across the intersection of ulica Narutowicza and Kościuszki today, I glance at the spot where the 'lily lady' sat leaning on the kerb. Sometimes I still see her there. Now I will never know what became of her or who she was. She is certainly somewhere in the other world, and perhaps she too looks down from there at that spot in the gutter.

The Occupation did not spare us strong impressions ... I lived through the Polish military campaign of 1939, I wandered on foot from Silesia [in the west] to Sarny [in the east], I saw many corpses and survived the aerial bombardment of communication arteries and cities and witnessed the flight of thousands of civilians to the east – into nothingness. But I remember the day of the exodus of the people of the Radom ghetto as if it were yesterday.

70. Even the Germans Protested

Elżbieta Kowalska

I am a native of Rzeszów, descended from a family that were merchants in what, before the war, was a small town. Our many acquaintances among our fellow-residents included Jews. I can remember names like Wang, Silber, Rejsner, Kesztecher, Gartnikel, Ungar, Grubner, Roszfalb, Weigel, Doctor Infelar, Doctor Darufes, Attorney Grojower and others. The Germans began persecuting the Jews systematically from the start of the Occupation and, as everywhere, finally set up a ghetto. I remember the boundaries of the ghetto, closed from the Main Square along ulica Mickiewicz, Szpitalna, Lwowska, Gałęzowskiego, Sobieskiego and Kopernika.

The thing that stuck most firmly in my mind and that I remember even today is the deportation of the Jews to the camps. First they began bringing Jews to Rzeszów from all the surrounding villages and small towns. I can remember hundreds of horse-drawn carts loaded, aside from people, with the most diverse sorts of possessions, from bedding to various sacks, pots and pans, washbasins, and so on. This enormous, unending influx of Jews increasingly crowded the ghetto.

I lived with my family on ulica Szopena, along which so-called work columns of Jews were marched early each morning under guard by SS men and Jewish Police. We saw the familiar faces of Rzeszów Jews among them. I remember how a Jew by the name of Roszfalb, whom we knew, jumped quickly out of a group returning one evening, dived through the street door of the house where we lived in a first-floor flat, and knocked at our door, asking for bread. Despite her fear, my mother quickly tossed some bread into the bucket full of rubble that he always carried home after work. He vanished and slipped back into the marching ranks. He repeated this practice several times, and then failed to appear one evening. I remember the knocking at the door from two children, perhaps four or five, who said in Yiddish jargon that they were hungry. I remember my mother being unable to bring herself to slam the door. She asked, 'Where are you from? Where do you live?' In reply we heard, in broken Polish, 'We live in back' – in the back corridor or courtyard of some building. They returned several times, got whatever food was at hand, and quickly ran off. Then came the time when they returned no more. They had obviously stopped being hungry.

I remember the moment when I was returning home at mid-day to the house on ulica Szopena. As I walked along aleja Pod Kasztanami, the Gestapo officer Flaszke was leading a Jew of 18 or 19 years old along the pavement, pushing him with the revolver he held and kicking him until the moment when the Jew fell to his knees before him, obviously begging for his life. Then, before my eyes, Flaszke gave him one last kick and shot him dead.

I remember perfectly the period of the deportation of the Jews to the camps in Bełżec and Auschwitz. I was walking near one of the gates to the ghetto, on the Main Square at the top of ulica Mickiewicza where you can see all the way down past Gałęzowskiego to the old cemetery. By chance, the SS men and Jewish Police guarding the gate opened it for some reason just as I was passing. It was only a moment, but I could see hundreds of Jews in dense ranks kneeling motionlessly on the street. That 'kneeling' lasted all night until the Germans began leading the first transport away the next morning. They walked from the Main Square past the parish church, down Moniuszki, and turned into Pułaskiego, which ended at the entrance to the siding at Staraniewo railroad station.

I remember that hot, sunny June day. I was having a lesson at a friend's first-floor flat, which had a long view. From the window I could look right down at the thousands of Jews carrying various objects including even washing tubs and pots and pans. They walked in rows of eight escorted by SS men with sweaty red faces and wild expressions in their eyes, who lashed out blindly with their rifle butts and fired at random into the ranks.

I can remember a certain 'snapshot'. A girl, perhaps a daughter, was leading by the hand an old woman, perhaps her mother, who could barely shuffle her feet. Behind them walked an SS man beating them with the butt of his rifle. There came a moment when the old lady could not raise her foot up onto the kerb. The SS man pulled the girl away and took aim at the old lady's back ... the fear was such that no one even looked round, no one flinched. They marched in double-time as the 'master race' commanded, and the whole street was strewn with corpses.

I remember: an old Jew dressed in black trousers, a black waistcoat and a white shirt with a yarmulke on his head, who could not keep up. A German shot him, and he fell and died resting on his hands and knees. Thus he stayed. When they reached the station where the goods train was standing, the people had to pass through a narrow gate in the chain-link fence. The Germans turned this into a shooting gallery. Driven with rifle butts, the Jews could not squeeze through the gate more than two or three at a time. Heaps of corpses grew on either side of the gate. After this 'transport,' those hundreds of corpses were stacked onto so-called manure wagons. Loaded to capacity, they were escorted by Jewish Police through the whole town to the Jewish cemetery in the district known as Czekaj and thrown onto piles. Rain fell in the night after the burning hot day of the first transport. There, in the Czekaj district, there were several cases of people who had not been 'finished off' being revived by the rain falling on the stacks of corpses. They managed to get out and crawl to nearby homes. Thanks to this, some of them probably survived.

The route of the transport had passed along the street where a German field hospital was located in the school dormitory building. And after that first, macabre transport even the wounded Germans submitted a protest to the *Kreishauptmann* [district chief] named Ehaus. The Germans made a 'humanitarian' show of the next transport. The Jews were led from the Main Square under normal escort and were even provided with a lorry. At the corner in front of the parish church, Ehaus himself and other Gestapo men 'tenderly' helped feeble Jews selected from the ranks up onto the lorry platforms with 'dignity and delicacy'. Among other things, I remember how such 'help' was extended to the Jew Ungar, the former owner of a fabrics shop. The whole comedy was painstakingly filmed by a Gestapo crew as a demonstration of their 'humanitarianism', which did not prevent them, a few streets further on, from using their rifle butts and shooting everyone who wandered into their rifle sights.

71. The Red Kerchief

Teresa Słocińska

The little girl clinging to her mother's hip shivered from terror and a strange overwhelming emotion that compelled her to stay and watch, even though she felt an impulse at the same time to run away and hide somewhere in the deepest concealment possible. She stood in the room with her mother, by the kitchen door, facing the window through which, across the street, she could see something that her child's mind wanted to reject, but which still fixed her gaze. The view out the window was the same as always: fences, the backs of houses and the barn on the next street and the steep hill that ran down towards ulica Górnicza, where the girl's house stood. They rode sledges there in winter, which was an act of courage since the almost perpendicular drop meant that each time the sledge reached bottom it landed with a crash that knocked the breath out of the rider. Little happened on the hill at other times of year. The neighbourhood children preferred playing in the hiding places in the waste ground around the nearby cable factory.

Now, it was different. Hugging her mother until it hurt, the little girl watched as three men climbed the hillside beyond the fence. The first and third were Gestapo functionaries and carried rifles. In the middle, stumbling and swaying, walked a young man with a red kerchief around his neck. The kerchief mesmerized the little girl, since it seemed to her to be endowed with an incomprehensible life of its own. It moved, fluttered and wrapped its pulsing, shining folds around the man's neck. Only after a moment did she realize that what she had taken for a kerchief was blood spurting from a wound in his neck.

The young man took several mores steps and then fell as one of the Gestapo men pushed him. The German walked towards the wall of the barn, then turned around and aimed his rifle at the man who lay on the ground. At that instant the girl pressed her eyelids shut and ducked behind her mother. She heard a shot. She understood what had happened. She thought that when she looked again, the world would be different – a man had been killed. But nothing had changed outside the window. The young Jew lay in the same position, reminding her of a rag doll she sometimes played with. The German calmly put his rifle aside, drew his pistol, and shot his victim in the head.

The little girl was me. I was 7 years old and saw every detail. The street was narrow and our window was just at the level of the scene on the hill. We had moved to ulica Górnicza when they began creating the Będzin ghetto – our old house on ulica Przeczna lay within its boundaries. The ghetto was established where the city's slums stood then, in a district of miserable houses erected by the poor from wood and the cheaply available local limestone. Our original house had been on the periphery of the district known as Warpa, and had been taken over by a German.

The bungalow on ulica Górnicza where we spent most of the Occupation lay not two hundred meters from the ghetto gate. A column of Jews on their way to the garment works was marched down the middle of the street past our window each morning. I remember that there was no way to catch the eye of any of them; they walked humbly, looking straight ahead, never glancing to the side. They carried their own spoons and forks for the meals they received at work. One day, mother found a fork lying in the street after they had passed. I have it to this day.

The liquidation of the Będzin ghetto lasted several days. The large Jewish population of the town constituted a majority of the inhabitants. The scene described above occurred in the first days of the liquidation. We saw other similar episodes. I still have this image in my memory: a Gestapo officer standing on the hill with his feet apart, aiming a pistol, and below, frozen in a posture of flight, a young Jew in a cap and a jacket too big for him. We were alone on the street – the two of them and me. I do not remember what I was doing there; I must have simply gone out to play. These were the last moments of the destruction of the ghetto and calm was slowly returning to ulica Górnicza. Yet I can remember the paralyzing fear that the fury of the Gestapo man would also extend to me and that he would want to kill me, too – although I already knew that I was not one of those whom they were hunting just then.

A widow with her three daughters lived in the building next to where this was happening. They had a German surname and had signed the *Volkslist* [to become a German]. People said that they had helped a Jewish boy who had sheltered in their doorway while fleeing. They had fed him and given him some clothes. Other *Volksdeutschen* [those who signed the *Volkslist*] also lived in that building, but as far as I know none of them denounced the woman.

I also want to recount what my mother saw during the destruction of the ghetto. Five young Jews including a girl took shelter in the storage locker belonging to tenants of a house in a nearby street, right near the entrance to the ghetto. Someone denounced them. They were pulled brutally out and shot on the spot. They were killed one by one with a bullet in the back of the head. The girl knelt, embracing the Gestapo functionary's knees, sobbing and begging for her life ...

'What do they want from people?' my mother repeated helplessly, 'What do they want?'

When the ghetto had been emptied, patrols were maintained for a certain time for the purpose of catching any possible fugitives. We could see such a sentry post from our kitchen window. The soldier carried a chair out from a former Jewish flat and then a table on which he lay his rifle. He sat for hours watching the buildings. After a while, a child wandered into sight from among the abandoned houses. The child could not have been more than 2 or 3 years old. Barefoot and dressed only in a shirt, it was crying from hunger and cold. Mother was sure that the soldier would shoot the child immediately. Instead, he went into one of the houses and came back carrying leggings, sweaters and little shoes. He dressed the child, picked it up and took it off somewhere. Mother did not know if what she was watching was some reflex of mercy, or simply the carrying out of an order. One thing was sure – the child's hours were numbered.

Years later she told me that, immediately after the establishment of the ghetto, a Jewish woman she knew (I do not remember how she had managed to communicate with mother) had asked her to take her child. Mother regarded this as impossible. Aside from the fact that the house stood right at the edge of the ghetto, its owner was a widow who, despite her Polish surname, cherished a fanatical hatred of Poles. She must have been a German woman who had married a Pole. Her son served in the *Wehrmacht* and frequently threatened that when he returned from the victorious war he would make short work of us. (The young German supposedly hanged himself when the war was over.) There were only three tenants – ourselves, the widow, and an old woman caring for her granddaughter, whose attractive mother was notorious for entertaining German officers at home. In this situation, any strange child would immediately have been noticed, with predictable consequences. Furthermore, my father was a Home Army partisan and was in hiding following an operation at that time, making us vulnerable to a visit and search from the Gestapo. And so we do not have a tree in the Avenue of the Righteous [in Jerusalem].

72. Why Should I Hide?

Alina Adamowicz

I am part of the generation that remembers those tragic years.

I am a Pole. Let me state at once that I did not witness any shocking scenes in that period and, unfortunately, I did not save anyone.

I was a young girl then, after all, and there was little I could do, but there are certain events and people that have remained in my memory and that I would like to tell about.

I lived at 5/7 Włochowska Road in the Warsaw suburb of Okęcie with my parents. A Jew named Kuperman owned the house. I cannot remember his first name. He had a wife called Raisa and a son who was a couple of months old. German soldiers began making frequent calls at his flat during the first winter of the Occupation. They usually came at night and stole various valuable objects.

Being on good terms with the Kupermans, my parents decided that the child should sleep at our flat so that no harm should come to him.

I remember Mrs Kuperman's helpless tears as she kept repeating: 'Is such a little baby to blame for being born Jewish? Why should he have to suffer?' I also remember trying to get the baby to stop crying because it was better if know one knew that he was in our flat. Although our neighbours were decent people, it seemed strange that the Germans had known where the Kupermans lived. This situation went on for some time, and then one day Mr Kuperman was summoned to Gestapo headquarters on aleja Szucha.

He told us about this, and I remember how my father tried to convince him not to go. Kuperman answered, 'Mr Bilicki, I'm a decent man. I haven't done anything wrong, so why should I hide? I'll go and clear this matter up.' He went, and never returned. I remember waiting for him, and later his wife's despair and tears. She moved soon afterwards to her parents' and we never saw her after the establishment of the ghetto.

A little while later, we and the rest of the tenants were evicted from that building. We missed it and often reminisced about it.

My second memory from that period concerns a girl called Pola Dubińska. She was a good friend and to this day I cannot get over losing her. I do not know how or when she died.

She was in the ghetto with her family, but she and her mother frequently managed to sneak over to our side and then they would stay with us. I know that they collected various scraps, mainly bread crusts, and threw them over the wall in sacks. At a spot on ulica Elektoralna, I helped them do this several times, but I could do no more for them because we too were very poor and usually hungry.

And at this point I must admit to something that depresses me even today. Pola came on some holiday, when everyone tried to have something a little better to eat despite the prevailing misery. My mother fried a couple of fruit pancakes and naturally shared them out among everyone, including Pola. And I remember wishing she hadn't come that day, and being somewhat cross with her. I hope that she didn't notice, but I will never forgive myself that thought.

Later she and her mother stayed with us for a day or two now and then, and then they stopped coming. I do not know what happened to them later. I tried to get into the ghetto through the Jewish cemetery once, but a Jewish policeman caught me and sent me back.

Pola had two sisters, Sima and Hela, but their features were too Semitic for them to cross over to the other side. I liked them very much as well. Even before the war, their family had been poor. Her youngest sister, Hania, was in the orphanage run by Janusz Korczak. Pola and I visited her several times, and I even saw the Doctor. Everyone at Pola's spoke with great feeling about how good he was and how well he took care of the children. I too therefore felt affection for him and was happy that I had seen such an exceptional man.

Now, why am I writing all this? Perhaps to be able to give vent on paper to my feelings, but above all so that something of these people remains behind.

73. Four Scenes

Tadeusz Ludas

I lived from 1925 to 1944 in a small eastern Polish town near the River Bug, a county seat. The famous *shtetl* of Belz was an integral part of this region and its ethnic mosaic. So was the town of Hrubieszów, which I shall be describing. This is where I was born. This is where I grew up, along with Jews, Ruthenians and my own kind. The Jews were the most numerous, supposedly ten thousand, more than 60 per cent of the population. I never checked this, but it must have been true. For the most part, the Jews were either poor or very poor. They worked at all sorts of jobs. They bought and sold whatever they could. They practiced every vocation and branch of the crafts. They were cart drivers, teamsters, estate agents, dealers. You could count the wealthy Jews on the fingers of one hand: the Orensztajns, Rappoports, Ajzens and Sasses.

The majority of the Jewish population lived in dilapidated slums located in the very centre of town, on streets like Łazienna, Rybna, Wodna and Gęsia, and the districts known as Prowale and Wojtóstwo.

In keeping with the multi-ethnic nature of the town, there was a Roman Catholic church, an Orthodox church across the street, and a synagogue or prayer-house a little farther along. There were also large cemeteries: the Roman Catholic and Orthodox ones on the edge of town and the Jewish burial ground downtown.

I too lived in a slum, a Polish one, but in the Jewish quarter. In this way and thanks to this, I grew up among the Jewish population. This surely accounts for my respect and unconditioned tolerance towards precisely this people. They were poor, but they did not reject me. I was also poor, and perhaps that is why I treated them as my brothers.

It has remained so until the present.

I was thus with them and together with them all the time. I took part in their daily life and in various ceremonies, including weddings and funerals. As a mute witness and against my will, I also took part in their ultimate destruction: the Holocaust.

Living as I did with the Jews, I had friends and acquaintances among them. One of the former, perhaps the closest, was a boy my age, Józef Hudys, the son of a cart driver who worked hard for his living. I was often a guest in their needy dwelling. Complete harmony and agreement, care for the home and family, and above all extraordinary religious devotion reigned there in spite of all their troubles.

And a general reflection: observing Jewish community life at close quarters and knowing their customs, I came to the conclusion that this community showed incredible internal solidarity, amicable relations among people, and a readiness to help the weaker.

* * *

The Germans came in September 1939. Several days later, the Polish army counter-attacked from the direction of Włodzimierz and drove the enemy back as far as Krasnobród (in the Solska forest).

The Bolsheviks entered Hrubieszów on September 21. Who turned out to give them an enthusiastic welcome? The Jews. This came as a complete shock to me. No one else but the Jews immediately put on red armbands, slung rifles over their shoulders, and stood guard in front of all the town's important buildings.

There stood my acquaintance Mosiek with a rifle in front of the mill, pretending not to notice me. So I said, 'Mosiek, a Jew like you with a rifle?' He replied, 'Don't you call me a Jew, Tadek. I can have you arrested.' And that was that.

The Bolsheviks were not in town long, but they managed to loot all the shops. They withdrew across the Bug River (as they had agreed beforehand with the Germans, we know today) and the Germans returned to Hrubieszów. A few Jews left with the Bolsheviks. The rest stayed where they were — in Hrubieszów.

* * *

I do not intend to use dates here, since I do not remember them. The history of the extermination and persecution of the Jews on the territory of the General Government is well known. Everyone knows that the Germans did not immediately embark upon the extermination of this people. It was an incremental tragedy. First, the Jews were deprived of their shops, workshops and so on. Then they were ordered to wear the Star of David and forbidden to travel without permission from the German authorities. Later, after the establishment of the *Judenrat* and the Jewish Police, they were forced to perform various sorts of work in groups for the Germans and the local authorities.

As I have mentioned, the rest of the population perceived the Jews as characterized by collective fellowship and solidarity. This all suddenly turned out to be untrue. I myself saw how the clerks in the *Judenrat* treated their own. For no good reason at all, the Jewish police were capable of mercilessly abusing their co-religionists with truncheons while a German gendarme stood by chuckling out loud with satisfaction at the sight of Jew mistreating Jew in a style that even the Gestapo would not have been ashamed of.

Such behaviour was truly difficult to understand, and even harder to accept as a totally indefensible reality, rather than a bad dream.

* * *

It is known that the Germans proceeded methodically. First, therefore, they organized the deportation of significant numbers of Jews in rail transports in the direction of Zamość – surely to Bełżec and Sobibór. Once the number of Jews had been reduced to a workable level, the Germans organized a real ghetto in Hrubieszów – with sentries and surrounded by barbed wire. They packed in the Jews who remained alive.

The wait for the next extermination operation was not long. They initiated the mass shooting of Jews in their local cemetery. They murdered them in broad daylight and in full sight, before the eyes of 'Aryan' onlookers, as if they wanted a large, uncaring audience.

The executions went on from morning to late evening for three weeks. I saw a great deal close up and at first hand. I was thus one of many eyewitnesses of this tragedy, and to this day have not been able to shake off the impression or in any way to forget those brutal events even for a moment. It was deeply shocking!

I lived just a few metres from the Jewish cemetery. Thus I know the details. Several days before the slaughter, the Germans knocked a fifteen-metre-wide breach in the cemetery wall, facing ulica Ludna, which leads to the centre of town. This breach was to function as the 'Gate of Death'. Earlier, they had ordered Jews to dig three large, deep, rectangular pits. Then it started ...

One day a continuous cannonade of machine gun fire could be heard from early morning. I ran to the breach and watched with horror as the Germans finished executing a group of a dozen or more Jews. At first I thought this was an isolated incident (I did not yet know that the pits had been dug). But I quickly realized that I was wrong. The noise had barely died away when the next group, including elderly people, women with children, men and young people, arrived from the direction of town.

The Germans had painstakingly prepared and organized everything.

The starring criminal role was played by the Gestapo agent known by all the local people as 'Blondie'. In those days, no one yet knew his real name. He was supremely brutal to everyone, Jews and Poles alike. The terror of Hrubieszów. Here are the details: Every so often, obviously scheduled in advance, a group of sixty or seventy Jews, guarded by one gendarme, arrived from town. They were all packed into a tight group around which a single strand of barbed wire had been run. On arriving at the cemetery, the group was halted ten or fifteen meters from the nearest pit. Next, a Gestapo agent unwound the barbed wire and shoved the first ten people towards the edge of the waiting pit. There, they ordered them all to kneel and immediately shot them in the back of the head. Some were finished off individually. Others were not, and those who did not fall into the pit were kicked into its maw by the Gestapo. And so it went on, and on … until the end! When one pit was filled it was covered with a layer of soil (this was done by the Jews) and a new one filled from the beginning. After they had been covered over, the pits trembled with the last remains of life and the spasms of death. From the depths of the next pit rose incomprehensible cries and the groans of the people dying there.

There was also a moment – I saw it with my own eyes – when 'Blondie' tore a small child away from its mother, grabbed it by the legs, and smashed its head against a wall until it ceased giving any sign of life. Such a child, after all, could not kneel at the edge of the mass grave, all the more so because its mother clutched it to her breast as she knelt, protecting it from death. So the slaughter went on and on. The Germans had to relieve each other every so often so that they could catch their breath and rest.

No one knows exactly how many victims were murdered during that act of annihilation. I think it must have been at least 1,500 to 2,000 Jews.

One Polish woman, Magnuszewska, a Hrubieszów resident, also lay in one of those mass graves. She simply had the very bad luck to have come to deliver a canister of milk to a Jewish family at the moment when they were being led away to the cemetery. Although she showed her 'Aryan' *Kennkarte* [I.D.], she was taken along and shot for rendering aid to Jews.

Of all that I have related above, one thing was appalling and completely incomprehensible to me then (today, I see things differently). I did, of course, realize that none of those unfortunate Jews had the least chance of any sort of defence. I also realized that they all had to die martyrs' deaths. Yet I could not conceive how these people, including those who were young and strong, men and women, could so passively allow themselves to be led to the slaughter by a lone gendarme like the proverbial flock of sheep (please excuse the simile), bound with a single piece of wire or, as sometimes happened, with string, without the slightest reflex of resistance, attempt at escape, or anything of that kind. This was simply incredible, atrocious and dreadful. But perhaps these people were really so permeated with fear that they felt nothing, not even that they were part of that macabre procession of death. Who can say?

After that criminal annihilation came a momentary calm. But a large number of Jews still remained in the ghetto. Now there was no doubt that a similar fate awaited them, except that no one knew when. Two acts had been played out, and the third and last remained.

It happened more or less a week later. But it took place completely differently.

The Germans designated the training ground of the pre-war Second Mounted Rifle Battalion as the place of death for the several thousand Jews who remained alive. The terrain was ideal for the purpose. It lay not far from town, but was secluded, and screened by a thick grove of trees from the paved Hrubieszów-Moniatycze route. It offered good approach roads and a lot of open space. German army lorries carried Jews and their families there for two days from dawn to dusk. They were in a hurry. There and back, there and back ran the lorries. One sustained scream of despair from the people on board filled the streets. They knew where they were going and why. The route of this funeral procession ran through half of the densely populated city, in the direction of Chełm Lubelski. And so, once again, everything happened before the eyes of many, many people. In town, the continual drumming of the machine-gun salvos could be heard. The last act of the drama of the Hrubieszów Jews was being played out, and it was played out with exemplary German precision.

It somehow happened that I never had any subsequent occasion to find myself in that place and therefore I do not know if there is any kind of monument. I do know that during the whole communist period the site was used for military purposes by the Fourth Cavalry Battalion, the Fifth and Ninth Infantry Battalions, and the Battalion concealed under the number 2122. That sacred place is probably still used by the army, and the commanders might not even know that they are training their soldiers on the mass graves of their Jewish brothers.

* * *

All the Jews had already been murdered. The city was abandoned. No one lived in the ex-Jewish houses. There was not a living soul in them.

From time to time, there were some individual Polish looters rummaging through the flats, attics and cellars.

It looked as if there had been a plague where the ghetto had been. Everything was frighteningly empty. Only the wind blew the piles of feather stuffing, scraps of rags and papers around.

It was just noon, one day towards the end of September. I do not know why, but on that day I decided to take a shortcut home from the vocational school I attended. I went through the very centre of the former ghetto. Halfway, I suddenly heard shouting in German. What did I see? The Gestapo ('Blondie' again) was leading four people, a Jewish family, out of the house opposite. The terrain was hilly and uneven at this point. I was standing several metres above, looking down at what was happening. I looked closer and went numb. I saw the family of my schoolmate and friend, Józef Hudys, whom I mentioned at the very beginning. At one point he noticed me and we exchanged glances, just for a fraction of a second. Beating and kicking them, the Gestapo functionary stood the whole family in a row against the wall of the house. His automatic suddenly barked and all of them, Józef, his father, his mother and his younger sister, fell, each in a different position. It was quiet, but nearby, right by the whitewashed wall, a light breeze stirred the stalks of red mallows. After that terrible sight, I began running as fast and as far as I could.

One thing is intriguing in all this. Why did fate precisely pick me out to be the eyewitness of the death of someone close to me and of his family, all the more so as this was the last execution and therefore the last act of the Holocaust in Hrubieszów? It was some sort of fate, an inexorable predestination. Because under normal circumstances I would never have been at that particular place, at that time and on that day. I usually walked a completely different route. And yet just then something directed me there to see a scene such as I had never in my life desired to see, and which has haunted me to the present. Or perhaps it was Józef who drew me there with his internal will and his very thoughts, so that I could see everything and remember it forever. In any case, it was certainly more than the normal sort of coincidence after which one can return without deeper reflection to everyday life.

* * *

Now to sum up. Did the Poles help the Jews of Hrubieszów in their hour of trial? I do not know. I never heard of any such cases. In my opinion, knowing the reality of the times, help from Poles to Jews was rather impossible and not always eagerly rendered. Did the Jews, or even a small number of them, have any chance of escaping from Hrubieszów, for instance to the forests, to the partisans? Decidedly not. That was because, during the period of the destruction of the Jews in Hrubieszów, groups of the Home Army and Peasant Battalion (there were no other partisan movements in that region) were involved in heavy fighting with the UPA, the Ukrainian National Army, for the survival of the Polish population of the southern part of Hrubieszów county.

I do, however, know of one case of Jews being sheltered in the Polish-Ukrainian countryside of the Modryniecki Forest, by one Czesław Baran.

74. What Good is Bread to Me?

Janina Margules

The camp in Stutthof operated longer than any other camp in Poland. Founded in the first days of September 1939, it was not liquidated until 10–11 May 1945. No one in Warsaw ever heard of it. It was mainly for 'criminals' from the Gdańsk coastal area. After a visit by Himmler in February 1942, it was officially designated a concentration camp. It met all the criteria. It had a gas chamber and a crematorium. It was systematically enlarged. The hands of the prisoners built the 'New Camp', which was also called the 'Jewish Camp'. From 100,000 to 120,000 people were officially registered as prisoners, but there were also whole transports marked for immediate extermination that were probably never registered. In 1944, Adolf Eichmann set about the final solution of the Jewish Question in Hungary. Jewish people from Hungary filled all the camps in Poland. The transports brought to Stutthof carried mostly women and children. They had been exhausted by long journeys in the cattle wagons and decimated by illness. Regardless of overcrowding, they were packed a thousand and more at a time into a single barrack. The corpses were carried out in the mornings. The heaps rose as high as the roofs. Then sledges pulled by people came along to gather up those regarded as dead. How many of them were still alive? There was an 'Aryan' barrack next to the Jewish 'death barracks'. Most of the prisoners were Polish women from the Warsaw Uprising [1944], with a few Ukrainian and Russian functionaries. On the other side was another Jewish barrack, surrounded by non-electrified barbed wire. The Jewish women in the new transport from Hungary were separated from their children. The mothers were on one side, the children on the other, and the 'Aryan' barracks in between. The new arrivals crowded against the fences on both sides, calling out in Yiddish and Hungarian. At a certain moment, one of the mothers spotted her daughter. 'Are you hungry?' she shouted. 'Do you want bread?' The little girl, who must have been nine or ten, shouted back, 'Mama, what good is bread to me? I'm going to the gas.' I was petrified – those children knew what awaited them. I looked at the mother. A grimace of suffering twisted her face. She looked at me and said, 'What are you standing there and looking at? You have the right to live, but my child must die.' Both barracks were vacated several hours later. We lined up for our evening roll-call. They counted us over and over, while I kept wondering constantly whether they had met yet, whether they had been allowed to die together.

75. The Holy Days

Maria Schaechter-Lewinger

The Holy Days were something special in childhood. All the children waited eagerly for the joys they promised. Jubilant or solemn, every Holy Day left its stamp on family life.

We loved Passover best of all, and the anticipation of the moment when the great baskets full of the Passover table settings appeared in the kitchen. Then we crowded tight around Mummy as she removed the porcelain from the packing. Treasures we had not seen for a year emerged from the protective wood shavings: little white bowls with serrated edges, tiny chalices with handles for the smaller children, decorated with gilt stripes and the word 'Pesach' written in gold, the great Seder platter, Daddy's silver cup, and many other wonders. The large coffee mugs were finally extracted from the bottom of the baskets. Each of them bore portraits of the Three Emperors in gold medallions. Decorations hung from their fine, colourful uniforms. Two Emperors, the Prussian and the Austrian, had beautiful, waxed moustaches, while the Russian Tsar flaunted a long, noble beard. Amid cries of rapture, the children tried to touch these mugs, pushing and elbowing until Mummy asked everyone to leave the kitchen so that she could wash these Holy Day treasures and set them in the glass-fronted cupboard.

Then the merry sound of the whisk at work filled the kitchen for a week. There were eggs and pieces of matzo everywhere. Bottles of red borscht fermented in the pantry.

The high point of the Passover Holy Days was the visit to the prayer house that my parents attended on ulica Szpitalna. We always importuned Mummy until she agreed, for the sake of peace, that we could wear stockings for the first time that spring, although the weather was not always warm enough. In our Holy Day best, we chased other children up and down the wide stairs of the synagogue. Knees pale from winter flashed beneath the folds of our skirts and our new sandals squeaked encouragingly. There was no end of laughter, squeals and joy. These were moments of true delight – the great delights of the first years.

Yet there were also solemn Holy Days. The most solemn of all was Yom Kippur. Mummy and the maid spent the whole day preparing supper. The fragrance of fish and raisin cake filled the flat. We ate supper hurriedly in the evening. Daddy put on his Holy Day suit, painstakingly cleaned his top hat, and was ready to leave. Having given her final commands in the kitchen, Mummy then called the maid into the bedroom to help lace up her corset. Daddy paced impatiently up and down the living room. From time to time he would pause at the bedroom doors and urge, 'We're going to be late for Kol-Nidre. We really will be late.' At last, Mummy emerged. She would be overheated and blushing as she ran after Daddy, who was already waiting on the stairs.

After the day of hurry and confusion, the flat fell silent. Darkness came, but no one turned on the lights. The candles in the great silver candelabra dwindled slowly down. Only the flame of the candle burning for the souls of the dead cast a weak flickering light towards the dark corners of the room.

The children sat gloomy and morose. They did not go to bed, because it seemed strange to undress in a dark room. They all waited patiently for their parents to return.

The familiar tread was finally heard on the stairs. Mummy always returned in tears and disappeared straight into their bedroom. Daddy, as was his habit, strolled around the living room for a moment humming fragments of the Kol-Nidre. The children crawled silently into their little beds. The Day of Atonement had begun.

The Kol-Nidre prayer was the most important event of the year for members of the synagogue. The discussions would continue for a long time over whether the cantor had interpreted the melody correctly. There were many pros and cons. My Daddy worried about this a great deal. He loved singing himself. He had a strong, beautiful tenor and our flat frequently echoed to his favourite arias. He decanted the tears of the clown from *Pagliacci* with a bitter laugh. Or: 'Rachel, my child', he sang emotionally, 'now I will lead you to the pyre ... I hear your complaints, full of bitterness' – his vibrating voice easily rose up the scale – 'why are you deaf to my suffering?' – and he evoked the full dramatic exaltation of the aria. At this moment, my childish fancy always suggested the same image: Father leading my beautiful, eldest sister, dressed in a flowing gown, by the hand towards a flaming pyre where she would be burned at the stake.

Daddy's most beloved repertoire also included synagogue songs. Professor Sperber's boys' choir sang at the prayer-house on Szpitalna. The young childish voices mixed with those of the men. On returning from prayers, Daddy would give the four youngest children lessons singing the religious songs. We all had good voices and our little choir readily picked up new melodies. Under Father's baton, my twin sister held a note in her clear soprano – *Veeyneynu sirenu* [A prayer: may our eyes see]

– which Father answered in his tenor – *Sirenu malchusecho* [may they see thy kingdom]. Then we all joined the chorus in unison. Singing together was a great comfort. Father stroked his blond moustache in satisfaction and apportioned praise. Seated afterwards at the festive dinner table, Father sometimes mused aloud about one of his daughters becoming a famous singer, an accomplished pianist, or perhaps even a great actress. And for himself? For himself, what he dreamed of most was being able to sing the Kol-Nidre one day in the synagogue.

It was 1942. My family had had to leave Cracow and we were living in a small town away from any frequented route. Life passed slowly, monotonously. All the family's energy went into acquiring food. We were always carrying something out of the house to sell. Potatoes, onions, a bit of flour, barley or peas replaced the things we had sold. It was becoming increasingly more difficult to get food, and we had less and less to sell.

Terrifying reports suddenly began reaching the little town from unknown quarters. The Germans were deporting all the Jews from the region, transporting people to their death, killing old people, women and children. Father did not believe it. 'What does that mean, killing?' he asked. 'Why should they kill me? I have never wronged anyone in my life.' But ever more horrifying news reached us, ever more insistently. A tight ring of danger surrounded the town.

Autumn came, bringing the New Year and Yom Kippur. The Jewish community no longer had a rabbi or a cantor. My father was invited to sing the Kol-Nidre. A small party of frightened Jews gathered at a prayer house located in a private dwelling on the periphery of the town. I followed, and stood where no one would notice me. 'My father's dream is about to come true', I thought. 'This dark room is hardly the synagogue on Szpitalna, full of lights and the faithful in their best dress – but Adonai is everywhere, after all.' Listening to the murmur of prayers, I waited.

'Kol-Nidre', Father intoned gravely. And then, and then …. I listened to his singing with pain and incredulity. What had happened to my father's beautiful, melodious voice? This was a weak, famished man singing his prayer to God. The melody rose and fell despondently and never managed to ascend towards the heavens. There was only sobbing, lamentation, complaint … My father's singing seemed like a powerless struggle with God in a final act of doubt, in a final cry of despair.

It was his last Kol-Nidre.

My father, *moriturus* …

PART SIX

TO HELP OR NOT TO HELP?

Introduction

This section focuses on the difficult decisions faced by many Poles, in a complex situation, when they looked upon the suffering of their Jewish fellow citizens. The potential cost to themselves and to their families was great, as discussed in the introduction to Part 4, but the guilt of not helping would consume them for many years.

Antoni Kewis (76) a member of the Polish underground in Warsaw, hesitates to intervene to save two Jewish children of four to five years, when two Polish policemen momentarily refuse to obey the orders of a German soldier to kill them, and never forgets the incident, forever suffering 'pangs of conscience'. As a boy, Jerzy Tomaszewski and his friends stare at a Jewish boy who has escaped from the Warsaw Ghetto as it burns (78), whilst Tomaszewski ponders upon the consequences of helping him. The next day it is too late, for the boy has disappeared. This stirring of his conscience played a role in Tomaszewski's becoming a leading scholar in the history of the Jews in Poland and of the problems of national minorities. From the 'Aryan' side Janina Allerow (79) tries to help starving Jewish slave-labourers in the Warsaw Ghetto, by filling bags with groats, sugar and lard and then stuffing them into the inner-tube (instead of air) of one of the tyres on a wagon driven into the ghetto, but the risk proved too great for this to be tried a second time. Later, she did manage to help, by providing 'Aryan' identity papers for a Jewish couple. Immediately after the war, Zofia Kolczycka-Flajszman (80) gives some bread to starving German children. Perhaps, she remembered that a German soldier had risked helping her family during the war. Another German, a foreman in a Gross-Rosen sub-camp is kind to Hanna Gumpricht (81), and turns out to be a Communist who looks forward to their liberation by the Soviet Union. Maria Goldman, a teacher, and her friend Hanna Czarnianka take risks to teach the children in the Warsaw Ghetto (82), and this very act preserves their sense of human dignity.

76. Pangs of Conscience

Antoni Kewis

Whatever it was that led me to walk along the edge of the ghetto fifty years ago, it was not an accident. Destiny directed me there so that I could be a witness to the cruelty of the Nazis. Not the only witness. It was hell there.

Closed in on itself, the ghetto had become defenceless. Almost every building was ablaze. A corpse hung on a balcony. A wretched, frantic woman with an infant in her arms appeared every so often, each time on a higher floor, on the balconies of one of the buildings on a corner. The fire drove her up to the fourth floor, the top floor. Then, still holding the child, she made a desperate leap into the abyss of flames.

I associated her decision with the sentence I had seen carried out on two children of four or perhaps five years of age. Someone must have sent those two children out of the ghetto. Leaving the small ghetto on the ulica Żelazna side was not particularly difficult, especially for small children, since the barrier there was made of barbed wire. German and 'blue' police patrols were the only deterrent to escape. And so it was that the two small children were caught by a German patrol. The Germans held the children and waited for a police patrol. When the police appeared, the Germans ordered one policeman to remove the manhole cover in the middle of the intersection of Żelazna and Krochmalna, and the other to throw the children into the sewer. When the second policeman stalled and then refused to carry out the order, one gendarme drew his pistol and threatened the policeman with it. Both policemen went grey in the face and one even heaved with nausea. Yet they carried out the order.

In their own eyes, the Germans thus avoided committing a crime. The 'Gott mit uns' [God with us] stamped on their belt buckles left their consciences clear; their dull, merciless faces also testified to this.

Before the sentence was carried out on the children, I took a look at the faces of the people around me. The majority were terrified women. I searched those faces for any sign that they would approve if I intervened to save the children. Perhaps the onlookers included a woman who expected that children fleeing the ghetto should be protected. There was a moment when it seemed to me worth trying a psychological gambit and attempting to intervene. I could see that the Germans (or perhaps they were Austrians) did not want to take the responsibility for the deaths of those two children on themselves. The policemen were also wavering. I spoke German. The work papers from the German Siemens firm that I carried offered me some protection.

And yet I hesitated. A whole range of doubts sprang to mind. Would I be able to manage the colloquial phrases needed for me to pass as a German? Would they decide to subject me to a thorough interrogation? How could I be sure that the whole scene was not being observed from the nearby German gendarmerie headquarters?

And furthermore, I had higher responsibilities; I worked with the Resistance Information Bureau and submitted reports on the German installations, including military ones, to which I was sent as part of my work for Siemens. The Resistance leadership had warned me to avoid any conflicts that could endanger clandestine assignments. That was what tipped the scales.

Over time, my experiences from occupied Warsaw faded.

Now, in my last years, these events keep coming back more frequently and causing me pangs of conscience. 'You should have saved the lives of those two children. You could have done it. But you were a coward. You thought only of yourself.'

77. The Great Deportation

Anna Lanota

When I recall the ghetto – and I try to remember those times as little as possible – what comes back to me above all are events from the so-called 'great deportation' of July and August, 1942 [in Warsaw]. I can see and hear everything that I went through then, and it seems to me that I am back there, talking to my family, running but unable to run away. I feel doomed. What I have written about below are several moments from that operation in 1942, as they come up from time to time in my memory.

THE WEEK BEFORE 22 JULY 1942

Dusk was falling. I was walking along ulica Biała. Szczęsny Zamieński, my cousin Stefa's husband, was escorting me. That was the first time I got a close look at the wall around the ghetto. In this particular place it was not a wall, but a whitewashed wooden fence. The 'Blue Police' stood there in a dense cordon and German patrols checked the terrain every five minutes, keeping an eye on the 'Blues'. The passage to ulica Biała was a normal board in the fence, slightly loosened. It hung by one nail. Next to it stood the Blue Policeman assigned to take bribes from the Jews and Poles crossing over. As we came near, a German patrol drove up. We withdrew, laughing and pretending to be a pair of happily chatting passers-by oblivious to everything that was going on. When the Germans were out of sight, we hurried up to the Blue.

'It's going to cost you', he growled.

We did not give him a *grosz* [a penny]. Szczęsny looked like a Resistance Movement member – and his appearance suited the reality. When he said, 'The lady wants to visit her parents, so please let her through', the Blue lifted the board without a word.

I managed to say 'Goodbye' to Szczęsny and hell swallowed me up. That was my first impression as I lifted the board and walked through. It was too dark to see anything. I could hear wailing voices. Someone tugged at my coat and cried, 'Give me some bread!' Someone grabbed at my suitcase. A multitude of hands groped me. I tried to shake them off, but it had no effect. The crowd around me suddenly took flight. Close, not more than a step away, I began to make out something in the darkness. A man had me by the arm.

'Have you come from the other side?' he asked. 'Have you? It's going to cost you.'

'I have nothing', I said. 'I'm going to visit my parents.'

He shined a lantern in my eyes and let me pass.

I ran down Chłodna towards Leszno. Crowds of people filled the street and the pavement. Beggars leaned against the walls. The whole street shouted in Polish and Yiddish, 'A piece of bread!' A corpse under a newspaper. I stood there, not knowing what it was. 'Never see a body before?' said someone, jostling against me. 'Get a move on!'

I counted more than a dozen corpses on the way home. Many children hurried among the adults: one was trying to sell some sort of rags, another a few sweets, another matches. Suddenly, I was bumped hard. Someone was trying to run off with my suitcase – a little urchin of eight. If I could only make it home, to my parents! I pulled my suitcase out of the boy's hands. It was not hard to do. I pushed my way through the passers-by and stumbled into ulica Leszno, stopping at number five.

24 JULY, NOON

My parents' little room was demolished. The pillows were ripped open; a pan full of soup sat on the hob. Scraps of books, clothing and photographs lay scattered on the floor. Empty.

'Mother!' I cried. 'Is anyone there? Is anyone home?'

I opened the door to the corridor: 'Is anyone there?'

A voice from the corridor: 'Quiet, quiet.' A woman with a child in her arms came in. 'They just left', she said. 'They took everyone from the whole building. They shot the old Goldbergs. I hid. Your brother wasn't here, but they took your parents.'

'Where did they take them?'

'To a lorry with a canvas top. They pushed everyone in. They drove off.' The woman looked in the pan. 'Soup', she said. She found a spoon, sat on the edge of the bed, and began eating it greedily. One spoonful for herself, one for the child.

'Want some soup?' she asked.

'No, I've got to run to the *Umschlagplatz*' [where the Jews were loaded into cattle cars for Treblinka]. I raced out.

'Don't go there. They'll catch you', she called after me.

I ran through the empty streets towards the Gdańsk Station. Gęsia Square – surrounded by Germans on all sides. Two lorries stood in the square. With the help of Jewish Police, the Germans were grabbing passers-by and forcing them into the lorries, screaming '*Los! Los! Schnell! Schnell!*' [hurry up, hurry up] the whole time. The Germans were angry, and perhaps drunk. They beat people with the butts of their Schmeissers. Some of the people they caught showed certificates that must have come from jobs in the workshops. They were sent in the opposite direction with a wave of the hand, and this same wave of the hand opened the cordon of Germans around the *Umschlagplatz* to let them out. As I ran disoriented across the square, a Jewish policeman caught me and shoved me into a queue standing beside a lorry. I looked feverishly around. The man standing ahead of me showed a piece of paper to a German who had come up and the German said, '*Los, geh dort*' [get going, over there], motioning for him to join another group standing near the cordon. I showed the German a piece of blank paper folded twice and he growled, '*Na schneller, dort*' [quicker, over there], while signalling at the same time to the sentries with his finger that they should let that group out. I went with them, running and pushing. We passed through the cordon. I would not go running back to the *Umschlagplatz*.

ULICA LESZNO, 25 OR 26 JULY 1942

I was in Hana Rabinowicz's room. Hana was my classmate at university. Her mother, a half-paralyzed old lady, lay on the bed.

Hana said, 'Mother, when our neighbour comes, I'm leaving with him. They're not doing anything to old people. Once I set myself up, I'll either come back for you or send someone to get you.'

The old lady replied, 'Alright, Hana, but somebody has to come to help me.'

Hana turned to me. 'Can you drop in on my mother? Just for a few days?'

Hana pulled out a knapsack from under the bed and began putting her things in it.

I drew her as far away from her mother's bed as I could and asked her, 'Don't you know that they'll take her away?'

Hana said, 'I know. To resettlement in the east, perhaps to Belorussia. To work. That's what's written.'

I asked, 'When did you start trusting the Germans? It's all lies. Stefka Dobrowolska rang up and said that railroad workers claim that cattle wagons, filled to capacity, are taking people somewhere north of Warsaw, not far away, and coming back empty. There's nothing there, no factory. Stefka thinks they kill them all there.'

Hana said, 'Don't tell me such silly things. I read the letter that the Kons got. Their friend writes that they're somewhere in Russia, that we should take warm things, that the people there are friendly, that they don't have to live in a ghetto. They're in barracks and they get lots of fresh air. I read it myself.'

She keeps packing her knapsack. She cuts a slice of bread. 'I'll leave this for Mama, and I'm taking the rest with me', she says.

A man comes in wearing a knapsack. He's holding a little boy by the hand. 'Are you ready, Hana?' he asks. 'Everybody's waiting for you. Leave the bread for your mother. Everybody who volunteers gets a whole loaf.'

I ask how he knows this.

'They're announcing it over the megaphones. Everybody knows.'

I reply: 'It's all lies, I know that for sure. Someone rang me from the Aryan side. They're deporting people to their deaths.'

The man spits on the floor. 'Take those words out of your mouth! Don't frighten the child!' His facial expression changes and he leans closer to me. 'How much did the Germans pay you to stir up discontent among the Jews?' he asks. 'Just so they have an excuse to hold a massacre in the ghetto. How much?' He points his finger at me.

Hana says, 'Leave her alone, Menachem. She's my friend. She's only repeating silly things she heard. Don't be silly,' she says, turning to me.

I say, 'You're the silly one. Menachem, listen to me.'

Menachem says, 'Are you coming, Hana? I'm off.' He walks out with the little boy. Hana kisses her mother, then embraces me and walks quickly out, carrying her knapsack.

1 OR 2 AUGUST 1942

I am at the so-called brush shop. Two rooms: in the first, a large table with more than a dozen men and women around it, gluing brushes. My brothers Mietek and Rysiek are there. I should not be there, since I have not got the required pass.

We whisper to each other. Mietek: 'We're getting out before they kill us here.'

I: 'Where? To the Aryan side? Four of you, without a *grosz*?'

Mietek: 'But we have friends there.'

I: 'No one has come to me with such an offer.'

Mietek: 'You can't wait for them to offer. They have no idea, or only the foggiest idea, of what's going on here.'

I: 'They have an idea. They read about it in the underground newspapers.'

Mietek: 'There's a great difference between an idea and really knowing. And how could they know that we're at the brush shop? How could they contact us here?'

There are shouts in the courtyard: '*Alle raus, schnell, schnell*' [Everybody out, quick, quick]. We hear shots.

Rysiek: 'Stay calm. They're not taking the brush workers yet.' We all go on working.

The shouts grow louder, then there are more gunshots and the sound of a child crying. The doors burst open and a woman carrying a small child rushes in. People quickly shift to make room for her at the table. A moment later, the Germans rush in, aiming their automatics at us. '*Los, schnell, schnell*'.

Rysiek stands up. '*Wir sind Arbeiter*' [We are workers]. He gestures at the table.

A German chuckles: '*Noch sechs Wochen wirst du hier sitzen*' [You'll stay here for another six weeks]. Another German pulls the little boy out from under the table. He holds him by the back of the neck, laughs as he kicks the door open, and throws the boy down the stairs. He shoots him. The Germans all walk out laughing.

When the boy's mother screams, they slap their hands over her mouth and hold her tight to prevent her from running outside. No one says a word.

15 AUGUST 1942

The window of the cellar beneath the shop is covered by a piece of plywood and a carbide lamp burns for light. It is crowded. A woman hushes a baby.

A woman: 'That little one's going to give us away. Please keep him quiet.'

A second woman: 'If I hear him crying again, you and he both will have to leave.'

The mother offers the child her breast.

A man: 'What are these women upset about? What's the difference? They'll murder us all sooner or later.'

Someone says, 'Pray, Jews. The Lord is almighty, the Lord of Abraham, Isaac and Jacob...'

There are footsteps outside the window and the praying stops. Someone whispers, 'Those aren't Germans.' We can hear someone coming down the steps to the cellar. There is a muffled knock. Someone says, 'It's Michał', and opens the door.

Michał Rojzenfeld enters: 'I've brought bread and a little milk and water.' He sets it down in the corner.

Someone asks: 'What's going on outside?'

Michał: 'The same as yesterday. They're deporting everybody except the ones employed in the workshops. They're killing old people on the spot. Children, too. They take people to the *Umschlagplatz* and load them into cattle wagons. I stood there for several hours disguised as a policeman. They're not taking the police yet, but their turn will come.'

'Where are they taking them?'

Michał: 'What does it matter? To their death.'

'When will it end, Michał?'

Michał: 'I don't know.'

Someone says, 'I want to see Hitler when they drag him through the streets in a cage, like an animal, with everyone spitting on him.'

We hear the sounds of soldiers in the street. Everyone freezes, and then the footfalls grow fainter.

Michał: 'Is Hanka here?'

I: 'Here I am.'

Michał pushes towards me. 'I've got 200 złoty for you. Go to the gate at ulica Żelazna tomorrow morning at five o'clock and give the Germans all your money. They'll either let you out or shoot you. Understand?'

'I understand.'

78. From the Cellar

Jerzy Tomaszewski

That Easter I frequently went out onto the balcony on the fifth floor of the building where we lived, and strained to see the smoke and flames of the Jewish district. Sometimes the wind carried a scrap of paper with Hebrew letters on it. Less often, I walked near Gdańsk Station [in Warsaw] with my friend from school. We exchanged the latest information and looked for the flags, red-and-white [Polish] and blue-and-white [Jewish], that were supposed to be flying somewhere nearby. In spite of everything, we were expecting a miracle – not that the fighters would win, but just that they would hold out for a few more weeks, or even a few more days. I suspected that, had he [been unlucky to have] encountered an evil enough scoundrel, my friend could himself have been on the other side of that wall. I never asked him about it – secrets are better kept when no one shares them – and energetically countered any suppositions inclined in that direction, even when voiced by my immediate family.

The smoke and flames of the Uprising marked the end of a district cordoned off by a wall and guarded by sentries, about which it was nevertheless hard not to know or think in Warsaw. The first contact with its realities was a ride on the tram that did not stop in the tragically overcrowded streets of the closed district. There were cases of people who had urgent business there jumping off the moving tram.

One morning, a boy from our form did not show up at school. He and his whole family had been taken to the ghetto the day before. The closed district seemed to be drawing nearer to us. Many years later I heard that he had survived and emigrated to Palestine.

The tram route was soon changed, the Occupation authorities closed the district off more hermetically, and yet it was still possible to buy various odds and ends in the shops that were rumoured to be produced behind the walls, in that district, about which it was hair-raising even to speak. Those trifling products somehow made the existence of the ghetto more familiar. But the terror of the district was to re-emerge at very close hand.

One afternoon in what must have been the early autumn of 1942, a boy sat in the basement of a building whose foundations had barely been poured in 1939. He could have been just a bit older than me, or he might have been younger; he was skinny, ragged, and wearing a hat that seemed peculiar to anyone living outside the walls; he was above all lonely and frightened. Facing the cellar stood our little pack of neighbourhood children. He knew the fate that awaited a Jew caught outside the ghetto. We knew the fate that awaited those who aided Jews.

The cellar lay close to the main street of the district, but many years would pass before pedestrians crowded its pavements. The opening where the boy sat gave onto a clay pit seldom visited by adults but ruled by the children from the houses in the vicinity. Today, the clay pit is gone, the once-vacant plot of ground has been developed and a department store stands where the cellar was, but in those days it was an out-of-the way place and therefore relatively secure.

We stood at the edge of the cellar looking at the boy who was helpless and full of dread at having been noticed. The boy looked at us, quaking from the cold and from fear. He had no idea who we were. And we, on the other hand, were afraid to approach him. We feared every one of the few pedestrians on the nearby streets. We knew that something had to be done, but we stood there helplessly. In the daylight, anyone who spotted him would know that he was a fugitive from the ghetto. There were indeed no Germans in the area (but could we be sure of that?). The Polish 'blue police' were dangerous enough, and even an innocuous-looking passerby could turn out to be a traitor. What about our friends? Our pack were all trustworthy, but there were rumours (later proved false) that one boy's parents were trying to get onto the *Volkslist* [to be registered as ethnic Germans].

He has to be hidden, I thought. But where, and how? Our small flat, one room with a kitchen in a large building, contained no hiding place. The whole building had been searched several times. The gendarmes had even checked whether anyone was hiding in the little crawl space above our door, which was the only imaginable place of concealment. The boy needed immediate help, and yet what could we do when we had no place to put him? Dusk was falling and it was time for us to go home. The group standing facing the cellar began slowly to melt away. I went home terrified, helpless and conscious of the tragedy playing itself out before my eyes.

The cellar was empty the next day. I have no idea what became of its temporary occupant. He may have risked a further search for a hiding place after night fell. Perhaps a passerby found him and took him in. I am certain – almost – that he was not arrested in that cellar, since someone in one of the surrounding dwellings would have noticed and it would not have remained a secret. On the other hand, it would have been foolhardy to inquire if anyone had helped him. I hardly suspected any of my play-mates of being an informer, but the best-kept secrets are those known only to the parties directly concerned.

Many months later I, too, huddled frightened in a cellar, although I was not so appallingly alone. Above all, we did not have the threat hanging over us that each stranger represented a peril. However, I could not stop thinking about the solitary, terrified boy exposed to the stares of a group of children, each of whom could, even without any ill will, if only through foolishness, bring about his death.

I am sometimes asked why I made the history of the Jews in Poland and the problems of national minorities into my field of professional interest. The memory of the little fugitive who could look forward only to death in the closed district and to whom the world outside the walls was no less full of danger, is a part of the answer. Jerzy Ficowski has written, 'I did not manage to save even one life, and so I wander through the cemeteries that aren't there [...] and rush, too late, to offer help that no one calls for anymore.' In the autumn of 1942 I was unable, or perhaps above all I feared, to help a stranger boy who was facing death only because his people had become the object of hatred. Yet there are others for whom help, perhaps, will not come too late.

79. The Blessed Fake Documents

Janina Allerow

I worked in Dłużyński's 'Zwój' spring factory at 58 ulica Żelazna, in the so-called 'Small Ghetto', until its liquidation. They renewed my pass each month. Aside from its normal production, the factory was required by the Germans to produce railroad springs for the needs of the *'Ostbahn'*. Since there was a shortage of workers, the Germans allotted us a small group of Jewish workers, men and women, numbering perhaps fifteen or twenty – I cannot recall. The Germans quartered them somewhere in the Praga-North district, not in the ghetto. The Germans transported them each morning to the *'wache'* or sentry-post on ulica Leszna, from where one of our employees led them to the factory. After work, one of us escorted them back to the sentry-post and turned them back over to the Germans. One day, it was my turn to act as escort. That was when a scene that I cannot forget occurred. The Germans had given the group a starvation ration of food that day – probably a little *ersatz* coffee and a handful of groats or a chunk of bread, I cannot recall. The sentry-post on ulica Leszna was the most heavily manned and the most brutal. It had crews of German, Jewish and Polish police, and higher-ranking officers, probably from the Gestapo, often came to inspect it. They were ruthless and bestial. So it was that day. After the group had been presented and the document with the names listed on it handed over, one higher-ranking German cracked his whip and screamed that all the bundles containing that unfortunate food should be dumped into the gutter. They called on me for help, but my explanations and the documents that I showed meant nothing to the Germans, who threatened me with their guns. That 'Übermensch' struck a pregnant woman who was begging for mercy. Once she had fallen to the gutter, he kicked her. (For the first time in my life, I went with a friend to get drunk in the nearest bar on the 'Aryan' side.)

We did what we could do provide some additional food for the miserable, terrified, undernourished Jews. We had a large, rubber-wheeled horse-drawn wagon (the horse also needed a pass) for making deliveries and picking up the steel that we used in production. The Jewish women working with us sewed narrow cloth bags. We filled these bags with groats, sugar or lard on the 'Aryan' side and then pushed them into the inner-tube (instead of air) in one of the tyres on the wagon. Our luck did not hold for long. Someone informed on us. We found out about this when we were returning to the ghetto one day with a 'loaded' tyre. They stopped us and lined us up beside the wall [of the ghetto]. The wagon was also parked there, with the 'loaded' tyre close to the wall. Providence, or luck, was on our side. They ordered the Jewish police to take off one of the tyres – but it was the normal one. Taking it off, taking it apart, and putting it back on took a long time. They let us go, but we did not try that ploy again. When we tried to rescue our engineer, a highly-skilled expert, from deportation at the *Umschlagplatz*, they proposed that we might like to join him [on a train to a death camp]. I think someone has a photograph of that famous square.

I managed to provide 'Aryan' documents to two people, a girl and a man. I had joined the Home Army [the main Polish clandestine army under the authority of the exiled government in London] and that was where I got two *kennkarten* [identity cards] bearing stamped photographs that I had supplied, made out in the names of deceased people from outside the city and even the province of Warsaw. I took those identity cards to the ghetto along with ink, so that we could add the fingerprints on the spot. It worked – they got out. I do not know how. I had no close contact with them; I only know that they got married. Many years later, I met her on a bus. She told me that he had died, and she had arranged all the necessary documents and would be leaving with her daughter for Denmark, permanently, in a few days' time. All that time, even on their post-war Polish documents, they had been using the surname from the papers I had given them.

It is a painful and disgraceful fact that a group of villains operated within the city of Warsaw whose specialty was finding people of Jewish descent in order to blackmail them. An engineer whom I knew ransomed himself once with money and a second time with his watch. The third time, he must have had nothing, for he seems to have been informed upon and shot at the checkpoint. Sad, isn't it?

80. A Particle of Humanity

Zofia Kolczycka-Flajszman

I remember something that happened in the Łódź ghetto. The commandant, Hans Biebow, had eczema. The German doctors were perplexed. My uncle, Samuel Neumark, was called for a consultation. They sent a car to the ghetto for him, and took him to 'the city'. The Germans were polite. As a fee, they gave him a packet of cigarettes. He identified the source of the condition and treated it. A year later, my Uncle Sam, his wife and their child received deportation orders. Sam asked Biebow, his former patient, for a stay of deportation. Biebow assured him personally that he would be going to a very good camp, and that he would be given a post as a physician there. Like all the others, the family was transported to Auschwitz, killed in the gas chambers, and burned.

Terrible famine and illness ravaged the ghetto. My mother doled out our daily portions. I suspected my mother and grandmother of giving my father and me some of their rations. We also had the dog that Tadek had left behind when he fled to Lwów. My grandmother often pretended while preparing our scanty meals that the soup had boiled over or that food had spilled onto the floor in some other accidental way. 'Too bad', she would say. 'The dog can eat it.' This happened often; she did it deliberately. She was a wise, calm, controlled woman. It always seemed to me that she liked Michał better. Only later would I understand that she favoured him because of his handicap. Before our 'resettlement' to the ghetto, my parents had decided to leave our more valuable possessions (our bedding and silverware) for safety with a friend of my father's, a Pole from Piotrków Trybunalski who, like my father, was a chemist. Mother (who had 'good looks') transported these treasures to him on an 'Aryans only' train. She was very frightened. Her fear must have been obvious, because when she got off the train a uniformed German came up to her, took her by the arm, and said, 'Don't worry, no one will harm you if you're with me.' That soldier later came to visit us at our home at 58 ulica Śródmiejska. He made friends with my father and brought us butter and other products that were hard to obtain. That was in the autumn of 1939. He disappeared some time later and we never saw him again. Perhaps someone informed on him for visiting Jews.

In August 1944, my healthy young mother and I faced the camp medical commission at Auschwitz. Only I was judged fit to be sent to Germany as a labourer. Many people told me later that my mother was sent to Bergen-Belsen. I spent a long time looking for her, but never found her.

This is what the Auschwitz medical commission looked like: the naked women had to march quickly down a gauntlet of uniformed Germans, one of whom indicated *Rechts* or *Links* [to the right or to the left] with his riding crop – to work or to the gas.

People died like flies in Auschwitz. There were hunger, filth, lice and overwhelming fear. The roll-calls that lasted for hours with the repeated counting of the living and the dead were torture. But German precision demanded that the numbers add up. Things were somewhat different at Bergen-Belsen. Living in huge tents, we had more 'freedom' and fresh air. It was warm then, a real Indian summer. The hunger was unbearable. I ate heather and grass. Our bread ration was microscopic. There were four of us girls, aged 16 and 17, who stuck together. I remember how we made a 'cake' of three thin slices of bread with beet marmalade between them when a girl named Sima had her birthday. Sima died of tuberculosis right after the war.

In April 1945, the Germans decided to use slave labour to help erase the evidence of their war crimes. They loaded us back into the cattle wagons and took us away. They left the wagons at the station in the town of Beelitz, near Berlin. The Americans celebrated Hitler's birthday on 20 April with an air raid. That station and our wagons were bombed. I got out alive, but bomb fragments broke my arm. Two-thirds of the women didn't survive. We fled into the woods. My friends bandaged my broken arm, making a sort of sling out of scraps of torn clothing. We slept in the forest, ate grass and tried to stay away from Germans. The Russians took the town on 23 April 1945. I cannot recall comparable joy at any other moment in my life. The Russians took us under their protection immediately. A soldier took us to the local hospital and ordered them to set my arm. It hurt terribly. They put it in plaster. The Russian screamed at the German doctor and even slapped him several times. 'This is for what you people did to children', he said. The Russians settled twenty-five of us, women and girls, in a deserted farmhouse. The adults cooked with groats, flour and sugar supplied by the Russians. We were eager to get back to our homes in Poland, but they advised us not to set out because there was still fighting in Berlin.

When they took us to the hospital after finding us hungry and bedraggled in the woods, we saw that the Germans had hurriedly evacuated all the patients. It was a suburban sanatorium town, like Otwock outside Warsaw. We found the kitchen. There were sandwiches and slices of white bread with cheese that had already been prepared for the German patients. Ignoring the warnings against eating too greedily, we stuffed ourselves and took more 'for later'. When we went outside, we saw hungry German children begging for bread. I gave some of mine to one of them. The other Jewish women did the same. I often thought about this afterwards. The small gesture revealed that, despite all I had gone through, a particle of humanity remained.

81. The Selection

Hanna Gumpricht

Here are some particular episodes that have stuck in my memory.

After the establishment of the ghetto in Łódź, my mother threw something over the barbed wire. In return, the same way, she got bread and sausage. Only we children received those delicacies. The smuggling ended soon – the Germans reinforced the sentries.

It was a beautiful day in the summer of 1940. We were living near the barbed-wire boundary of the ghetto. I was alone in the flat when I heard shooting. Thinking of my father, I ran into the street and saw him slumped with his left hand over his right shoulder. I ran to him and managed to help him home. When he sat down, I saw the blood. I could not speak for fear. Then I started screaming. Mother ran in. Father had to go to the hospital for several weeks. His right arm was paralyzed.

Summer passed, then autumn and the cold winter. My parents managed from time to time to find work carrying something or cleaning.

Strangers brought father home one day. He had collapsed in the street and been unable to rise. He was swelling from the hunger. After several weeks of hallucinations, he died in his own bed.

He was one of the first victims of hunger, humiliation and despair. There would be thousands.

THE SUMMER OF 1942

There was a *'Sperre'* [a curfew] – no one was allowed outside. The Germans closed off our street. Mother decided that we would hide in the attic. We were on our way up the ladder when a policeman appeared and ordered us out into the street, where the Germans were holding a selection. Those deemed incapable of working had to get into the wagons. They selected my brother and me. Mother and my sister ran after us. All four of us ended up in the Poor Hospital on ulica Łagiewnicka. The patients had already been deported. I recall the semi-darkness, the cries of infants, an atmosphere of unreality.

A distant cousin of ours was employed there as a nurse. I found her. She must have known what our fate was. Terrified to find us there, she had us moved to a two-room suite where, she said, there would be another selection the next day. The room was packed and more people crowded outside the doors. The SS men came very early in the morning and ordered everyone to line up. Mother whispered, 'Children, pinch your cheeks so that the colour will come into them.' My brother did not want to do it and would not allow anyone to touch him. When our turn came, the SS man's finger stopped on my brother and then pointed to the door. My brother walked out. There was an awful silence!

After a certain time, the handful of us who had survived the selection were taken to a building near a pond that had once been an old people's home. The weather was lovely.

They released us in the late afternoon. The streets of the ghetto were deserted and there was a deathly silence broken by my mother's crying and shouting, 'Where's Hesio? They've taken my son!'

1944: THE LIQUIDATION OF THE ŁÓDZ GHETTO

I cannot say how long we hid in the attic. We had neither a watch nor a calendar. Mother had decided that we would not report to the evacuation point. At night, we looked for vegetables that had been left in garden plots. We found some beets, carrots and potatoes. These treats had to be eaten raw. In the end, mother decided that we would report. Where they evacuated us, we would at least get work. Here, we were starving to death.

THE RAMP [IN AUSCHWITZ]

Mother had preternaturally acute eyesight and intuition in those days, and she noticed that the SS men were separating all people who held each other's hands or had their arms around each other. She whispered, 'Keep apart. Each one of us will walk alone.' The SS man who stopped her asked, 'How old are you?' She answered, 'Thirty' (she was 35). He signalled for her to go to the side that, as it turned out, offered some hope. The same with us. We were together. We looked around and saw the sign, *Arbeit macht frei* [Work makes you free]. Barbed wire, barbed wire, barbed wire ... and human skeletons in striped camp uniforms. Enormous eyes full of hunger, terror and madness. Where exactly were we?

We were standing in line, naked. All around stood the uniformed *Übermenschen*. They motioned for some people to leave and others to stand off to the side. Mother was sent 'off to the side'. The SS man asked me, 'Are you healthy?' I said nothing. From the corner of my eye, I could see mother's knees buckling. Suddenly, as if it came from very far away,

I heard my sister's quavering voice: '*Gesund, gesund*' – healthy. 'Off to the side', said the SS man. We walked towards mother.

Herr Fürster, my foreman at the Gross-Rosen sub-camp in Mittelsteine, was the only one to whom we *Häftlinge*, we prisoners, could put a name. He called us girls by name and said '*Frau*' [Mrs] to the older women. He brought me sandwiches and bread, which mother divided into portions. One night, he took advantage of the brief absence of the *Aufseherin*, the female SS guard (of whom he said '*sie ist dummer wie dumm*' – she's dumber than dumb) to invite me to his room. He had brought a thermos full of hot cocoa and china cups and saucers from home. He served me the fantastic hot beverage, saying, 'Hania, I just wanted you to have a little taste of home'. He often ordered me to load things from one crate to another, no doubt so that I would not become fatigued from operating the machine. He once ordered me to do so and added that I should be sure to share what I found at the bottom of the crate with the other girls. What I found was loaves of bread: our foreman had heard that we had been deprived of food rations for the day because of some infraction – and this was his reaction.

Another way of sparing me labour for the Third Reich was by 'repairing' my machine, even when there was nothing wrong with it. During these acts of sabotage, he asked me about my family and our lives. He also told me about himself, including the fact that he was a communist and had had all his teeth knocked out by the Nazis while he was in prison. He kept me up to date on the situation in Europe. Once, I heard him say, '*Hani, ist gut, die Russen sind schon da*' [Good news, Hana – the Russians are almost here]. Another time, he sighed, '*Armes Deustschland*' [Poor Germany].

We were transferred to Graffenort, another Gross-Rosen sub-camp, in April 1945. There, we had to carry huge stones. We must have derived strength from the threat of being beaten or killed. We also dug ditches.

On 7 May 1945, we were led out of the camp towards Glatz [Kłodzko], which the Germans had already evacuated. We were sent back to the camp. The bars from the windows lay on the floor and there was not an *Aufseherin* left. The Red Army arrived the next day. A crowd from the neighbouring camps assembled in the square to greet the liberators. The *Marseillaise* was sung, mixed with the *Internationale*.

> Today's feeling of freedom is unimaginable,
> The awareness of time restored.
> Experiencing the world anew.
> Hope...
> The return to a home that no longer exists.

82. Clandestine Teaching

Maria Goldman

Of the numberless images that crowd the memory, I shall choose the chapter about my work. In other words, I shall answer the question: What did you do in the ghetto?

As a secondary-school Latin teacher, I had one desire and one option: to teach. All education was strictly forbidden in the ghetto and therefore punished automatically. Nevertheless, the young people longed for any sort of substitute for school, and their parents were prepared to deny themselves everything, up to and including food, to ensure their children's education. Groups of young people of a similar age therefore coalesced in the search for a teacher and guide. I reached an understanding with Hanna Czarnianka (whose name I deliberately cite so that it will not vanish into total oblivion), who was adept in the mathematical and scientific subjects. I took upon myself the lessons in Polish, French, Latin, history and geography. Hanka taught mathematics, physics, chemistry and biology. The groups varied, but were made up of two, three or at the most four people. Larger groups were impossible because of the problem of finding rooms. We had no school premises. The lessons had to be held in a different flat each time, and since we all lived in indescribably overcrowded conditions, it was hard to come up with chairs or a larger table. I was sharing a sublet room, perhaps twelve metres square, with my mother, my aunt and my 12-year-old cousin, where there were two 'permanent' beds, two cots that unfolded at night, a tiny cooker set into the heating stove for preparing food, and a cord hanging from the lamp with an immersion heater on it for boiling the coloured liquid that we referred to as tea. There was a tiny table in one corner, with two small chairs.

That was my 'home' and my 'classroom' on the days when I hosted the lessons. Conditions elsewhere were similar. In July and August, Hanka and I sometimes managed to hire a miserable, neglected little courtyard with a scraggly bush where our youngest pupils of reading and writing could run and play. We called it 'summer camp'.

The problem of textbooks was as critical as the problem of premises. No shops in the ghetto sold books. Textbooks passed from hand to hand – worn-out, borrowed by the day or the hour, uncovered in old Warsaw homes, copied out by hand, given by one child to another.

The young people learned eagerly. They came beaming to lessons. They wanted to be together, to work as a group like all pupils, and they drank in knowledge about a world they did not know. They dreamed about the future.

My pupils included two 10-year-olds, one of whom, like quicksilver, never skipped a chance to touch something, shift something around, give something a push, break something. His innocent tricks moved me. Both those boys died in the deportations.

Not all the lessons were paid. The fees did not suffice to satisfy either my mother's hunger or mine. Sometimes, when I was racing from one lesson to another, terribly tired, with everything all mixed up in my mind, I had to battle the temptation to buy myself one of the sweets that were sold in the ghetto by the piece. To this day, the sight of a sweet is a symbol for me.

Hanka died in August 1942 (during the big *aktion*). She was an active member of the Resistance Movement. All of our classes fell apart in those days. We were all trying to save ourselves.

I do not know the fate of my pupils. Sometimes I see their faces, and I still love them as I did once.

Glossary

Appelplatz	roll-call square
Arbeitsamt	Labour Office
Arbeitslager	work camp
Aufseherin	female SS guard
Ausweis	identification-card indicating employment
Bahnschutz	railway police
Bekanntmachung	announcement
Einsatz- kommando	detachment of the
einsatzgruppen	(mobile forces) of the SS with the task of eliminating Jews
Endlösung	'Final solution' euphemism used by the Nazis for the elimination of the Jews
Gimnazjum	grammar school
Häftlinge	prisoners
Judenrat	Jewish council established by the Germans to supervise the ghettos
Kampfgruppe Reinefarth	unit under the command of SS Lt-General Heinz Reinefarth, assigned to the Wola district of Warsaw to suppress the Rising of 1944
Kennkarte	Identification card
Kinderheim	children's ('home') barrack
Kreishauptmann	district chief
Kriminalpolizei	criminal police
Lyceum	'liceum' in Polish – secondary school
Metsiya	Yiddish, *metsie:* a 'find' or a 'bargain'
Morgs	Polish: Morg, morga – unit of land measure (5,600 sq. m.)
Mussulmann	In the camps' slang: a starved person on the brink of death
Oberka	female SS overseer
Ordnungsdienst	Jewish police in the ghettos supervised by Polish guards and armed German police
Ostfront	the Eastern Front
Rottenführer	low ranking SS officer

Schulrat	school council
Sperre	curfew
Szaulis	'rifleman' in Lithuanian. Units of these fascist Lithuanian police were used to fight the Polish Home Army partisan units and participated in actions oppressing Jews
Umschlagplatz	collection point in the Warsaw Ghetto where Jews were gathered for deportation to the Treblinka extermination camp
Volksdeutsche	ethnic Germans living in Eastern Europe
Volkslist	register of ethnic Germans in Eastern Europe under Nazi rule
Wache	sentry-post
Wachmeister	sergeant-major
Wehrmacht	German armed forces

Index of Place Names

Arnold Daghani's
Memories of Mikhailowka
The Illustrated Diary of a Slave Labour Camp Survivor

Deborah Schultz and **Edward Timms** (Eds)

Arnold Daghani (1909-85) came from a German-speaking Jewish family in Suczawa, then in the Austro-Hungarian Empire, now Romania. His understated narrative of his experiences in the slave labour camp at Mikhailowka, south west Ukraine (1942-43), presented here in its first English book edition, provides a day-by-day account of the chilling experiences of Jewish slave labourers. It is written in a compelling style and illustrated by watercolours and drawings that Daghani made secretly in captivity and smuggled out of the camp and a Romanian ghetto. It includes an extraordinary account of the couple's escape and the shooting of over three hundred prisoners.

The uniqueness of Daghani's Holocaust testimony lies in his role as an artist which led to his (and his wife's) escape from the camp and their survival. The camps in Ukraine have been under-investigated and the diary provides significant material. It was used as the basis of investigations in the 1960s into war crimes in the slave labour camps in Ukraine, helping to bring attention to the region and providing some form of recognition for those who suffered there. This richly illustrated and scrupulously edited book is distinguished from more conventional Holocaust memoirs by focusing on fundamental questions of historical testimony and the problems of representation in both words and images. Daghani's diary is contextualized on the basis of wide-ranging new historical, archival and art historical research in essays that document the artist's attempts to achieve justice and reconciliation. They locate the diary in relation to contemporary issues on migration and statelessness, genocide and trauma, self-reflection and memory. The diary is both art and document, addressing how we understand and construct history. It enables readers to engage with the Holocaust via the viewpoint of an individual, making statistics more meaningful and history less distant.

2009   256 pages   2x8 page plate sections
978 0 85303 638 8   cloth   £45.00/$75.00
978 0 85303 639 5   paper   £18.95/$32.50

Antisemitism: The Generic Hatred

Essays in Memory of Simon Wiesenthal

Michael Fineberg, Shimon Samuels and Mark Weitzman (Eds)

Dedicated to the memory of the 'conscience of the Holocaust', Simon Wiesenthal, to whom it offers a number of personal tributes, this book brings together essays by a wide variety of authors on antisemitism and related forms of intolerance, racism and xenophobia. Starting from the idea that antisemitism constitutes a paradigm case of collective and individual hatred, it examines some of the reasons why it has prospered over the ages and persists in our time, even after well-nigh universal condemnation of the Holocaust. Some authors see it as a virus, always ready to develop and spread, wherever Jewish difference is resented; others emphasize that the antisemitic myths are not grounded in reality but depend rather on a fabrication, an imagined being to whom every kind of vice and perversion can be attributed. Jews, Gypsies, Kurds, Armenians, Tutsis: they can all be made to fit the bill.

Simon Wiesenthal believed not in vengeance but in justice for the victims and played a pre-eminent and, at times, lonely role in tracking down individual criminals and bringing them to trial. But he knew that was not enough. The contributors to this memorial volume, representing a range of cultural, religious and disciplinary perspectives, share that view. They know that so long as the Jewish stereotype is vested with legitimacy, the fight against antisemitism can never be won. Nor can it be defeated so long as it is fuelled by crisis in the Middle East, which has allowed some people to give expression to their antisemitism while denying it, by treating the State of Israel not as a state, with its own particular problems and shortcomings, but as a kind of reified Jew. These are some of the issues addressed by the authors of the essays presented here, along with others, such as antisemitism as a determinant of Jewish identity and the possibility of forgiveness for the perpetrators of genocide. The book thus seeks to understand and learn from this particular paradigm of hatred and to suggest ways of countering it, in the name of the core values of a common humanity.

2007   376 pages
978 0 85303 745 3   cloth   £40.00/$75.00
978 0 85303 746 0   paper   £19.50/$35.00

Jewish Refugees in Switzerland during the Holocaust
A Memoir of Childhood and History

Frieda Johles Forman

This is the first English-language memoir of the Jewish refugee experience in wartime Switzerland focusing on children's experiences and daily life in the refugee camps. The author integrates her memories of a refugee childhood with archival and historical research, including interviews. Fleeing the Nazis, the author's family was among the 25,000 Jews who sought refuge in Switzerland. The refugee camps were administered by Swiss government authorities with a peculiar mix of rigidity and compassion. Torn from a Jewish world that was fast disappearing, the refugees created a remarkable cultural life in the camps including educational programmes for children and adults, vocational training, art classes for children, newspapers, theatre productions, religious programmes, music, lectures and study groups.

Paying particular attention to the experiences of women and children, the author explores the response of the Swiss Jewish community, and interviews some of the men and women who dealt with the refugees including former welfare workers, camp administrators and foster families. Research in the archives of the Swiss government as well as of Jewish organizations uncovers a treasure trove of official documents, along with refugee correspondence, photographs and children's art created in the camps. Original French, German and Yiddish documents are translated into English for the first time to reveal the heated public debates about Switzerland's refugee policy and about the treatment of Jewish refugees.

2009   144 pages   8 page plate section
978 0 8530 3961 7   cloth   £40.00/$26.50
978 0 8530 3951 8   paper   £14.99/$59.95